THE RUSSIAN REVOLUTIONARY MOVEMENT IN THE 1880s

The book deals with the various revolutionary groups active in Russia in the 1880s. The first chapter attempts a definition of Populism, examines the main strategies on which revolutionary activity was based in the 1870s, traces the development of the main organisations of that decade and discusses their relationship to the prevailing theories. The three following chapters examine the history of the organisations of the 1880s in the light of this discussion and against the background of a reactionary political atmosphere, cultural stagnation, despondency in the intelligentsia, and industrial development. Separate chapters are devoted to each of the main categories into which groups might broadly speaking be divided – those adhering to or sustaining the tradition of Narodnaya Volya; Populists opposed to political terrorism and intent on patient propagandistic activity, and miscellaneous related groups; and groups leaning in the direction of Social Democracy. Considerable attention is devoted to such subjects as the growth of circles in the higher educational institutions; attempts at propaganda in the working class and the armed forces; views on organisational matters and on the relative importance of 'political' and 'economic' objectives and forms of struggle; and attitudes towards the peasantry, terrorism, the development of capitalism in Russia, and Western European Social Democracy. The early political activity and sympathies of Lenin are also discussed at some length. The conclusion assesses the significance of the organisations of the 1880s in the larger history of the Russian revolutionary movement.

The main importance of the book should be threefold. Firstly, it should provide a brief general history of the Russian revolutionary movement in a little-known phase. Secondly, it demonstrates that the 1880s represent not what they are usually perceived to be in the history of the revolutionary movement – that is, a vacuum between the dynamic Populism of the 1870s and the rise of Social Democracy in the 1890s – but a period of intense activity that kept alive the revolutionary tradition in unfavourable conditions. Thirdly, it reveals that there was no clear-cut divergence between Populism and Social Democracy, rather that theoretical allegiances were in general extremely confused and that the early groups that are usually described as Social Democratic, in particular, are of a much less clearly defined Marxist orientation than is generally supposed.

THE RUSSIAN REVOLUTIONARY MOVEMENT IN THE 1880s

DEREK OFFORD

Lecturer in Russian
University of Bristol

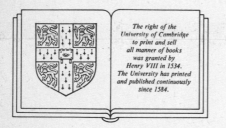

The right of the
University of Cambridge
to print and sell
all manner of books
was granted by
Henry VIII in 1534.
The University has printed
and published continuously
since 1584.

CAMBRIDGE UNIVERSITY PRESS

Cambridge
London   New York   New Rochelle
Melbourne   Sydney

Published by the Press Syndicate of the University of Cambridge
The Pitt Building, Trumpington Street, Cambridge CB1 1RP
32 East 57th Street, New York, NY 10022, USA
10 Stamford Road, Oakleigh, Melbourne 3166, Australia

First published 1986

Printed in Great Britain at the University Press, Cambridge

British Library cataloguing in publication data

Offord, Derek
The Russian revolutionary movement in
the 1880s.
1. Revolutionists–Soviet Union–History
–19th century   2. Soviet Union–Politics
and government–1881–1894
I. Title
322.4'2'0947   DK240

ISBN 0 521 32723 7

Library of Congress cataloguing in publication data

Offord, Derek.
The Russian revolutionary movement in the 1880s.
Bibliography:
Includes index.
1. Populism–Soviet Union–History–19th century.
2. Socialism–Soviet Union–History–19th century.
3. Revolutionists–Soviet Union–History–19th
century.   4. Soviet Union–Politics and government–
19th century.   I. Title.
HX313.036 1986   322.4'2'0947   86-17636

SE

FOR MY MOTHER AND IN
MEMORY OF MY FATHER

❧ CONTENTS

Preface   page ix
Note on dates, transliteration and use of Russian terms   xv
Glossary   xvii
Map of European Russia in the 1880s   xviii

1   RUSSIAN REVOLUTIONARY POPULISM
     BEFORE 1 MARCH 1881   1
The theory and spirit of revolutionary Populism .   1
Revolutionary strategies: Lavrov, Bakunin and Tkachov   8
Revolutionary organisations and activity in the 1870s   16
The movement from 1879 to 1 March 1881: Chornyy Peredel
     and Narodnaya Volya   26

2   NARODNAYA VOLYA AFTER 1 MARCH
     1881   36
The aftermath of assassination   36
The party regroups its forces   39
The pogroms and the attitude of Narodnaya Volya towards
     them   43
The ascendancy of 'Jacobinism' in the Executive Committee
     and the party's organisation in the armed forces   46
The workers' groups of Narodnaya Volya in St Petersburg and
     provincial cities   51

The dispute between the 'old' and 'young' Narodovoltsy in 1884 — 56

Orzhikh's attempt to rebuild the party in 1885 — 63

A. I. Ulyanov and the plot to kill Alexander III in 1887 — 69

Attempts to revive Narodnaya Volya in 1888–90 — 75

3 'POPULISTS', 'MILITARISTS', 'CONSPIRATORS' AND OTHER GROUPS IN THE 1880s — 77

Russian culture in the 1880s — 77

'Militarists' and student groups in Moscow and St Petersburg — 82

Student groups in Kharkov — 87

Student circles in Kazan and the network of Fokin and Bekaryukov — 90

The student movement and the disturbances in Kazan in 1887 — 95

V. I. Ulyanov (Lenin) and his role in the student movement in 1887 — 99

The symposium The Social Question compiled by Populists in Kazan — 107

Fokin's circles in Kiev in the second half of the 1880s — 112

Bekaryukov and workers' circles in Kharkov and Rostov — 114

4 THE BEGINNINGS OF RUSSIAN SOCIAL DEMOCRACY — 117

Attitudes to Marx and Engels in Russia before the 1880s — 117

Marx's and Engels' views on Populism — 120

Plekhanov and the 'Emancipation of Labour' group — 125

The Blagoyevtsy — 131

The 'Morozov strike' of 1885 — 138

Tochissky's 'Association of St Petersburg Artisans' — 141

Fedoseyev's activity in Kazan in 1888–9 — 145

V. I. Ulyanov at Kokushkino and in Kazan, 1888–9 — 149

The labour movement and student circles in St Petersburg in the late 1880s — 155

Conclusion — 161

Key to abbreviations used in notes and bibliography — 171

Notes — 173

Select bibliography — 197

Index — 208

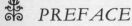 *PREFACE*

The purpose of this work is to examine the course of the revolutionary movement in Russia in the 1880s. An attempt is made briefly to describe the main revolutionary organisations and groups, together with their thinking and activity, to indicate their complexion and inter-relationships, to assess their contribution to the movement as a whole and to discuss the way in which they reflected its fortunes.

It is perhaps as well at the outset to enumerate the problems, all of them of perennial importance to Russian socialists, to which the revolutionaries of the decade had to address themselves. What was the relationship of Russia to Western Europe and, in particular, how did her path of economic development compare with that of the West? Was it the peasantry or the proletariat which would provide the main revolutionary force in Russia, and what was the relationship between the peasants, who constituted the vast majority of the population, and the emergent working class of the towns? What should be the respective roles of the intelligentsia and the masses in revolutionary activity, and would revolution come about at the instigation of the former or of the volition of the latter? Should revolutionaries strive primarily to secure economic improvements in the condition of the masses or to transform political institutions? Was revolution an imminent or a distant prospect, and what should the tempo of the movement be? By what means would the goal be best promoted – by cautious and thorough propaganda or by militant agitation, even armed struggle against the authorities? What sort of revolutionary organisation was it desirable or necessary to create, given the ideals of the revolutionaries and the nature of the society in which they were operating? And last, but never least in the thinking of the Russian intelligentsia, what moral considerations impinged on all these problems?

These were the main questions which to a greater or lesser extent exercised the minds of all Russian socialists in the 1880s. In order fully to understand the way in which revolutionaries of that decade approached them, however, we need to see their thinking and activity against an earlier background, for the movement of the 1880s represents in the main a final and decadent phase of the revolutionary Populism which had its roots in the 1860s and its heyday in the 1870s. In the first chapter a preliminary attempt is therefore made to describe Populist doctrine (which is perhaps best seen against a rather broader cultural canvas than is generally sketched in histories of the revolutionary movement), to outline the most important revolutionary strategies on which practical activity was based, to chart the rapid growth of revolutionary organisations in the 1870s, and to draw attention to the main modifications made to strategy and tactics in that decade in the light of practical experience in a harsh reality. It was the theoretical premisses of Populism – which proved very durable – and a reverence for certain forms of struggle tested in the 1870s that revolutionaries of the 1880s inherited; and in a sense their history is a history of struggle with that heritage as well as with the régime they despised.

The revolutionary Populism of the 1860s and the 1870s has been very thoroughly studied. All who are interested in the movement of those decades are indebted to the Italian historian, Venturi, whose monumental work on the subject, written some thirty years ago, remains unsurpassed in any language.[1] A further readable, though more popular, survey was provided at approximately the same time by Yarmolinsky. More recently the Polish historian of philosophy, Walicki, has made important contributions to the discussion of major Populist thinkers. In the Soviet Union – where vigorous research into the pre-Marxist phase of the revolutionary movement was abruptly curtailed in the early 1930s – much attention has been devoted to Populism by scholars of the post-Stalin period and useful monographs – by Levin, Tkachenko, Itenberg, Volk, Sedov, Tvardovskaya and others – have now appeared in Russian on the major organisations of the 1870s. The movement of the 1880s, on the other hand, has never been examined in any work in English – or Russian – except in the most selective way. Yarmolinsky and Volk have a few pages on the decline of Narodnaya Volya after 1 March 1881. There is a very brief – though

valuable – article by Utechin on various organisations other than
Narodnaya Volya which were active in the 1880s. Several historians, both
Soviet and Western, have explored the circumstances in which Lenin began
his revolutionary career in the late 1880s and have examined the plot to
assassinate Alexander III, in which Lenin's elder brother was involved in
1887. Baron's major study of Plekhanov deals comprehensively with the
émigré Social Democrats of the 'Emancipation of Labour' group. Another
American historian, Pipes, devotes some contentious pages to the St
Petersburg labour movement of the mid and late 1880s. And a number of
Soviet historians, notably Polevoy and Kazakevich, have studied those
groups of the 1880s which may to some extent be seen as pioneers of Russian
Social Democracy (though the degree to which these groups developed a
specifically Marxian socialism has often been greatly exaggerated). But the
picture which emerges from these sources of the Russian revolutionary
movement of the 1880s is neither coherent nor entirely accurate, for it is
fragmentary and creates the misleading impression that groups were
isolated, inactive and few.

The 1880s could be characterised, it is true, as a period of failure and
despondency in the ranks of revolutionaries, as in Russian intellectual and
cultural life in general. Populism was in decline and revolutionaries
fumbled for alternative paths to socialism. All the same, the history of the
movement during that decade does deserve to be known, and not merely in
order that a large lacuna should be filled, for, firstly, it is only when set
against the decline of the 1880s that the exploits of the revolutionaries of the
1870s and their contribution to the movement in its broadest perspective
come sharply into focus – only then do on the one hand the delusiveness of
their ideals and on the other their capacity to inspire others, both the
shortcomings and the quixotic virtues of revolutionary Populism, become
fully apparent; and secondly, and more importantly, the revolutionaries of
the 1880s make their own contribution to the movement as a whole. It was
in this decade that attention shifted from the countryside to the towns, in
practice if not often in theory. Developments in organisation and tactics
were made which to some extent ran counter to previous theory and
practice and provided models and even foundations for the new generation
of revolutionaries who were to operate in the more propitious climate of the
1890s. Greater attention began to be paid to the theoretical preparation of
the revolutionary. Moreover, the organisations of the 1880s served as both
a training ground for revolutionaries of the following decade and a bridge
between the Populism of the 1870s and the reanimated movement of the

1890s. It was in this milieu that a new wave of the revolutionary movement gathered its at first unsuspected force and that many revolutionaries, the young Lenin included, made their first acquaintance with socialist thought, gained their earliest experience of illegal activity and began preparing for a revolutionary vocation.

The primary sources available for a study of the revolutionary movement in the 1880s are sufficient, if not abundant. The theoretical writings of the major revolutionary thinkers who were influential at the time are preserved, mainly in posthumous collections or selections of their works. Also extant are the journals of the main revolutionary organisations, many of the pamphlets, proclamations and programmatic documents written by their members, the correspondence of individual revolutionaries and their testimonies to the police (which were often understandably evasive or misleading but sometimes entirely 'frank' and usually forthright on matters of theory or principle). A great deal of all this material, as well as transcripts or summaries of the trials of many revolutionary groups, has been published in anthologies or in journals devoted largely to elucidation of the history of the revolutionary movement (*Byloye, Golos minuvshego, Katorga i ssylka, Krasnaya letopis', Krasnyy arkhiv, Letopis' revolyutsii, Proletarskaya revolyutsiya*), the majority of which sprang up in the Soviet Union in the decade following the triumph of Bolshevism. We have in addition the memoirs of former revolutionaries themselves. Admittedly, the fallibility of memory – many of these accounts were written more than forty years after the events described – and the frequent desire of memoirists to paint their past in colours acceptable to readers in another time require one in many instances to treat these writings with caution. Nevertheless, memoirs remain the greatest source of first-hand material on the movement which has been available to me. They may be supplemented by various official documents which, although less sensitive to the niceties of revolutionary theory and sometimes liable to confuse various groups operating independently of one another, are extremely informative on points of fact. Of particular use are the reports of police investigations into the revolutionary movement which were compiled by clerks of the Ministry of the Interior during the 1880s and which are now housed in the Central State Archive of the October Revolution (TsGAOR) in Moscow.

A few remarks need to be made, too, on the scope of my study. The selection of dates within which to concentrate one's attention inevitably has an element of arbitrariness, and a particular decade may not completely embrace a given stage of some movement or historical process. The distinct phases of the Russian revolutionary movement, in so far as phases can be distinguished clearly from one another, do not coincide entirely with the decades of the second half of the nineteenth century, although certain decades have come to be associated with various social and intellectual moods and a predilection for particular forms of revolutionary activity. Roughly speaking, the 1880s do coincide with what has variously been described as the 'decadent' period of revolutionary Populism and a 'preparatory' period prior to the emergence of Social Democracy as a powerful force in the 1890s, and the decade is associated in particular with the phenomenon of *kruzhkovshchina* (the formation of circles, *kruzhki*) for the purpose of 'self-education' or theoretical preparation; but it could not be said that by the end of the decade the decline of Populism was complete, or interest in self-education exhausted, or the ascendancy of Marxism assured. All the same, I have for two reasons excluded from consideration events which took place from 1890 on. Firstly, it seemed important to sketch in some detail the events of the 1880s, which are so little known, and indeed a study much larger than the present one would be required if adequate coverage were also to be given to the in any case more familiar developments of the early 1890s, such as the most intensive activity of the Brusnev group in 1890–2, the rapid development of the labour movement in St Petersburg in those years, the proliferation of Marxist circles in the early 1890s, Lenin's stay in Samara from 1889 to 1893 and his study of Marxism there, the responses of revolutionaries to the famine of 1891–2, and the new enthusiasm for agitation in the factories at the beginning of the 1890s. Secondly, the developments to which I have devoted most attention – the decline of Populism in all its forms, the growth of interest in the urban workers, the increasing concern to build secure organisations and undertake careful preparation – are sufficiently clearly apparent by 1889–90 for us to be able legitimately to treat those years as a divide no less distinct than 1879, which marks the first crisis in revolutionary Populism, and 1881, the year of both the triumph and defeat of the Populists' terrorist wing.

Finally, it is a pleasant obligation to thank those whose help has enabled me to complete this study. I am grateful to the staff of the British Library, the School of Slavonic and East European Studies of London University, the London School of Economics, the Lenin Library and the Central State Archive of the October Revolution in Moscow, in all of which I have received much assistance, and to Professor Sedov of Moscow State University, who gave generously of his time in 1972–3 when I was a British Council Scholar in the Soviet Union working on the doctoral thesis out of which the present study has grown. Most of all I am indebted to the late Professor Leonard Schapiro, of the London School of Economics, who supervised that thesis and who on many occasions after its defence in 1974 gave invaluable encouragement and advice (though responsibility for whatever faults and errors the work may contain lies, of course, with me alone). Warmest thanks are due, too, to Mrs Anne Merriman and Mrs Barbara Case, who have at various times contrived with good humour and much skill to convert difficult manuscripts into typescripts of high quality, and to Keith Lloyd for his final meticulous perusal and improvement of that typescript. And last, but by no means least, I thank my wife for the patience and toleration she has mustered over the many years it has taken me to bring this study to completion.

NOTE ON DATES, TRANSLITERATION AND USE OF RUSSIAN TERMS

DATES

Unless otherwise indicated, dates given in the text are in the Old Style, that is according to the Julian calendar which was used in Russia until February 1918 and which in the nineteenth century was 12 days behind the Gregorian calendar used then, as now, in Western Europe. (New Style dates are indicated by the abbreviation NS.)

TRANSLITERATION

The method used in the text, notes and bibliography is that of *The Slavonic and East European Review*. In the text, however, the name Gertsen and the place name Kiyev are rendered in the commonly accepted forms Herzen and Kiev respectively and for the sake of simplicity no indication is given of soft signs in Russian words (hence Kharkov, Zemlevoltsy, etc., instead of Khar'kov, Zemlevol'tsy). In the notes and bibliography soft signs are everywhere transliterated.

USE OF RUSSIAN TERMS

The names of the following revolutionary parties have been left in their Russian forms:

Zemlya i Volya	Land and Liberty
Chornyy Peredel	Black Partition
Narodnaya Volya	People's Will

So, too, have the names of supporters of these parties, which are rendered in Russian with the suffix *-ets* (plural *-tsy*). Thus:

Zemlevolets	*pl.*	Zemlevoltsy
Chernoperedelets	*pl.*	Chernoperedeltsy
Narodovolets	*pl.*	Narodovoltsy

This suffix may also be attached to surnames in order to denote a person or persons associated with a particular individual; hence Nechayevets (*pl.* Nechayevtsy – member or members of Nechayev's group), Chaykovets (Chaykovtsy), Blagoyevets (Blagoyevtsy), etc.

Words denoting the body of thought associated with the parties listed above and indicated in Russian by the suffix *-chestvo* (equivalent to English -ism) are also left in their Russian form; hence Zemlevolchestvo (doctrines of Zemlya i Volya), Chernoperedelchestvo, Narodovolchestvo.

Titles of Russian journals have been left in their Russian form but (with the exception of the journals *Zemlya i volya*, *Chornyy peredel* and *Narodnaya volya*) are also translated when they first occur in the text. Titles of books in Russian, French and German are given in English whenever they occur in the text.

❦ GLOSSARY

artel'	workers' association
bashi-bazouks	Turkish irregular soldiers notorious for their brutality
bosyaki	drifting workers
buntari	Bakuninist agitators
druzhiny	armed bands
dvorniki	concierges
gimnaziya	grammar school
intelligént(y)	member(s) of the intelligentsia. The word implies commitment to some political, social or moral cause as well as intellectual interests and education
izba	peasant hut
kruzhki	circles
kruzhkovshchina	meticulous study in self-education circles
kulaks	wealthy peasants
meshchane	members of the lower middle class
mir	communal assembly
moujiks	peasants
odinochki	lone individuals
pervomartovtsy	those involved in the assassination of Alexander II on 1 March 1881 (*pervoye marta*)
poddyovka	man's long-waisted coat
raznochintsy	people of varied social origin, mainly from the lower middle classes or the lower clergy, who assumed a new prominence in the ranks of the Russian intelligentsia after the Crimean War
sermyaga	coarse, undyed cloth, or caftan of this material
zemlyachestvo	society of students from same town or district
zemstvo	elective district council

European Russia in the 1880s

CHAPTER ONE

✤ RUSSIAN REVOLUTIONARY POPULISM BEFORE 1 MARCH 1881

THE THEORY AND SPIRIT OF REVOLUTIONARY POPULISM

The history of the Russian revolutionaries of the 1880s is in a sense a history of their struggle with the heritage of the Populists of the 1870s as well as with the régime they despised, for while they remained for the most part deeply affected by the same beliefs as their predecessors and strove hard to preserve those beliefs, nevertheless they were forced increasingly to admit that the bitter campaign of the previous decade had brought the dream of socialist utopia no nearer to realisation and they had consequently to carry out modifications to revolutionary strategy and tactics in the light of their practical experience in a harsh reality. As for those among them who decided at an early stage to explore new channels, even they had first to reckon with the established Populist canon before they could effectively strike out on their own. It is important at the outset, therefore, briefly to re-examine the basic premisses of the Populism of the 1870s, for they provided a powerful source of inspiration for the activists of the 1880s and gave resilience to the revolutionary movement in that difficult decade, and yet at the same time their survival posed problems with which the activists had to grapple.[1]

Implicit in the Populist credo which had finally evolved around 1870 were perhaps as many as six fundamental and inter-related assumptions. Firstly, the Russian peasant commune was an egalitarian and democratic institution and would serve as a basis for socialism in Russia. Secondly, the Russian peasant was instinctively socialistic, or at least he had qualities which made him amenable to socialist collectivism. Thirdly, given these advantages, Russia could bypass the capitalist stage of economic development currently afflicting the advanced nations of Western Europe and thus pass directly from a semi-feudal condition to socialism. Fourthly, the educated man had a compelling moral responsibility to devote himself to the task of transforming his society in the name of the socialist ideal. Fifthly, the individual – or at least the individual who belonged to the ranks of the intelligentsia – possessed, as did his nation as a whole, the freedom and the capacity to exercise a significant degree of control over his own destiny. And, sixthly, the forthcoming revolution would not only promote the interests of the popular masses but would also give expression to their wishes and even be carried out mainly by them. The classical exponents of Populism thus defined were Lavrov, Mikhaylovsky and Bervi-Flerovsky, though Bakunin, broadly speaking, shared most of the assumptions enumerated above and even Tkachov, for all his isolation among the revolutionaries of the 1870s, subscribed to some of them.

It cannot be too strongly emphasised that by the 1880s these assumptions had acquired in revolutionary circles an apparently self-evident plausibility that made attempts to dislodge them seem hazardous, if not indeed sacrilegious. They had about them an incontestability that came partly of the fact that they had been incessantly repeated over a long period by thinkers of various persuasions (some of whom did not even have any connection with the revolutionary camp). The closely inter-related views held by the Populists on the peasant commune, the nature of the Russian peasant and the historical path being followed by their nation, for example, were not novel in the 1870s, but dated back to the 1840s and originally owed something to the politically conservative German aristocrat, Baron von Haxthausen, who had depicted the commune as a bulwark against the 'pauperism and proletarianism' of the modern West,[2] and to the Slavophiles, who fondly believed that the Russian masses still preserved the familial spirit and brotherly love supposedly characteristic of pre-Petrine Muscovy. In the same decade Bakunin, already embarked on his career of revolutionary agitator, had also begun to eulogise the masses, in whom, he claimed, the 'energy and future life of Russia' lay, and to predict that these masses would soon reveal themselves in all their 'virginal beauty' through a 'great' and 'salvatory' 'tempest'.[3] Herzen, in a series of essays written between 1847 and 1854 and aimed in the first instance at a public in Western Europe, had put forward a brand of 'Russian socialism' that was essentially similar to Bakunin's, though more moderate in tone. Anxious to demonstrate that 'Europe', such as it was, had 'completed its role' and that the time had now come for the Slavs to make their contribution to history, Herzen extolled the supposedly instinctive socialism which he thought found expression in the peasant commune, a miniature republic which had existed since time immemorial, democratically governing the internal affairs of the rural community and ensuring equitable use of the common resources. Russia's 'youth' as a nation, moreover, made it conceivable to Herzen that this inherent 'socialist element' might mature, for Russia had thus far remained immune from the capitalist development that would have undermined the commune. Russia might therefore arrive at socialism without passing through all the phases of Western European historical development; or at least she would pass through such phases only 'in the same way that the foetus passes through the inferior stages of zoological existence'.[4] Chernyshevsky, the main tribune of the young *raznochintsy*, took a more restrained view of the commune, which he saw as a feature of the existence of all peoples at a primitive stage of their development rather than as 'any mysterious characteristic' exclusive to the Slavs. And yet he, too, believed that the commune might serve as an 'antidote' to the Western ill of proletarian misery and in the late 1850s argued, as Herzen had done, that Russia might proceed directly from a semi-feudal condition to a form of socialism based on the existing peasant commune without undergoing a protracted intervening phase of capitalist development.[5] In the same period Dobrolyubov endorsed the belief that the peasant masses were the 'real Russian people' and described them as serious-minded, practical, endowed with a moral purity lacking in the idle aristocracy and fit for the role of free citizen after the abolition of serfdom.[6] Publicists such as Bervi-Flerovsky and Mikhaylovsky – whose writings exercised a very great influence on Populist revolutionaries[7] – therefore had numerous and venerated predecessors when at the end of the 1860s and the beginning of the 1870s they argued that the Russian people, in preserving the communal system of land-tenure, had shown 'incomparably more tact and common sense' than their Western European counterparts and that Russia might undertake an 'unprecedented experiment' and evolve on her own 'some combination of social forces more or less distinct from those which prevail in the West'.[8]

It was not only the wide currency given to these notions about the Russian people and the commune and Russia's historical path by Russian *thinkers*, however, that accounted for the vitality and tenacity of Populism and made it still credible to revolutionaries in the 1880s, for by the 1870s these notions were on one level merely expressions of a mood that extended

far beyond the confines of socialist publicism. Intellectual and artistic
endeavours in different fields were to an unusual degree interdependent in
Russia in the second half of the nineteenth century. The radical intelligentsia was small, concentrated in St Petersburg and sustained in a state of
excited anticipation by its sense of beleaguerment. The work of its representatives often had a strong utilitarian bias and reflected a shared determination
to introduce civilised values into a benighted society. It is therefore
understandable, though the point is often overlooked, that disciplinary
distinctions – the borders between publicism, philosophy, sociology and
political economy, historical and ethnographic scholarship, and imaginative literature – were more than usually blurred, and even painting and
music reflected current social and political preoccupations. The osmosis of
ideas on the common people between publicism and imaginative literature,
for instance, proceeded steadily from the late 1850s on. There emerged a
substantial school of young writers – Golitsynsky, N. I. Uspensky, Levitov,
V. A. Sleptsov, Reshetnikov, Nefyodov, Naumov, Zasodimsky and others
– who, together with the poet Nekrasov, described conditions in the
countryside and on the factory floor in unembellished and often heart-
rending terms. Painters such as Perov, Repin, Myasoyedov and Kramskoy
also began to treat the masses in their work with compassion and respect,
pointing up the continuing social inequality of post-reform Russia or
hinting at the supposed strength of the common man. Even some
composers (notably Musorgsky) attempted, under the guidance of the critic
Stasov, to express the elusive spirit of the people, freely introducing folk
songs and motifs into their works and treating the peasant mass as a mighty
historical force. There was great interest in the ethnographer Maksimov's
sketches of peasant life and in Mordovtsev's surveys of peasant rebellions in
Russian history. Finally, numerous writers, following the example of
Shchapov, made studies of the schism in the Russian Church and of the
resultant communities of Old Believers, whose sobriety, industriousness
and civic spirit seemed to give grounds for believing that the Russian
people were capable of governing themselves democratically if freed from
the interference of the state.[9] It would be wrong, of course, to see all these
writers and artists as precursors of the Populist revolutionary movement in
any strict theoretical sense. But their images, particularly those of
Nekrasov,[10] did imprint themselves indelibly on the minds of subsequent
revolutionaries, for whom their works for long remained almost textbooks
on the life of the masses. More important, they evoked sympathy for the
masses and fostered the impression that the key to Russia's destiny was to be

found there, among the common people. In their way, then, artists, ethnographers and historians, no less than the socialist thinkers and publicists, helped first to generate the revolutionary movement in its Populist phase and then to sustain it.

There is a further factor which helps to explain both the emergence of Populism as a revolutionary doctrine at a fairly precise date, in the late 1860s and early 1870s, and its resilience even after practical experience would have seemed to militate against a continuing defence of Populist views on the peasantry and the commune, namely fear of the development of capitalism in Russia. It is no coincidence that the assertion by Bervi, Mikhaylovsky and other publicists of the possibility of an autochthonous historical development for Russia was accompanied by condemnations of the capitalist mode of production which operated in the West. Admittedly, deep-seated hostility to capitalism had long since been widespread in Russia, even among conservative thinkers, who often harboured the aristocrat's disdain for the bourgeois or the country squire's distaste for the industrial townscape. But among the socialist intelligentsia of the 1860s and 1870s tirades against the capitalist West, and against England in particular, became commonplace and acquired a new vehemence. These condemnations, moreover, derived vigour and authority from the knowledge which Russian publicists were now beginning to gain of the study made of Western capitalist society by Marx and Engels. The title chosen by Bervi for his major work, *The Condition of the Working Class in Russia* (1869), suggested an indebtedness to Engels' work on the English proletariat. A young political economist, Ziber, wrote a scholarly dissertation on the theories of Ricardo which relied on Marx's analysis and was discussed by Mikhaylovsky, who himself reviewed Marx's *Capital* in 1872.[11] And, more clearly than any other work, the first Russian translation of the first volume of *Capital*, begun by Lopatin, completed by Danielson and published in 1872, allowed Russians to glimpse the fate that might befall their own country if capitalism established itself there. The matter had great topicality for them, too, for economic processes threatening the survival of the commune were becoming more apparent in the Russian countryside, where the richer peasant, appearing to offer a helping hand to the needy, was in fact subjecting them to a new, economic form of dependence and voraciously accumulating property and capital. Russia was in the condition of an embryo, it seemed; indeed the whole country, one 'huge embryo' of the modern industrialised capitalist West, was pregnant with capitalism, as the publicist Yeliseyev put it, borrowing an image from Marx.[12] Thus

Populism – an assertion of Russia's independence from Western European historical development – began to flourish at precisely the moment when Russians became more fully acquainted than ever before with the operation and effects of Western European capitalism and when, too, they detected clear signs that the seeds of a similar order were also sprouting in Russian soil. And the hope that Russia might still avoid capitalism – a hope deftly translated by publicists into an assumption that such avoidance was indeed historically possible – was not abandoned as the feared economic and social changes proceeded. On the contrary, Russian radical publicists and their revolutionary disciples clung even more tenaciously to it – and to the related faith in the Russian peasant – as the only guarantee of socialism in Russia in their time.

If we turn now to those premises of Populism which concern not so much the peasant as the revolutionary intelligentsia – that is to say the moral responsibility of the *intelligént* and his freedom of action – then we again find that crucial statements were made at the end of the 1860s, but that the power and authority of these statements were greatly increased by their compatibility with the mood of the times and with a longer-established and rich cultural tradition.

It was important to the theoreticians of classical Populism to free ethical and sociological speculation from the jurisdiction of the supposedly infallible scientific method invoked by the radicals of the early 1860s, especially Chernyshevsky. Those radicals, by their attempt to explain man's behaviour as a product of environment or physiological factors over which he had no control, had tended, albeit unintentionally, to deprive man of the freedom to change his society, and consequently of the moral responsibility to do so. Such determinism, however, was deeply disturbing to thinkers of a slightly later period, who were alarmed by the advance of capitalism and impatient to transfrom society in accordance with their own ideals. They wished to assert that man did have the freedom to make moral choices and to change his society; indeed, they demanded that he do so. Thus Mikhaylovsky, in his long essay 'What is Progress' (1869), argued that the objective point of view obligatory in the natural sciences was 'quite unsuitable' in sociology, in which man was himself the subject of study as well as the student. Perhaps the sociologist could only arrive at the truth, Mikhaylovsky suggested, if he put himself in the position of the sentient beings he was examining, if he tried to think their thoughts, suffer their sufferings and shed their tears. At any rate he could not help but make moral judgements. While not wishing altogether to abolish the objective method,

Mikhaylovsky did therefore demand that the subjective method serve as a 'higher control'.[13] Even more important for the Populists than Mikhaylovsky's essay were Lavrov's *Historical Letters* (published in serial form in 1868–9 and in a separate edition in 1870), which acquired, to judge by the accounts of memoirists of the period, an almost evangelical significance in revolutionary circles.[14] Having attempted, in the same spirit as Mikhaylovsky, to establish that history is a field of human enquiry at least as important as the natural sciences and that a subjective method, unacceptable in the latter, is inevitable and legitimate in it, Lavrov proceeds in his fourth 'letter', entitled the 'price of progress', to frame a vigorous appeal to the intelligentsia to pursue the ideal of social justice. An enormous price had been paid by the toiling majority of mankind, Lavrov argued, for the conditions which had made possible the development of the privileged 'critically thinking minority' who cherished that ideal. A member of the educated minority might absolve himself from a share of the blame for the sufferings of the masses only if he began at once to repay his debt to those masses by attempting to translate his ideals into practice. No excuses for inaction, no self-doubt, no scholarly work divorced from society's real and immediate needs, no fears about the possible futility of heroic deeds by solitary individuals could relieve the *intelligént* of this obligation.[15]

These pleas for social concern and a resolute crusade on behalf of the masses had an intrinsic power, to be sure; but they could hardly have enjoyed such widespread popularity and lasting influence had they, too, not given expression, in sociological terms, to a mood that had broader cultural sources. They echoed the sentiments of literary heroes with whom Populist revolutionaries, as we know from their own testimony, were no less familiar. The conception offered by Mikhaylovsky, Lavrov (and Bervi, too) of the *intelligént* moved by conscience to dedicate himself to a social cause corresponded to the portrait of the 'positive hero' (or heroine) of imaginative literature, who from the beginning of the 1860s had supplanted the ineffectual 'superfluous man' so prominent in the fiction of the Nicolaevan period. This 'positive hero' invariably embodied some permutation of three qualities which were to be deemed indispensable to the revolutionary: an ability to rise above the philistinism of his environment; a morality which was altruistic, at least in practice if not in theory;[16] and the practicality and resoluteness needed to translate convictions into action.[17] The most celebrated early incarnations of the 'positive hero' or 'heroine' are Turgenev's Insarov and Bazarov, in *On the Eve* (1860) and *Fathers and Children* (1862) respectively, and the 'new people', Lopukhov, Kirsanov,

Vera Pavlovna and Rakhmetov, in Chernyshevsky's novel *What is to be done?* (1863). The type also finds embodiment in a sense in Sokolov's popular work *Renegades*, first published in 1866 and republished in 1872, in which the stoics, early Christians, sectarians, utopians and socialists are all presented as beings of superior moral calibre who chose to live outside the imperfect societies into which they happened to have been born. And he, or she, reappears, often as a pilgrim to, or propagandist among, the people, in a further spate of works (for instance, Bazhin's *History of an Association* (1869), Mordovtsev's *Signs of the Times* (1869), Omulevsky's *Step by Step* (1870), and Kushchevsky's *Nikolay Negorev, or a Successful Russian* (1871)) that were produced in precisely those years when interest in the peasantry was also reaching a new height. Nor was inspiration for prospective revolutionaries to be found exclusively in prose. It could be drawn, too, from the poetry of Nekrasov, who exhorted his readers to contemplate chivalrous exploit and seemed to invite heroic self-sacrifice. Even the painter Kramskoy, in his canvas *Christ in the Wilderness* (1872), captured the pervasive sense of yearning for suffering in some noble cause.

Thus the revolutionary Populism which took shape in the period 1868–72 was much more than a set of bare sociological, economic and philosophical propositions and the strategic and tactical deductions that might be made from them. It was made up not only (perhaps not so much) of certain specific ideas for which objective validity might be claimed, but also of a strong emotional component and an expansive quixotic spirit. Its objective appears in retrospect to have been not merely a revolution in the material condition of the impoverished Russian peasant, for whom the Populists expressed an unconditional love and compassion, but also a revolution in the moral condition of the relatively affluent *intelligént*, with his almost religious thirst for some grand redemptive feat, *podvig*, through which he might sacrifice himself for the larger good. Populism was, then, a consummate expression of fears and hopes, guilt and aspirations that ran deep in the Russian intelligentsia, and as such it had an intensity and a vitality that sustained it long after its theoretical premisses had first been called in question.

REVOLUTIONARY STRATEGIES: LAVROV, BAKUNIN AND TKACHOV

The Populist credo that has been outlined gave rise in the early 1870s to certain strategies which underpinned the activity of revolutionaries in that decade, and since these strategies, taken in conjunction with the revolution-aries' practical experience, continued to serve as the main starting-point for discussion in revolutionary organisations throughout the 1880s as well, they, too, need to be briefly examined here. By far the most influential strategies were those of Lavrov and Bakunin, but it is important also to take account of the views of Tkachov, for we shall have to consider in due course the extent to which some of his challenging assumptions affected the thinking of revolutionaries after 1879.

Like many of his contemporaries Lavrov believed that it might soon become impossible to implement socialism in Russia in the foreseeable future if capitalism were allowed to develop freely there. Under a limited constitutional monarchy the Russian bourgeoisie, which at present had no traditions or unity, would become strong, while the masses would be further debilitated by 'all the vampires of the new civilised Russian capitalism' which sucked their blood.[18] The revolutionary was therefore urged to turn his attention immediately to the Russian countryside – for it was 'not from the towns but from the villages' that the Russian revolution would come[19] – and to inculcate in the peasant the socialist consciousness that would enable him to transform Russian society before the march of capitalism and its attendant class struggle had become irresistible. This the revolutionary would do by means of propaganda, not agitation. That was to say he would promote an understanding of socialism by exploring present conditions in their broadest perspective rather than by dwelling on specific or local grievances. He would appeal to the few rather than the many, since only the actions of a minority were governed by the rational precepts which it was the purpose of the propagandist to expound.[20] Having won staunch adherents among the masses in this way, the revolutionary would retire into the background (though he would of course still share the fortunes of the masses in the ensuing struggle),[21] for the revolution itself – and this was a point of cardinal importance to Lavrov – would have to be carried out from below, by its prospective beneficiaries, the masses themselves. Russian society should be reconstructed, Lavrov insisted, 'not only with the people's welfare *in view*, not only *for* the people, but also *through the agency* of the people'.[22] Socialist ideals should not be imposed on the masses from above by a small minority claiming to represent the people's interests. Revolutionaries should not plan to take the reins of central government themselves and to issue decrees, attempting to mould a better society as a potter shapes soft clay. In all instances where 'consciousness' had been imposed on the masses by a minority alien to them a new breed of exploiters had come to power over the bodies of those who had built the barricades.[23] It was consistent with this distaste for authoritarian socialism that Lavrov should argue for the gradual elimination of the state (although he did concede in his book, *The State Element in the Future Society*, a weighty utopian treatise published in 1876, that the state might for some time remain a necessary evil).[24] The revolution that Lavrov envisaged was, therefore, in the terminology of the time, an 'economic' rather than a 'political' one. Lavrov was concerned primarily to promote a new social structure by transferring ownership of the means of production from the privileged minority to the masses rather than by handing over the administrative apparatus to a new government. Like early Western European socialists, such as Fourier and Robert Owen, he was sceptical of the value of political machinations and, like many of his own compatriots, such as Kropotkin and Tolstoy, was inclined also to view political power as a corruptive influence on those who exercised it.

Both the Populist's traditional faith in the Russian peasant and his chivalrous morality were implicit in Lavrov's revolutionary strategy. Advocacy of revolution from below rested after all on the assumption that there could be found in the ranks of the masses in general administrators quite as able as those from the educated class[25] and that the Russian masses in particular had 'strength', 'energy' and 'freshness', as their uprisings and the withdrawal of the sectarians among them into communities of their own seemed to demonstrate. Lavrov affirmed, too, that the practice of communal land-tenure was the 'special ground' on which socialism might be built in Russia, and that the *mir* might become the 'basic political element' of the future society.[26] And in an article of 1875, published in a revolutionary journal, he urged on the revolutionary the same moral purity and integrity with which the 'positive hero' of imaginative literature and the 'critically thinking' *intelligént* of the *Historical Letters* had been endowed. 'Social-revolutionary' morality, he argued here, demanded the renunciation of self-indulgent pleasure, the strict limitation of one's material needs, and the cultivation of the capacity to derive enjoyment from contributing to the common well-being.[27] Nor were these moral considerations without their practical implications for revolutionary tactics. The revolutionary was warned not to jeopardise the 'moral purity of the socialist struggle'. He did not have the right in his struggle for social justice to stain his banner with a single drop of blood needlessly shed or to attempt to hasten the revolution with dishonest propaganda,[28] for justice and truth could not be promoted by gratuitous violence or deception, an end could not be attained by the use of means that were incompatible with it. Indeed, even Lavrov's strategy, as well as the tactics he commended, were in the final analysis dictated by such moral considerations. Revolution had to be implemented from below because authoritarian government and compulsion could not inaugurate an era of freedom.[29] Thus Lavrov's approach to revolutionary activity – as it was outlined in the journal *Vperyod! (Forward!)*, which he and a number of young supporters produced in emigration between 1873 and 1877 – accorded well with the general mood of the radical youth in Russia at that time, though his advice that the prospective propagandist prepare himself for work among the masses by painstakingly acquiring almost encyclopaedic knowledge[30] entailed a gradualism that was bound to be unattractive to impatient activists.

Those who craved a more robust approach to revolutionary activity than that commended by Lavrov tended to turn instead to Bakunin, who in the last years of his life had a greater impact than ever before on the youth in Russia (though he, too, like Lavrov, remained in emigration until his death). Bakunin's violent rebelliousness, his glorification of revolt – and indeed his personal example as a revolutionary of international renown – had no less inspirational value than Lavrov's appeals to conscience at a time when the revolutionary tide in Russia was gaining its early momentum. His view of man, as it has been aptly described, as 'in some sense, self-creating, as choosing to be what he is'[31] also accorded well with the current faith in the ability of the *intelligént* to mould his own character and help to reshape his nation's destiny. Most importantly, his anarchism, his view of the state in all its forms as 'the likeness of a vast slaughterhouse or an enormous cemetery' where 'all the best aspirations, all the living forces of a country' were sacrificed and interred,[32] was congenial to socialists who believed that the revolution should be 'social' and 'economic' rather than 'political'.

Since he considered revolutionary dictatorship to represent only a continuation of the former 'rule over the majority by a minority in the name of the supposed stupidity of the former and the supposed intelligence of the latter',[33] Bakunin agreed with Lavrov that revolutionaries should not seek to change society from above but should induce the people to establish or promote their own forms of free association from below.[34] Like Lavrov again, he urged the intelligentsia to move closer to the masses, indeed he, too, suggested that it was in merging with the masses and living for them that the destiny of the intelligentsia now seemed to lie. The object of Bakunin's going to the people, however, was to be very different from that of Lavrov, for the masses, in Bakunin's conception, were not a blank sheet of paper on which the *intelligént* might inscribe his own favourite thoughts. On the contrary, the people had untainted ideals of their own. Free of the 'religious, political, juridical and social prejudices' ingrained in the West and embodied in its law, the Russian common people would create 'another civilisation', a 'new faith and a new law, and a new life'. The task of the intelligentsia, therefore, would merely be to help the people to express their will, to realise the ideals they already nurtured but of which they were perhaps not yet fully aware.[35]

This broad strategy found its definitive expression in Bakunin's tract *Statism and Anarchy*, or rather in an essay printed together with it in 1873 under the title 'Appendix A', which was very widely circulated among Russian revolutionaries of the 1870s – the police found it in the course of their searches in almost every centre of revolutionary activity[36] – and made a profound impression on that generation of activists. The intelligentsia, Bakunin argued in 'Appendix A', was not in a position to teach the masses anything of use or to predict how they would and should live on the morrow of the revolution. No one from the ranks of the intelligentsia could formulate and present to the people that prerequisite for successful revolution, an ideal which would give the uprising sense and purpose. It was therefore futile to open 'sociological departments in the countryside'. The peasant would not understand the propagandists and in any case the government would not allow the propagandists to operate. And yet conditions were not unpropitious for revolution. The common people lived in poverty and servitude. And, most importantly, they did themselves possess an ideal on which social revolution could be based. (Indeed, if they had not possessed such an ideal, Bakunin wrote with a confidence that would have been impossible a decade later, then one would have had to give up any hope of revolution in Russia.) This ideal comprised three elements: firstly, the assumption universal among the masses that the land belonged to those who worked it; secondly, the belief that the right to use the land rested not with the individual but with the whole commune, which divided the land periodically among its members; and, thirdly, a 'quasi-absolute autonomy, communal self-government, and, as a result of that, the downright hostile attitude of the commune to the state'. Unfortunately other factors at present distorted this threefold ideal and complicated and delayed its implementation, namely the 'patriarchal quality' of peasant life, the 'engulfment' of the individual by the *mir*, and popular faith in the Tsar. Revolutionaries who went to the people should attempt to break down these obstacles to the development of socialism in the countryside rather than to communicate any ideal formulated by the intelligentsia. They should also, of course, foment the hostility which Bakunin supposed the masses to harbour towards the state, cultivating a sense of strength and solidarity among the scattered rural communities. The people, then, did need assistance from the intelligentsia, but only in order that they might fulfil their own ideals in the aftermath of a general peasant revolt.[37] That they would prove able to accomplish this task Bakunin did not doubt, for he seemed to ascribe to them his own innate rebelliousness. They possessed, in addition to their instinctive socialism, a proclivity to brigandage, which Bakunin idealised, and a tendency violently to sweep away authority in uprisings of the sort led by Stenka Razin and Pugachov, by whom Bakunin had long been fascinated.[38]

The third major strategist of the 1870s, Tkachov, had an influence that was only negligible in that decade,[39] but his ideas were to take on a new significance once the strategies of Lavrov and Bakunin had been tested. Despite the strong deterministic strand in his thought Tkachov, too, posited considerable freedom of action for the revolutionary. He tended to belittle the importance of individuals in the making of history, firstly by asserting, like Marx, that man and his culture were shaped by environment and in particular by economic conditions and, secondly, by denying that ideas in themselves had much effect on historical development.[40] And yet at the same time he doubted whether history was governed by laws as rigid as those of the natural sciences, acknowledged in man a critical faculty which enhanced his capacity to effect social change, and conceded that for a minute minority there do exist 'passions of a higher order, passions aroused by moral ideals', which might prompt men to accomplish 'great deeds'.[41] These deterministic and voluntarist tendencies coexisted uneasily in an important review, published in 1868, of a book dealing with peasant movements in sixteenth-century Germany. Economic 'principles' governed social orders and it was not possible to disrupt their orderly logical development, Tkachov argued here in his deterministic vein; consequently, anyone trying to accomplish far-reaching social change by quickening or slowing the operation of that principle was doomed to failure. Quite different, though, was the case of one who sought entirely to alter the governing principle of his society, to replace it with a new one, to accomplish, as Tkachov put it, a 'historical leap' from one social order to another. That ambition, like those of the leaders of the German peasant revolt, was not in the least utopian.[42]

Like the Populists, again, Tkachov argued that conditions in the 1870s were exceptionally propitious for Russian revolutionaries but would rapidly become less so. The Russian state, unlike its Western counterparts, did not represent the interests of any social class and had no foundations or support in the social structure, he contended in an 'open letter' to Engels in 1871; it merely hung 'in the air'. Thus, although it gave an impression of might at a distance, the state was so weak, Tkachov believed, that it could easily be overthrown.[43] However, capitalism was developing in the wake of the emancipation of the serfs, and as a powerful, conservative class of peasant landowners and farmers and a commercial and entrepreneurial bourgeoise took shape and gathered strength, so the chances of a violent revolution would become increasingly 'problematical'. Revolutionaries could therefore not afford to wait. '*Now* or not at all quickly, perhaps *never*!' Tkachov declared (though the slogan was hardly incisive!).[44] The time had come to call the revolutionary intelligentsia to action, and both the title and the programme of the journal set up by Tkachov in Geneva, *Nabat* (*The Tocsin*), twenty numbers of which came out between 1875 and 1881, emphasised the urgency.

What distinguished Tkachov so sharply from the vast majority of his contemporaries in the revolutionary camp, however, was his wholly unflattering view of the Russian peasantry and his formulation of the role of the intelligentsia in the making of the revolution. Since the psychological condition of a society's members was a product of their economic position and environment, the oppressed majority in Russia, Tkachov stated in an early article *à propos* of Reshetnikov's stories, was 'coarse, savage and brutal' and bound to remain so until it ceased to be poor.[45] Admittedly, dissatisfaction with the prevailing order made the masses 'always *ready* for revolution'; indeed, an 'oppressed, exploited people, deprived of all human rights' was and 'always must be revolutionary'. Age-old slavery and oppression had taught them patience and silent obedience. Their energy had atrophied. Even the most outrageous wrongs could not shake them out of the stoical passivity with which they had encased themselves like a snail within its shell.[46] Thus, if the people were left to themselves, Tkachov stated unequivocally, they would never effect a social revolution. The Russian *intelligént* would be confronted with the same peasant 'with his petrified principles, with his immovable conservatism'. There was therefore no reason for him to do obeisance to the people, and senseless phrases about the '*popular genius*' should be expunged forthwith from the revolutionary lexicon.[47]

Tkachov's relatively unflattering view of the Russian peasant masses dictated a revolutionary strategy diametrically opposed to those put forward by Lavrov and Bakunin. In the first place, it was clear that if the prevailing economic conditions dulled the peasant mind and if the masses were incapable of seizing the initiative, either in the present or when their best interests were carefully explained to them in the future, then propaganda of the type advocated by Lavrov was merely wasteful of time and resources.[48] In the second place, if the peasants had no ideals of their own on which a socialist order might be based, then even the elemental revolt favoured by Bakunin would not be sufficient to produce a genuine and stable socialist society. In any case, since they were so passive some 'external push', some 'unexpected collision', would be needed to force them out of their rut.[49] Revolution could not be anticipated, therefore, from below; on the contrary, it would have to be carried out from above, by the intelligentsia, or rather by that small section of it which understood the true nature of the masses. Certainly the minority should not neglect to kindle the smouldering discontent constantly present among the masses; but it should also be sure to give any popular rising the form and direction which the minority itself considered desirable. Moreover, the minority, with its capacity to change the course of history, would itself decide when the moment was propitious. Nor could the untutored masses be left to themselves to reorder society even on the morrow of the initial turmoil. The intellectual and moral authority of the intelligentsia would not be exerted, Tkachov argued unashamedly in the programme of *Nabat*, unless the intelligentsia itself wielded political power. A true revolution, therefore, could only take place in the event of the seizure of state power by the revolutionary minority. The conservative state would have to be transformed into a revolutionary one. The minority, having secured power, would re-educate the majority and implement a series of economic, political and legal reforms from above.[50]

In preparation for the *coup d'état* the minority should immediately set about organising their own forces rather than squander time and resources on activity among the masses. They would have to bring to their ranks a degree of discipline and organisation shunned by the freedom-loving majority of the revolutionaries of the early 1870s. Success would be ensured only by centralised 'tight, solid, strictly disciplined organisation', as decisive and single-minded as a military force.[51] Tkachov criticises contemporaries who squeamishly eschewed these organisational principles and pays tribute to the conspiratorial organisations founded in the 1860s by Ishutin and Nechayev. He also commends the utilitarian morality associated with these groups.[52] His revolutionary minority, the 'people of the future' convinced of the 'rectitude and sanctity' of their cause, would not be fastidious in their choice of methods,[53] but, like Machiavelli, would approve that which brought nearer their goal and deprecate that which hindered its attainment.[54] This moral relativism, however, together with Tkachov's dismissal of the peasantry as a more or less brutish mass, his advocacy of revolution from above (that is to say, the imposition of the will of the minority on the majority), his demand that the revolutionary combat the state and himself wield political power, and, lastly, his acceptance of the need for a coercive spirit within the revolutionary organisation, inspired deep hostility to 'Jacobinism' or 'Blanquism' (as Tkachov's strategy was designated) among the great majority of the revolutionaries of the 1870s. Indeed, so antithetical was 'Jacobinism' to the Populist outlook that it is tempting to view a desire to negate it as a final formative influence on Populism.

REVOLUTIONARY ORGANISATIONS AND ACTIVITY IN THE 1870s

The socialist circles which arose in Russia at the beginning of the 1870s for the most part gave quite faithful expression to the principles advanced and the attitudes reflected in the publicism of the period and in the strategies of Lavrov and Bakunin. For example, the so-called Chaykovtsy – members of a circle which sprang up among the students of St Petersburg and which had connections with circles of similar complexion in Moscow, Kiev, Odessa and Kherson – deplored Nechayevan authoritarianism and shunned hierarchies and strict discipline, preferring instead a loose, informal organisation bound together only by the mutual respect and trust of its members.[55] Such organisational laxity was characteristic of a period in which the socialist circle tended to be seen not so much as a clandestine political society but rather as a 'family of men and women . . . closely united by their common object', or a '*knightly order*' charged with the mission of working a social miracle.[56] For these revolutionaries it seemed more important to renounce bourgeois values than to protest against the political order or fight for political freedoms, the usefulness of which, in Russian conditions, the Chaykovtsy seriously doubted.[57]

Also entirely in keeping with the mood of the early 1870s was the enthusiasm of the Chaykovtsy for propaganda among the workers in St Petersburg, which began in earnest in 1871 and continued relatively unimpeded by the police – perhaps because, being novel, it was not at first detected by them – until arrests began to decimate the society in 1873.[58] No longer did it seem premature to attempt to stir the masses, as Kropotkin argued in a lengthy programmatic document for the Chaykovtsy, for it was felt that there were 'dissatisfied elements' among the people, that their respect for the Tsar was decreasing and that they were ready to revolt.[59] Indeed, revolutionaries began to harbour the most optimistic expectations and some militant *buntari*, as the Bakuninist agitators were known, anticipated revolution in as little as three to five years.[60] By the spring of 1874 the urge to forge at last a close relationship with the masses had become irresistible and the scattered attempts at propaganda in factory and countryside gave way to the historic 'going to the people'. Some 2,000 young men and women now descended on factories and villages through-out European Russia, taking jobs as teachers, clerks, doctors or midwives, carpenters, joiners, dyers, cobblers, masons or farm labourers, and trying to acquaint peasants and workers with socialist teachings, or haranguing them on their want of land and the burden of taxation, or simply engaging them in conversation or teaching them revolutionary songs. In the course of this frenzied activity distinctions between the supporters of Lavrov and Bakunin were lost; 'agitators' differed from 'propagandists' perhaps only in that they went about their work 'with more fervour and less circumspec tion'.[61] All displayed a similar zeal, which assumed almost religious proportions. Participants compared themselves to the first Christians, who had renounced the world in which they lived and dedicated themselves to struggle with evil.[62]

It is most important when tracing the subsequent course of the revolutionary movement in Russia to bear in mind the full extent of the failure of this 'going to the people', which by the autumn of 1874 had petered out with the arrest of some 1,600 persons, and to appreciate the reasons for that failure. Not only had a large number of the movement's freshest young forces been lost; still more important, perhaps, was the fact that the propagandists and agitators had failed to create unrest even on a local scale. To some degree, of course, the disorganised nature of the 'going to the people' accounts for the *débâcle*. It was as if the zealous spirit which gave the movement its intensity also precluded a realism and practicality which might have made it more successful. The authorities, it is true, saw the most energetic individuals, such as Kovalik, Rogachov and Voynaralsky, as ringleaders in a conspiracy; but in fact the movement represented a spontaneous awakening of conscience and lacked central

direction, consisting merely of innumerable individual initiatives. Moreover, in their haste to spread their message, the propagandists in general
spent very little time in any one locality, with the result that few strongholds
were established which would serve as bases for future activity. Revolutionaries 'flitted across Rus'', wrote one participant in a letter produced at the
trial of the propagandists, but 'nowhere did they settle'.[63]

A far more disturbing cause of failure than the lack of organisation in
revolutionary ranks, however, was the disappointing response of the
people themselves. Admittedly, some propagandists claimed that they had
found sympathisers among the peasantry, or at least that they had been
heard willingly by an unaffected audience.[64] Furthermore, criticism of the
landowners, the *kulaks*, local officials and the priesthood does seem to have
been well received.[65] But from all accounts of the pilgrimage to the people in
1874 it is clear that there were formidable obstacles confronting revolutionaries in the countryside. The belief persisted among the peasantry, for
example, that the Tsar had the interests of the people at heart and, generally
speaking, criticism of the monarch did not find approval. It was widely
rumoured that the Tsar himself would order the partition of the land among
all, regardless of their social position.[66] The propagandists complained, too,
that the peasant's mind was filled with prejudice and superstition and that
religious beliefs still exercised a powerful influence on him. Sometimes the
peasants blamed themselves for their misfortunes. They had to endure
'hardship, offence and foul treatment', one propagandist was told, because
they themselves were 'drunkards to a man' or had 'forgotten God'.[67] Even
among the sectarians, whom many revolutionaries regarded as particularly
promising material for their propaganda, fatalistic submissiveness often
produced complete indifference to social and political issues.[68] The poor
benighted people lived in ignorance, were indifferent to the well-being of
the *mir* – the affairs of which were surrendered to a small group of *kulaks*
and their assistants – and seemed more susceptible to rumour than to
reason.[69] Women in the peasant community appear to have made the least
favourable impression: they revealed the most servile and conservative
attitudes and some of their remarks drove even the patient propagandists of
1874 to exasperation.[70] Sometimes the people were inattentive: conversa-
tions did not 'really sink in' or what was said went 'in one ear and out of the
other'.[71] The propagandists' attempts to make themselves acceptable to
peasant audiences proved to have been ill-founded. There was reason to
suppose that literacy and the manner of the educated class inspired respect
rather than suspicion, as the propagandists had anticipated. Indeed, the

unkempt appearance which the radical youth had carefully created, their worn and tattered clothing and plebeian hair-styles, tended to debar them from entry to the *izba* rather than to earn them the peasants' trust.[72] And on occasion the propagandists found the peasants downright hostile and were betrayed by them to the police.[73]

The lesson of 1874 was not quickly absorbed, however, for the premisses on which Populism rested were too deeply entrenched to be undermined by one disaster, whatever its magnitude. Thus peasant revolt remained the objective for the 'Pan-Russian Social-Revolutionary Organisation', known more informally as the 'Muscovites', a group made up of an improbable combination of young Russian noblewomen, Georgian socialists and Russian workers, who hoped, like the Chaykovtsy, to reach the peasantry through the urban workers and who established circles in Moscow, with connections in other towns of the industrial heartland, in 1875–6. The 'Muscovites' also reaffirmed hostility to the Jacobin ambition to impose socialism on the people by force, and in their rules expressed both the customary antipathy to centralist organisational principles and the common belief in the paramountcy of 'moral duty' as the binding force in a revolutionary group.[74]

Even the organisation Zemlya i Volya (Land and Liberty), the nucleus of which emerged in St Petersburg towards the end of 1876 and which in practice helped to give the movement a new direction, remained faithful in theory to the traditions of Populism in its classical period.[75] The second sentence of the first draft of the organisation's programme, for example, reiterated two fundamental Bakuninist principles: firstly, the organisation had to give expression to the ideals of the people themselves; and, secondly, the Russian people were socialist in character.[76] Other shibboleths were repeated, too. Whereas in the West the factory question was paramount, in Russia revolution would emanate from the countryside, and it was therefore the leaders of the great peasant rebellions who should be emulated.[77] Again, capitalism was not an inevitable stage on Russia's historical path and might indeed be bypassed, for history was not a 'uniform mechanical process'; even Marx, Plekhanov wrote, had not wished to put mankind on the 'Procrustean bed of "general laws"'.[78] Most importantly, faith in the revolutionary potential of the peasant was undiminished. Reference was made to the mass of 'large- and small-scale movements' and to the religious sects and gangs of brigands, groups which reflected the continuing determination of the people to protest against the existing order.[79] Everywhere there was 'combustible material', and in the event of local disturbances the peasantry always seemed to produce its own leaders. It could be inferred, therefore, that the failure of the 'going to the people' in 1874 was due not to the unrevolutionary nature of the masses but to the inability of the revolutionaries to speak a language comprehensible to the peasant. Since the peasant masses were not 'colourless' and 'inert' and could not be pushed in directions chosen by the intelligentsia, propagandists had been wrong to assume that they should inculcate their own ideal upon them.[80] Thus the strategy commended by Lavrov gave way to that advocated by Bakunin, and the change was associated with a shift from supposedly European methods to apparently Russian ones. Revolutionaries had not gone far enough when in 1874 they had abandoned 'German' clothes for the peasant *sermyaga* in the hope of winning acceptance among the people. They should now cast off, too, the foreign form with which their socialism was invested.[81]

In accordance with all these assumptions, the Zemlevoltsy again went dutifully to the people in the spring of 1878, although they did now attempt to establish settlements in the countryside instead of flitting from one locality to another. They also concentrated their efforts to a greater extent on the Volga region, which they identified as both the cradle of the great peasant rebellions of the past and the principal modern refuge of those who sought a life free from governmental persecution for their heterodox religious beliefs.[82] All the same, only in one case did Bakuninist agitators score a significant success in the second half of the 1870s. In 1877, at Chigirin in the Ukraine, Stefanovich, Deych and others, mindful of the widespread loyalty of the peasants to the Tsar, set about preparing a peasant force for an armed uprising by the stratagem of distributing false manifestos, purporting to come from the Tsar, in which the peasants were urged to revolt against the landowners; hundreds had joined the agitators' *druzhiny* before a drunken peasant exposed the conspiracy.[83] Elsewhere, though, the peasant remained impassive and in general the *buntari*, for all their anti-intellectualism and their insistence on 'propaganda by deed' and 'Russian' methods in preference to 'propaganda by word' and 'Western European' methods, had no more appeal to the peasants than their predecessors.

While uttering theoretical commonplaces about the peasantry, however, the Zemlevoltsy did also make organisational innovations which took proper account of the lack of political freedom in Russia. The principles of tight organisation and secrecy, so repugnant to earlier groups, began to win acceptance, largely as a result of the efforts of Oboleshev and, in particular,

Aleksandr Mikhaylov, who by his own admission had been impressed by the views on organisation advanced by a group of Jacobins whom he had encountered in Kiev.[84] Thus Zemlya i Volya evolved in the course of 1877 into a centralised and disciplined secret society. The new organisational principles were enshrined in a set of rules definitively formulated in 1878. Among the 'basic principles' enumerated in these rules were some, it is true, which had long been accepted by Russian revolutionaries, such as the absence of private property among a group's members. But the insistence that the minority be subordinated to the majority, that the individual member yield to the wishes of the circle as a whole, would have found no favour with the immediate predecessors of the Zemlevoltsy, nor, of course, would the clause which stipulated that the end justified the means. The libertarian principle which had inspired the Chaykovtsy was breached too by a clause requiring the establishment of a 'basic circle' (probably thus designated in order that the more natural but still contentious epithet 'central' could be avoided) which would have 'control' of the activity of all other circles and each individual member of the organisation. Further clauses defining the obligations and mutual relations of members of the 'basic' circle affirmed the new spirit of centralisation and authoritarianism. Clashes between individual members of the 'basic' circle, for example, would be resolved by a 'court of arbitration', the decision of which would be binding. The 'basic' circle was empowered to order any individual, chosen by a majority of its members, to undertake any assignment for which there were not already enough volunteers. Any member wanting to leave his group or change his role in the organisation had to give the 'basic' circle at least two months' notice of his intention and was not entitled to leave his position until that period had expired. Members of the 'basic' circle who had particularly important connections in the organisation were forbidden to take part in dangerous ventures which might increase the likelihood of their arrest. And, if it were proved that any member who had left the circle was betraying its secrets, then, according to one version of the rules, he would be killed.[85]

The practical activity of the Zemlevoltsy, as well as their organisational principles, acquired an emphasis rather different from what Lavrov or Bakunin had envisaged. For one thing, certain Zemlevoltsy, particularly Plekhanov, had for some time been conducting propaganda in small circles in most of the industrial regions of St Petersburg, and their growing interest in the urban workers was indicated by the increasing amount of space devoted to the labour movement in their publications in 1878–9. Plekhanov attempted to come to grips with the question of the role of workers in the Russian revolutionary movement in an article printed in the party's journal in February 1879 and pointed out that the workers had been deeply affected by socialist doctrines, even though revolutionaries had hitherto paid relatively little attention to them.[86] That was not to say that the Zemlevoltsy rejected the view held by other Populists, such as the Chaykovtsy and the 'Muscovites' before them, that the urban workers should be seen as an extension of the peasantry rather than an independent revolutionary force. These workers were merely the 'flower of the rural population', younger and bolder than those who remained in the countryside it was true, but still peasants at heart.[87] The Zemlevoltsy had differences of opinion, too, with labour leaders such as Obnorsky and Khalturin (to whose North-Russian Workers' Union[88] the Zemlevoltsy sent propagandists) and in particular they did not share the workers' belief in the importance of political freedom.[89] Nevertheless, it was perhaps not to have been expected that revolutionaries who remained Populists in their outlook should devote so much attention to the urban workers – who constituted only a minute proportion of the Russian mass as a whole – or that they should, relatively speaking, enjoy such success among them.

Furthermore, in the towns to which many of them had been forced by their failure in the countryside to retreat, the Zemlevoltsy also began to discover new means of promoting their revolutionary objectives. They resorted increasingly to agitation, that is to say the advertisement of particular grievances or the use of certain occasions to voice protest, gain wider support and increase animosity towards the authorities. Thus they were quick to associate themselves with renewed unrest in the higher educational institutions in the winter of 1877–8, devoting much space in their journal to the disturbances and printing proclamations in support of the students.[90] They also took opportunities to mount political demonstrations, such as the gathering of students and workers that was organised in December 1876 outside the Kazan Cathedral on Nevsky Prospect (the main street of St Petersburg/Leningrad) to honour the memory of political prisoners who had died in exile.[91] And, paradoxical as it may seem, the movement was further invigorated by the trials of revolutionaries who had been arrested, particularly by the trial of the 'Muscovites' (known as the 'trial of the 50') and the trial of some of the propagandists arrested in 1874 (the 'trial of the 193'), which took place in February–March 1877 and between October 1877 and January 1878 respectively. The revolutionaries gained widespread public sympathy both as a result of the passing of savage sentences by the courts and the transparent idealism of the defendants, whose speeches, printed on clandestine presses and widely circulated, constituted a further form of revolutionary agitation.[92]

Besides student disturbances, political demonstrations, perorations in court and the distribution of leaflets drawing attention to all these forms of agitation, there was one further tactic to which revolutionaries began to resort in the second half of the 1870s, namely 'disorganisational activity', as the programme of Zemlya i Volya described it[93] – that was to say, various forms of terrorism. The violence began in 1876 in Odessa with the shooting of a police agent who was left for dead, his face disfigured by sulphuric acid, and was in the first instance directed at individuals who threatened the safety of revolutionaries (spies, the police and officials responsible for their detention, prosecution and punishment), but it quickly escalated as each side, authorities and revolutionaries, carried out reprisals for the attacks they had suffered. Vera Zasulich's attempt of January 1878 to kill General Trepov, the governor of St Petersburg; Kovalsky's armed resistance to arrest in the same month in Odessa; the attempt of Osinsky and others the following month to kill a public prosecutor, Kotlyarevsky, in Kiev; Popko's killing of a secret police officer, Geyking, in May 1878, also in Kiev; Kravchinsky's stabbing to death of Mezentsov, head of the secret police, in August 1878 in St Petersburg; and Goldenberg's fatal wounding of Prince D. N. Kropotkin, governor of Kharkov, in February 1879 – these were the main, but by no means the only, manifestations of the new militancy.

It is possible to identify a number of reasons for this rapid growth of terrorism in the second half of the 1870s. Firstly, terrorism was a welcome alternative to the activity that had preceded it, for it produced more obvious results than propaganda. It provided an outlet for energies frustrated in the countryside. Secondly, in its initial phase, in 1878, terrorism represented rather a logical application of the belligerence characteristic of the Bakuninist wing of the revolutionary movement. (Significantly it was from the south, where the *buntari* were most numerous, that many of the early advocates of violence emanated.) Thirdly, the authorities undoubtedly encouraged violence by meting out draconian punishment for trivial offences and by making martyrs of those who did take up arms against them. (It was no coincidence that the wave of terrorism immediately followed the end of the last of the major political trials of 1877–8.) And, fourthly, the tense and even exalted mood of many revolutionaries may well have been heightened by the martial atmosphere of the southern cities during the Russo-Turkish war of 1877–8. Here there was plentiful evidence of the new hardships being endured by the masses, the suffering of the sick and wounded, and the incompetence and corruption of Russian official-dom. Even the Turkish enemy, it was felt, could be no more cruel and despotic than the Russian authorities, whom the Zemlevoltsy constantly described as, or even compared unfavourably to, *bashi-bazouks*.[94]

The motives advanced by the terrorists themselves for their actions, as opposed to the possible historical causes of the growth of terrorism, tend to confirm that the new form of struggle, in its early stages, was a more or less spontaneous response to the revolutionaries' own failure, to official persecution and to the government's incorrigible indifference to the well-being of the nation. Far from proceeding according to any preconceived rational plan, the terrorists acted on confused impulses, explaining their deeds in terms of self-defence, vengeance, revolutionary justice and defence of the honour of the party. Vera Zasulich, wrote Klements in a proclamation, had heroically defended the rights of the down-trodden and thus helped to 'bridle' unpunished 'arbitrariness'.[95] Kovalsky, to judge by a proclamation *à propos* of Zasulich's attempt which he drafted shortly before his arrest, was simply filled with indignation and felt that only death was suitable for cruel tyrants like Trepov.[96] Kravchinsky, in a pamphlet with the vengeful title *A Death for a Death*, explained in similar fashion that he had killed Mezentsov because the police chief had trampled on the dignity of others and seemed subject to no law. Revolutionaries, placed by the government in the position of people in primitive, savage societies, would themselves defend 'human rights'. Mezentsov was killed, moreover, not as a matter of principle but in retaliation for specific 'crimes' which Kravchinsky enumerated. And in a passage typical of attitudes towards terrorism in this period Kravchinsky explained that it was not in any case the government but the bourgeoisie which the revolutionaries saw as their main enemy. The demands put by Kravchinsky at the end of his pamphlet – an end to persecution for the expression of political convictions, an end to official arbitrariness and an amnesty for all political prisoners – were therefore very limited. Terrorism was not expected to win more.[97] Similarly, the leading article of the first number of *Zemlya i volya* described terrorism as a 'system of mob law and self-defence'; terrorists were 'no more than a protective detachment' whose purpose was to safeguard the organisation from the enemy.[98] Further references to 'capital punishment', 'execution' for various 'crimes', rightful vengeance and 'self-defence' were made in the revolutionary journal and in a proclamation concerning the killing of Kropotkin, which, significantly, had followed the appearance of a pamphlet, *Buried Alive*, describing the harsh treatment of political prisoners in Kharkov gaol.[99]

It is important to bear in mind when examining the course of the revolutionary movement after 1881, however, that although the early motivation of terrorism might have been mainly retributive new, more extravagant claims began to be made for the tactic as the terrorist acts became more frequent and their impact more resounding. Tikhomirov, for example, attempted to incorporate terrorism into the traditional Bakuninist view of the path to revolution in Russia. Revolutionaries should try to give their party the same standing among the people as the Tsar enjoyed there. It was necessary to stir the peasant and arouse him to protest and in so doing make him more receptive to socialist propaganda.[100] Morozov went even further, glorifying terrorism as not merely a means of revenge and self-defence but as one of the best agitational weapons in present conditions. The terrorists were described by Morozov as the free among millions of slaves; in future, when passions abated, people would bow down before them and consider them holy. By killing their enemies they might make their party into a 'whole and indivisible force' and would endow themselves with the authority necessary if they were to carry the masses with them. By striking at the heart of the government apparatus, finally, they would administer a severe shock to the whole political system. To carry out political assassinations was to wage 'revolution in the present'.[101] Other Zemlevoltsy, too, having come to accept the need for 'political struggle' (that is to say, for contest with the régime as opposed to attempts to persuade the masses to change the economic order from below) logically turned their attention to the autocrat himself, and began to look on tsaricide as a panacea for all Russia's ills. Killing the sovereign would, of course, satisfy the thirst for revolutionary justice, for the Tsar, as the person ultimately responsible for all lawlessness and himself the most lawless of all, merited 'execution' more than any of his officials.[102] But the Zemlevolets Solovyov – who helped finally to establish political terrorism by his attempt on the life of Alexander II in April 1879 – seems also to have hoped that the assassination of the Tsar might deepen the country's economic crisis and jolt the masses, among whom discontent was now believed to be very serious.[103] And other advocates of the tactic began to speak of wringing concessions from government.

THE MOVEMENT FROM 1879 TO 1 MARCH 1881: CHORNYY
PEREDEL AND NARODNAYA VOLYA

The growth of terrorism and its use for purposes that were conceived of as
primarily political created a tension within Zemlya i Volya between those
who advocated the new tendency, on the one hand, and those who wished
to pursue a more traditional Bakuninist strategy, on the other. Disputes
now divided the editorial group of the party's journal – Morozov,
Plekhanov and Tikhomirov – and led to the inauguration in March 1879 of
the 'leaflet of Zemlya i Volya', which served as a vehicle for the expression
of the views of Morozov and his supporters.[104] In the spring of 1879 those
who were determined to continue the terrorist struggle, even if opposed by
a majority within the party, formed a group of their own within Zemlya i
Volya and took over first the appellation 'Executive Committee', previously used by Osinsky's Kievan group, and then the title 'Freedom or Death'
which perhaps reflected the new belief that the winning of political freedom
(*svoboda*, not *volya*) was a desirable objective. Finally, in June, a conference
was held at Voronezh (preceded by a meeting of the advocates of terrorism
at Lipetsk) in an attempt to resolve the differences that had arisen within the
organisation. No one wished to bring about the disintegration of a party
which had achieved much and within which all had shared certain ideals,
and some conciliatory resolutions were therefore passed concerning the
composition of the journal's editorial group and the allocation of the party's
funds. But unity was precarious and from the autumn two factions operated
independently: Plekhanov and his supporters (Akselrod, Aptekman,
Deych, Popov, Preobrazhensky, Stefanovich, Zasulich and others, the
'countrymen' as they had been dubbed on account of their preference for
activity among the peasantry) under the banner Chornyy Peredel (The
Black Partition); and the advocates of political terrorism (Barannikov, Vera
Figner, Frolenko, Grachevsky, Kolodkevich, Kvyatkovsky, Aleksandr
Mikhaylov, Morozov, Oshanina, Perovskaya, Tikhomirov, Yakimova,
Zhelyabov, Zundelevich and others) under the banner Narodnaya Volya
(The People's Will).[105]

It must be emphasised that Chornyy Peredel was from the outset
relatively ineffectual and not merely because it immediately suffered severe
setbacks – leading members were arrested in Moscow and Kiev and the
party's first clandestine printing press was seized by the police early in 1880,
whereupon Plekhanov, Deych, Stefanovich and Zasulich emigrated – but
also because it had a rather limited appeal in Russian socialist circles in the

years 1879–81. Plekhanov's attribution of past failures not to the hostility or indifference of the peasant towards the revolutionary but to the ineptitude of the propagandists and agitators themselves[106] had a hollow ring. The goal of 'economic' revolution in the countryside which he was determined to pursue was too elusive, and in any case Chornyy Peredel did not seem capable of pursuing it vigorously. Most important of all, Plekhanov's prediction that the new political tendency would be unproductive seemed unconvincing, even disrespectful to terrorism's early martyrs. It is not surprising, therefore, that a number of prominent revolutionaries of long standing, such as Perovskaya and Zhelyabov, who were basically in sympathy with the aspirations of Chornyy Peredel, should have joined the ranks of Narodnaya Volya instead, on the grounds that the Chernoperedeltsy failed to undertake any important rural venture of the type they favoured or that the programme of Narodnaya Volya seemed more appropriate at the given historical moment.[107] And, indeed, even some of those who did at first align themselves with Chornyy Peredel soon began to defect to Narodnaya Volya, whose programme, as the authorities regretfully noted, attracted most of the persons who belonged to the 'criminal association of that time'.[108] For instance, one group of 'Populists' – the term was now applied to Chernoperedeltsy in order to distinguish them from Narodovoltsy – announced in December 1880 that they had come to the conclusion, after prolonged activity among the masses, that it was not possible at the present time to build an organisation of conscious revolutionaries in the countryside and spoke of the need for some 'push', such as a *coup d'état*, if the people were to rise against their oppressors.[109]

Nor were those revolutionaries who escaped arrest and remained loyal to Chornyy Peredel altogether unaffected by the recent development of combat with the government. Some of them now declared that they did not 'unconditionally' repudiate 'political' struggle: 'Please do not think, comrades,' wrote Aptekman in the first number of *Chornyy peredel*, 'that I am in general opposed to a constitution, opposed to political freedom';[110] it was merely a question of where one's priorities lay. Plekhanov himself, by the beginning of 1881, had come to propose a new balance between agitation for the improvement of economic conditions, on the one hand, and the political task of organising a conscious revolutionary party among the masses, on the other: the demand for political freedom would be an 'integral part of the sum total of immediate demands' made by such an organisation.[111] Thus history, Plekhanov admitted, was pushing on to the 'path of political struggle' even those who had recently opposed the adoption of that course.[112] Even some revolutionaries who continued to repudiate political struggle, such as Kovalskaya and Shchedrin (founders of a 'South-Russian Workers' Union' in Kiev) defended terrorism in its 'economic' form, that is to say the killing of individuals such as factory owners who were deemed directly responsible for hardship among the masses – a tactic which, they reasoned, might give the masses the confidence to express their discontent.[113]

Narodnaya Volya, in contrast with Chornyy Peredel, immediately developed into a determined and dynamic revolutionary force capable of undertaking very wide-ranging activity.[114] During the most celebrated period of the party's history, between June 1879 and 1 March 1881, Narodnaya Volya assisted, founded or brought under its control workers' circles in St Petersburg, Moscow, Odessa, Kiev and Kharkov and circles in the armed forces in St Petersburg and the nearby Kronshtadt naval base; conducted agitation among the students of the country's higher educational institutions; set up and operated clandestine presses (on which were printed five numbers of a journal in the party's name and two numbers of a paper specifically for the workers, entitled *Rabochaya gazeta* (*Workers' Paper*), as well as numerous leaflets and proclamations); and, most importantly, mounted a prolonged terrorist campaign which culminated, after a number of unsuccessful attempts, in the assassination of Alexander II on the bank of the Yekaterininsky Canal in St Petersburg on 1 March 1881. By these means, and especially by means of their terrorist campaign, the Narodovoltsy proceeded greatly to deepen the political crisis in the 'upper spheres' of Russian society, a crisis which the terrorists themselves had significantly helped to precipitate and of which Narodnaya Volya was in a sense the product.[115]

As in the period of Zemlya i Volya, the terrorists became ever more intoxicated with their tactic and advanced further justifications for it as the momentum of their campaign increased. Certainly the old motif of retribution was not forgotten. In a proclamation of 1879, for example, the Executive Committee (which was in practice the body that controlled the party's operations) spoke of tsaricide as execution of a tyrant for crimes against his people and insisted that Alexander deserved to die for all the innocent blood he had shed.[116] But more often and more clearly now, Narodovoltsy affirmed that they wished by attacking the government to win political freedom and a constitution which would guarantee it. Although there was no evidence in recent Russian or Western European history to suggest that this aspiration was a realistic one, it was enshrined in a clause of the programme of the Executive Committee which demanded 'complete freedom of conscience, speech, press, assembly, association and electoral agitation'.[117] Mikhaylovsky emphasised the importance of political freedom in the two eloquent 'political letters' which appeared in the second and third numbers of *Narodnaya volya*.[118] The letter sent by the Executive Committee to the heir to the throne, after the assassination of Alexander II, reiterated the demand,[119] and Narodovoltsy generally stated it too in the speeches they made at their trials, often with a promise that the party would lay down arms the moment concessions were made. Very soon after the formation of their party, however, Narodovoltsy also began to make more extravagant claims in defence of their terrorism. They hoped they might ignite what the assassin, Grinevitsky, in his testament described as the 'combustible material' in the towns and countryside, that is to say spark off a popular uprising.[120] They might even overthrow the autocracy altogether. Thus they began to speak of lifting from the people the yoke that crushed them and of clearing the road of the obstacle which had impeded their attempts to reach the masses.[121] Before they could begin to work profitably among the people they would have to 'break the government itself'.[122] 'Delenda est Carthago!' ('Carthage must be burned!') proclaimed the leading article in the first number of *Narodnaya volya*;[123] the main enemy would have to be eliminated before any improvements could be expected. An aptly military image explained the apparent deviation from the road to a social revolution implemented by the masses themselves. The ultimate goal of the Russian army during the recent war with Turkey had been Constantinople; but the army had had to encamp at Pleven for almost six months, 'because without taking Pleven they could not move beyond the Balkans, they could not leave in their rear an army capable of cutting off all their communications'.[124] Violence, it seemed, had become a means to many ends.

To what extent, though, had the Narodovoltsy moved further than the Zemlevoltsy away from the old Populist ideals? Undeniably their position differed from that of most prospective revolutionaries a decade earlier in several important respects and as a result they stood much closer to Tkachov. Firstly, of course, they were unashamedly waging a 'political' struggle, confronting the autocracy directly (rather than turning to the countryside in the hope of inciting economic revolution there) and demanding political freedoms as a prerequisite for the resumption of effective propaganda among the peasantry. They even conceded that the revolution itself, as opposed to the preparations leading up to it, might have to have a political character: a document written early in 1880, which outlined their plans for preparatory work, revealed that they were willing to contemplate an insurrection and seizure of power.[125] Secondly, Narodnaya Volya represented a further development of the centralist and conspiratorial principles towards which Zemlya i Volya had moved and which were even more necessary in an organisation dedicated to political struggle with the government. In Russia, where political agitation could not be conducted openly, the Narodovoltsy reasoned, the central revolutionary organisation could not consist of elected representatives but had to take the form of a 'secret society' exercising control over the groups on its periphery. It was therefore a hierarchical organisation that the rules of the Executive Committee described.[126] Thirdly, the party's attempt to secure support in the armed forces represented a novel step in the history of Populism, for it was only with the advent of 'political' struggle against the autocracy that the support of the military began to seem valuable, indeed essential.[127] Fourthly, like Tkachov, the Narodovoltsy were quick to admit – as the Chernoperedeltsy were not – that work in the countryside was in present circumstances unproductive. The peasants had not responded to socialist propaganda as it had been hoped they would: they had deceived the 'rosy hopes' of the propagandists as cruelly as the Tsar had deceived the peasant. This passivity was attributed partly to the fact, Tikhomirov supposed, that any mass was 'inert and cowardly' and inclined to prefer the most appalling but familiar present to the 'unknown and hazardous future',[128] and partly to the fact that the peasant's mind was indeed dulled by poverty and oppression and filled with myth and superstition,[129] as Tkachov had contended. In any case the authorities, by deploying so many informers and police in the countryside, had ensured that the socialist would be reported, searched and arrested, no matter under what guise he conducted his propaganda. It was therefore considered pointless for the revolutionary to remain in the countryside, beating against the people 'like a fish against ice'.[130] Lastly, the Narodovoltsy advanced certain views on social relationships in Russia that were also reminiscent of those expressed by Tkachov, particularly in his 'Open Letter to Engels'. They argued that the relationship between the state and society was not the same in Russia and Western Europe. The Russian government was not a 'commission of representatives of the ruling classes, as in Europe, but an independent organisation existing for its own benefit'. Since it represented no class interests, moreover, the autocracy had insecure foundations: it was a 'colossus of iron on feet of clay'[131] and might therefore be easily toppled.

Thus it was optimistically declared that the *ancien régime* was living out 'its last days'; if no one came forward to deal it the final blow it would 'die a natural death'.[132] The intensification of official vigilance and the increase in the number of arrests of revolutionaries seemed only to confirm that the 'rabid monster' was in its 'death throes'.[133] Not that the revolutionaries could afford to postpone their attempt to take advantage of the government's enfeeblement, for the bourgeoisie, which was as yet weak and dependent for its welfare on the favour of the autocracy, might quickly grow strong if capitalism took root in Russia. It was therefore essential to fell the autocracy before the bourgeoisie reached political maturity. And if the Narodovoltsy shared these last sentiments with most other revolutionaries of their generation, nevertheless even the terms in which they counselled haste were reminiscent of Tkachov, who had particularly laboured the point: 'Now or never', warned Tikhomirov.[134]

Tkachov himself was delighted with the developments he saw taking place inside Russia from 1878 onwards. The organisation of revolutionary forces for battle with the government, the 'disorganisation and terrorisation' of the authorities, the creation of 'executive' and other committees – these were the 'basic demands' put forward in *Nabat* and seemed to Tkachov to signal the triumph of his ideas.[135] The Narodovoltsy, for their part, however, far from seeking the guidance of one who considered himself their mentor, rejected overtures made to them by the Jacobin émigrés through Morozov in 1880. Morozov's extreme glorification of terrorism and his dissatisfaction with the centralist organisational principles favoured by the Executive Committee made it difficult for him to co-operate for long with the party he had helped to found. At the beginning of 1880, therefore, he went abroad, where he was joined by Romanenko, a revolutionary previously active in the south of Russia, particularly in Odessa, where he had been a student. In the course of 1880 both Morozov and Romanenko penned short pamphlets demanding the systematic use of terrorism and predicting the revelation of socialism on the far shore of a sea of blood.[136] These views were not congenial to the Executive Committee, which may have planned to publish a rejoinder to Romanenko's screed in *Narodnaya volya*,[137] but they did bring Morozov and Romanenko close to Tkachov and his 'Society for the Liberation of the People'. Talks were held and a note despatched to St Petersburg in which the Jacobins proposed federative relations with Narodnaya Volya and joint publication of a journal whose editorial board would include Tkachov. They also promised to make part of their funds available to the Executive Committee 'without any formal obligations' other than that both parties should publish a statement to the effect that they had 'nothing against one another'. This advance, however, was coolly received. In May 1880 the Executive Committee replied through Tikhomirov that it did not need the Jacobins' money – although it was privately admitted to Morozov that the party's financial position was bad – and that Narodnaya Volya would neither consent to participation in a joint publication nor make any concessions on points of principle.[138]

It is possible that the Narodovoltsy were reluctant to do business with Tkachov because they believed that the Jacobins' organisation was not a going concern. They may also have feared lest they should give their critics firmer grounds for accusing them of Jacobin sympathies. But more probably their rejection of alliance with Tkachov was motivated by sincere distaste for Jacobinism. The Narodovoltsy were not of Tkachov's generation; they were not pragmatic 'men of the 60s', but belonged to that idealistic generation which had rejected the morality of Nechayev and had 'gone to the people'. Even when they had themselves resorted to 'political' struggle they considered their programme very moderate by comparison with that of the Jacobins. They had effected a synthesis of the two extremes represented by the Jacobins and Chornyy Peredel, extremes which laid one-sided emphasis on the 'political' and 'economic' facets of revolutionary struggle respectively.[139] Only Oshanina among the prominent members of the Executive Committee before 1 March 1881 was known to hold Jacobin views – she had received her political education in the 1870s in Oryol under the supervision of Zaichnevsky, one of the first major exponents of 'Jacobinism' in Russia – and memoirists make a point of mentioning the fact,[140] from which one may infer that these views were exceptional. Indeed, she herself admitted that at the time of the formation of the Executive Committee she alone among its members was not a 'Populist'.[141]

In the main, too, the Narodovoltsy of 1879–81 stressed that they wished to continue the tradition of the movement in the preceding years rather than to repudiate it. They had made an 'essential correction' in their programme when in 1879 they reviewed the Sisyphean labours of the decade that was coming to a close, but not a volte-face. In fact, they saw themselves at first not so much as a new party but rather as one wing of the old one. Their new journal would follow the principles laid down in *Zemlya i volya*; and, although they could not keep the title Zemlevoltsy, because they were no longer representative of all who had gone under that name, nevertheless 'Land and Liberty' remained their 'motto' and their 'slogan'. They still cherished the title 'Populist', which they conferred upon themselves in the first sentence of their new programme. Most importantly, they continued to insist that revolution must express, as the name of their party implied, the 'people's will'. And far from contemplating the protracted exercise of power, they envisaged the convocation of a constituent assembly, 'freely elected by universal suffrage', through which the people would express their will and order their affairs as soon as the existing government was overthrown. Like many revolutionaries during the 1870s, they pointed to the survival of the self-governing commune, to the persistence among the peasants of the belief that the land belonged to all who cultivated it, and to the independence of fugitive and sectarian communities, as evidence that socialism was feasible if the people were indeed allowed such self-expression. And the government's refusal to allow the people this right of self-expression was criticised by the Narodovoltsy as bitterly as its economic policies which kept the masses destitute.[142]

Nor did the Narodovoltsy entirely dismiss the masses as a revolutionary force or lose sight of the traditional Populist mission among them while they were waging their terrorist campaign. The programme of the Executive Committee stressed the need to secure popular support and the party's agents were advised to watch the mood of the masses and detailed questionnaires were compiled to help them assess it.[143] And as soon as conditions seemed to become more propitious in the autumn of 1880 (when crop failure and famine in some Volga provinces and the rising price of bread and growing unemployment in the towns caused some unrest) the Narodovoltsy allocated more resources to work among the masses, particularly the urban workers, than they had considered it useful to expend there a few months before.

It would be wrong, therefore, to see the Narodovoltsy as having forsaken libertarian Populism for Jacobinism in the first year and a half of their party's existence. Popular rule remained their unalterable ultimate objective. They did believe, though, that no single course of action – be it political terrorism, organisation of an insurrection, or propaganda among the armed forces or the urban workers – should be followed at the expense of all others or preclude reversion to another. The party should not repeat the mistake of the supporters of Lavrov and Bakunin, who had naïvely gone to the people with *a priori* assumptions which dictated the pursuit of one course of action and one course only. It should not be governed by bookish theory, wrote Tikhomirov in the first number of the journal in 1879; it should set itself ends which were 'concrete' and 'realisable' and choose the 'means' which were most effective 'at the given moment'. More than a year later the point was made again: revolutionary tactics should be flexible and answer the needs of the changing situation; only 'revolutionary doctrinairism' made plans 'for ten years ahead'.[144] It was this willingness to countenance various courses of action that enabled revolutionaries with diverse backgrounds and affiliations to co-operate easily within the Executive Committee (disputes are said to have been rare before 1 March 1881).[145] The former Chaykovtsy, Perovskaya and Zhelyabov, the southern *buntar'* Frolenko, the Jacobin Oshanina, and Zundelevich, who was said to have Social Democratic sympathies,[146] were all prepared to bury differences in order to further the revolutionary cause in any way they could, so long as the weakness of the government seemed to present them with an unprecedented chance of success.

In a sense this conception of the party as a fighting organisation which had to adapt itself to constantly changing circumstances was a reaffirmation rather than a betrayal of old ideals. If the old faith in the peasant, which lived on in Chernoperedelchestvo, was weakened (though not altogether extinguished) in Narodovolchestvo, the other basic premiss of Populism, reliance on the self-willed and self-abnegating revolutionary hero, came to the fore in it. The Narodovoltsy had overcome the 'passivity' which seemed to have been the undoing of their predecessors and which of late had apparently gripped even the masses as well as peaceful socialists, and they derived a 'heroic' quality from their determination to fight without sparing themselves, to lay down their own lives in the struggle.[147] They should not be compared to some of their near contemporaries, such as the French anarchists Auguste Vaillant and Emile Henry, who threw bombs into crowded cafés simply because the class enemy was there, or Ravachol, who combined a pedestrian knowledge of anarchist theory with a pure criminality which led him by turns into smuggling, counterfeiting, housebreaking and murder. Nor was the emphasis in Narodovolchestvo where it lay in Tkachov's Jacobinism, that is to say on the seizure of political power by a minority. On the contrary, far from being cynical advocates of violence or revolutionary dictatorship, the Narodovoltsy answered very precisely to Dostoyevsky's description of the typical young Russian idealist, published in 1880 in *The Brothers Karamazov*: an honest nature, demanding truth and yearning for some great exploit (*podvig*) in which all, even one's life itself, might be sacrificed.[148] And thus they remained firmly in a broad and long-established tradition, as indeed the association of both Mikhaylovsky and Lavrov with their party would seem to indicate. They did not discard the classical Populist conception of Russia's distinctive historical path; and they gave vigorous expression to the perennial quest of the Russian intelligentsia for the translation of noble ideals into action.

By 1881, then, revolutionaries in Russia had come empirically to a number of conclusions or been driven by circumstances into positions that they had not foreseen. The need for tight organisation was widely (though by no means universally) accepted, as was the inevitability of 'political' struggle. The failure to rouse the peasantry in the countryside and the vigilance of the authorities there had compelled the revolutionaries to concentrate their forces in the towns, where they found the urban workers more receptive than the peasants had been and where agitation could also be effectively conducted. They had adopted, and become enamoured of, violent means of struggle. And yet it is very doubtful whether these shifts signalled any substantial change in the basic assumptions with which most Russian revolutionaries had set out ten years before. Populism, in its broad sense, remained resilient, indeed it had been strengthened by the achievements, or at least the endeavours, of its representatives in the 1870s. And throughout the 1880s revolutionaries were by and large to remain faithful to it, sometimes attempting to apply it in novel ways or to resort in practice to new tactics, but only rarely and very cautiously questioning the basic premisses and assumptions on which it rested.

CHAPTER TWO

❧ *NARODNAYA VOLYA AFTER 1 MARCH 1881*

THE AFTERMATH OF ASSASSINATION

The assassination of Alexander II on 1 March 1881 was perhaps the major triumph of revolutionary Populism, for a long and determined campaign had been crowned with success and an example provided of what could be achieved by revolutionaries with boldness and dedication. And yet at the same time it also represents a failure and marks the beginning of Populism's long decline.

Initially, of course, supporters of the régime were hardly disposed to draw comfort from the events of March 1881, nor were revolutionaries inclined to view them pessimistically. Court circles feared further attempts at tsaricide. Pobedonostsev, the new Tsar's former tutor and now his mentor and close adviser, urged Alexander III to lock the door of his bedroom at night and to look under the furniture before retiring.[1] Fearful for his safety in the capital, Alexander tended to immure himself in the austere royal palace at Gatchina some thirty miles to the south-west of St Petersburg. And such was the fear of further acts of terrorism that Alexander's coronation did not take place until May 1883, more than two years after his accession to the throne. The Executive Committee of Narodnaya Volya, for its part, made the extravagant claim that the assassination had been greeted with sympathy and even with glee by an 'enormous' number of people.[2] Mikhaylovsky is said to have believed that revolution was now at hand.[3] And undoubtedly the death of Alexander II helped to slake that thirst for vengeance which had been growing among the revolutionaries throughout the previous decade. But the assassination did not achieve any of the other objectives declared by the terrorists. The 'combustible material' of which Grinevitsky had spoken in his testament[4] was not ignited by the killing: no uprising occurred, nor indeed was there any popular disturbance on a scale sufficient to threaten the security of the institution of autocracy. The new Tsar would not accede to the demands for a general amnesty for political prisoners and for the convocation of a popular assembly which were put to him by the Executive Committee in the rather mild letter written with the help of Mikhaylovsky in the days following the assassination.[5] Moreover, he quickly and indefinitely shelved Loris-Melikov's proposals – which Alexander II had approved on the morning of 1 March – for the establishment of commissions, consisting of local representatives, who would discuss legislation before its submission to the State Council.[6]

The assassination of Alexander II, then, did not precipitate revolution or impel the government to carry out reforms. On the contrary, it inaugurated one of those periods of grim reaction with which the history of tsarism is punctuated. The new ruler revealed strong attachment to traditional values, narrowly interpreted. A devout Orthodox, Alexander III was wont to record his attendance at divine services in his diary and neatly add them up at the year's end for his edification.[7] Even the fact that he wore a full beard – he was the first Russian monarch of the nineteenth century to do so – attested to stolid respect for native custom and opposition to Western innovation. This staunch conservatism was combined with an intellectual mediocrity which facilitated Alexander's manipulation by his mentor Pobedonostsev, Chief Procurator of the Holy Synod throughout the reign, a relentless opponent of constitutionalism[8] and himself the author of the manifesto of 29 April 1881 in which the new Tsar's determination to defend his absolute power was affirmed.[9] The more liberal advisers prominent in the reign of Alexander II, such as Loris-Melikov, Abaza, the Minister of Finance, and D. A. Milyutin, Minister of War, resigned or retired, to be replaced by men of frankly reactionary views like the Pan-Slavist Count Ignatyev, Minister of the Interior until May 1882, and Count D. A. Tolstoy, who occupied that post from 1882 until his death in 1889. Much of the legislation inspired by these men (for example, the laying-down, in 1882, of new provisions relating to censorship; the closure of the journal *Otechestvennyye zapiski* (*Notes of the Fatherland*) in 1884; the setting-up, in 1885, of a Nobles' Land Bank from which members of the gentry could take out loans on favourable terms; and the establishment, in 1889, of the office of land-captain, conferring extraordinary local powers on members of the nobility) was designed to buttress the old social order, not to soften its harsher aspects or lessen its inequalities.

It is worth bearing all these factors in mind when tracing the history of Narodnaya Volya after 1 March 1881, for against the background of an exceptionally reactionary – and stable – régime, the weakness of the assumptions on which the party had based its terrorist campaign is starkly apparent. The autocracy was not as frail as the Narodovoltsy had supposed; it could not be bludgeoned into making political concessions, let alone toppled altogether. Nor were the masses in a state of latent revolutionary ferment. And yet such was the enthusiasm the Narodovoltsy had generated for terrorism that none of them seems to have questioned its usefulness in the light of its failure to achieve any of the party's declared objectives. Indeed, the prestige that the first Narodovoltsy had won by their militancy and by their willingness to sacrifice themselves for the revolutionary cause continued to inspire others to emulate them throughout the 1880s. The party's revolutionary strategy, devised ostensibly to meet rapidly changing needs during the crisis of 1879–81, came to be treated with a reverence that made it fundamentally unalterable. Thus the pronouncements of the later Narodovoltsy, far from demonstrating the flexibility of which their predecessors had boasted, tended to interpret the programme of the first Executive Committee more or less uncritically as a blueprint for revolutionary activity for the foreseeable future.

However, if the glamour of terrorism made revolutionaries reluctant to abandon the theory which had originally served as its justification, or even to incorporate innovations in the party's programme, nevertheless several factors did begin to make themselves felt after 1 March which tended to undermine Narodovolchestvo. Firstly, the failure of the party to arouse the masses by means of terrorism produced an element of desperation in some quarters of the party. Secondly, the loss of many of the old leaders and the emergence of new ones caused unprecedented stresses within the Executive Committee and combined with the unproductiveness of the assassination to encourage a strengthening of the 'Jacobin' element of the party's doctrine. Thirdly, the party's epigones began to learn in practice that propaganda among the urban workers was a more rewarding activity than the terrorism which had previously provided the main *raison d'être* of Narodnaya Volya, although it did prove difficult to incorporate this discovery in the existing theory of Narodovolchestvo. And, fourthly, the success of the police, with the help of betrayals and 'frank testimonies' on the part of arrested revolutionaries themselves, in destroying the party's groups in the major cities had the effect of driving the remnants of Narodnaya Volya into increasingly remote parts of European Russia, where their effectiveness was bound to be greatly diminished.

THE PARTY REGROUPS ITS FORCES

The capacity of Narodnaya Volya to inflict on the government further blows as damaging as the assassination of Alexander II was rapidly impaired after 1 March. Rysakov (a young member of the party's workers' organisation and one of the bomb-throwers on 1 March) soon began, in the vain hope of saving himself from execution for his part in the killing, to divulge to the police all he knew of the revolutionary organisation. Assisted by Rysakov's copious depositions, the police made further arrests among the party's leaders, taking Perovskaya, Kibalchich (who had made the bombs used on 1 March), Isayev (another of the party's technical experts and a member of the Executive Committee), Sukhanov (another member of the Executive Committee and prominent in the party's organisation in the armed forces), Frolenko and Yakimova in the course of March and April. Zhelyabov, Perovskaya and Kibalchich, together with T. Mikhaylov (another member of the team of bomb-throwers on 1 March), Rysakov himself and Gelfman (who had been in charge of the flat which served as headquarters for the attempt on Alexander's life) were brought to trial in March, as there was sufficient evidence to support the charge of tsaricide against them. With the exception of Gelfman, who was pregnant, they were publicly hanged on 3 April. Frolenko, Isayev, Sukhanov and Yakimova, together with Barannikov, Kolodkevich, Aleksandr Mikhaylov, Morozov, Trigoni (a southern member of the Executive Committee who had been arrested in February 1881), and Kletochnikov (who from January 1879 until his arrest in January 1881 had worked as a clerk for the Third Section passing invaluable information on police investigations first to Zemlya i Volya and then to the Executive Committee of Narodnaya Volya) were tried together with ten others in 1882. Sukhanov was executed by firing squad and the others sentenced to long terms of imprisonment in harsh conditions which many did not survive.

The majority of those Narodovoltsy who eluded the police in March and April 1881 were forced to flee from St Petersburg in order to avoid arrest. No one, however, left the northern capital with gladness or pretended that the exodus was tactically or psychologically desirable, for St Petersburg was the political and administrative centre of the Empire, the main residence of the autocracy and the seat of the government on which Narodnaya Volya had resolved to wage its assault. Without a strong base there the party's capacity to accomplish the 'political' tasks which it had set itself would be greatly impaired. Again, St Petersburg was the main industrial centre of tsarist Russia. Partly because it was the seat of government, partly because of its favourable geographical position offering egress to the Baltic, it attracted many of the foreign investors whose capital to a large extent financed Russian industrial development at this time. The various industrial regions of St Petersburg – the harbour region, Vasilyev Island, the Petersburg and Vyborg districts and the Narva region around the Obvodnyy Canal – therefore accommodated a substantial and growing working class, in which Narodnaya Volya had established a firm base, but with which the Executive Committee, with its departure for Moscow, now lost contact. Moreover, with its relative proximity to the West and the amenability of its intelligentsia to alien ideas, which in tsarist Russia were almost inevitably subversive, St Petersburg also had a symbolic significance as the fount of political opposition to the autocracy and of a radical intellectual tradition. It had been the scene of the Decembrist revolt in 1825, the home of Belinsky during the final and politically radical phase of his publicistic career in the 1840s, the location of all the major journals in which the critics of the régime had outlined their accusations and formulated their own proposals, the city in which the young generation of the 1860s had constructed its utopias and conducted its experiments in new communal ways of living, and the background against which nihilists like Dostoyevsky's Raskolnikov had pondered the rejection of the old values and morality.

By contrast, Moscow, the city to which Narodnaya Volya now transferred its headquarters, was quite unsuitable as a base from which to launch an attack on the central government. It was also at the centre of an area in which light industry, particularly textiles, with a substantial proportion of women and children in the labour force, prevailed over the heavy industries – metal-working, engineering, armaments, ship-building and the railways – in which revolutionary propaganda tended to be best received; and its enterprises were in any case of a smaller scale than those in St Petersburg. Finally, Moscow had distasteful associations for the revolutionary camp. As the seat of the Grand Princes who had cast off the Tartar yoke and gathered in the Russian lands it was regarded as the spring from which autocracy drew its inspiration. Nowhere were Russian Orthodoxy and the national traditions venerated by Slavophiles and reactionaries felt to be more staunchly preserved. As if in recognition of this fact Pobedonostsev gave the title *Moscow Collection* to his conservative treatise on the principles of virtuous government, although it was in St Petersburg that he held office. Thus in retrospect it is tempting to see the retreat of the Executive Committee from St Petersburg to Moscow as marking the beginning of the party's long decline. The absence of the Executive Committee from the northern capital weakened the party's *raison d'être* and was before long to become a source of tension within the party's ranks.

By the summer of 1881 most of the leading Narodovoltsy had gathered in Moscow. Oshanina and Tellalov (who had laid the foundations of the party's groups among the workers in Kharkov and then in Moscow) had been joined there by Grachevsky, Tikhomirov, Korba (the daughter of an engineer from Tver province, who had been a member of the Executive Committee since January 1880) and Bogdanovich (a member of the Executive Committee who had acted as proprietor of the cheese-shop on the Malaya Sadovaya in St Petersburg, from which Narodovoltsy had tunnelled in order to mine the road Alexander was expected to use on 1 March). Two other revolutionaries who were based in Moscow, Lebedev and Martynov, had also been drafted onto the Executive Committee. These Narodovoltsy continued to speak in terms that would have been approved by captured comrades of the great task of 'bridling despotism' and replacing unlimited monarchy with 'universal representation'.[10] The installation of a clandestine press in Moscow in the spring enabled the party to issue more leaflets and to publish in the autumn the sixth number of *Narodnaya volya*, at the beginning of which appeared a short statement again defining the prime objective of terrorism as the acquisition of political rights. The statement was prompted by the death in September 1881 of the American President Garfield from wounds inflicted by an assassin in July. The Executive Committee offered its condolences to the American people and protested, in the name of the Russian revolutionaries, against the use of violence in pursuit of political ends in countries in which the 'freedom of the individual' made it possible legally to express diverse political opinions. In such countries, where the president was freely elected and the people's will the source of law, 'political assassination' was a manifestation of that same coercive spirit that the Narodovoltsy were trying to banish from Russia.[11]

Meanwhile those who wished to continue to work among the masses watched attentively for signs of unrest. Shortly after the assassination of Alexander II a document was drawn up enumerating the questions which should be answered by agents trying to define the grievances of the peasants and to measure their discontent.[12] In the party's journal a correspondent from Saratov province noted with satisfaction that local peasants had shown interest in documents recently distributed by the party's agents, while another correspondent, from Voronezh province, reported that the 'antagonism between estates and especially between the peasants and the landowners' had greatly increased of late.[13] Others considered, if their memoirs are to be believed, that the assassination had won them respect among the urban workers and that the workers expected the party to strike again. The propagandists, led by Tellalov, did indeed make some headway among the masses in Moscow, where by the autumn of 1881 they are said to have been operating in about thirty factories and workshops in a network embracing more than a hundred workers, and in St Petersburg, where an attempt was made to revive the organisation decimated by the police following the testimonies of Rysakov. Preparations were made for the printing of a further number of *Rabochaya gazeta*, the formation of fighting units for the protection of the organisation was again encouraged and a police agent was killed in St Petersburg at the instigation of one of the party's propagandists. Towards the autumn the party's efforts among the workers were assisted by another bad harvest, rising prices and industrial crisis.[14] There was also some unrest for the party to exploit among the students. In Moscow 'disorders and disturbances of the most deplorable nature', as official circles saw it, followed the attempt of some students to collect signatures and donations for a wreath to honour the memory of Alexander II. The list of signatures was torn up by students sympathetic to the revolutionaries and those who had conceived the plan were noisily denounced at a student meeting.[15] Shortly afterwards one of the radical student leaders, Viktorov, took advantage of the public defence of a doctoral dissertation to make a speech, prepared with the help of leading Narodovoltsy, in which he argued that many great reforms in history had been preceded by bloody events.[16]

The activities in which surviving Narodovoltsy were engaged after 1 March 1881 in Moscow and St Petersburg, however, were clearly of very little significance when measured against the grandiose ambitions nourished during the first phase of the party's activity. And before long, ideas began to emanate from the centre of the party which underlined the sense of frustration many activists must now have been experiencing.

THE POGROMS AND THE ATTITUDE OF NARODNAYA VOLYA TOWARDS THEM

It was in the response of some Narodovoltsy to the anti-Semitic violence that erupted shortly after the assassination of Alexander II that the party's frustration first found public expression.

When assessing the attitude of revolutionaries to this violence it is important to emphasise that the pogroms, more than two hundred of which were recorded in the course of 1881 and 1882, did not have the elemental character of the great Russian peasant revolts of the seventeenth and eighteenth centuries. Admittedly, the Russians often displayed hostility towards the Jews – official legislation which held Jews in a position of social inferiority and tended to force them to make a living as unproductive middlemen encouraged this hostility[17] – and in many places it was therefore not difficult to turn the local masses against the alien minority. But there are strong indications that from the very first outbreak of violence, when on 15 April 1881 a horde rampaged through Yelizavetgrad in the Ukraine, the pogroms were quite unspontaneous. According to the account of an American journalist, Harold Frederic, who made a study of the subject at the time:

> a band of young men from St Petersburg – young students, clerks, and ne'er-do-wells generally – was travelling about the country, and invariably appeared in a town a day or so before the outbreak of the riot. These *agents provocateurs* did their work too clumsily. They grew inflated by their success, and appeared on the streets blowing whistles, marching in step, and otherwise calling attention to their organisation.[18]

There is no doubt but that the pogroms took place with the connivance of the authorities, for in many instances local police and troops failed to come to the assistance of the victims of the attacks. Indeed, it is even probable that the violence was inspired in official circles by xenophobic conservatives who had for one reason or another fallen into disgrace under Alexander II, but who now, with a monarch more malleable and sympathetic to their views, had increased opportunities not only to defend the cherished autocracy but also to persecute what was alien. Foremost among these conservatives was Count Ignatyev, who, while ambassador at the Porte from 1864 to 1877, had sedulously fomented unrest among the Balkan Slavs and had tried to persuade them that Russian intervention on their behalf against the Turkish infidel could legitimately be expected.[19] Pan-Slavic ambitions had ultimately been thwarted by the anxiety of other European powers, especially Britain, lest they should be faced with a strong Russia in the Balkans; but nationalistic dreams impossible of fulfilment on a European scale could at least be revived at home. Thus Ignatyev – who was appointed Minister of the Interior shortly after the first pogrom, an eminence to which he rose precipitously from the ignominious position of Governor-General of Nizhniy Novgorod – is alleged to have attempted to extort a million roubles from the Jews of St Petersburg and, on their refusal to succumb to this blackmail, framed the 'May Laws' of 1882 which confined Jews living in the Pale of Settlement to the towns, suspended their mortgages and leases on landed estates and their powers of attorney for managing them, and forbade them to conduct business on Sundays and the principal Christian holidays.[20] At the same time the Jews themselves were held responsible for the violence against them. Thus Ignatyev alluded in a circular of 1881 to Jewish control of trade and commerce and Jewish ownership of much landed property and claimed that the Jews had conspired to exploit the indigenous population.[21] Finally, official currency was given to the fallacious notion that Jews constituted the predominant element in the revolutionary camp. In fact, only one of the *pervomartovtsy*, Gelfman, was Jewish, and the Executive Committee of Narodnaya Volya, before the assassination of Alexander II, contained only three Jews out of thirty-one revolutionaries: Tellalov, who operated among the workers in Moscow until the summer of 1881; Zlatopolsky, who never played an influential role at the meetings of the Committee; and Zundelevich, who was arrested early in the party's history, in 1879. Nevertheless, provincial officials quickly took their cue and began, in the words of Harold Frederic, to circulate 'the most shameless lies about the Nihilists being entirely composed of Jews, and about fresh Israelitish plots for the murder of the new Tsar'.[22]

What is of particular interest in connection with the pogroms for the student of the revolutionary movement, however, is the fact that even though the anti-Semitic violence lacked spontaneity and was officially sanctioned and associated with anti-revolutionary propaganda certain Narodovoltsy themselves began to lend credence to the rumours concerning the exploitation of the Russian people by Jewish usurers and to interpret the pogroms quite simply as the beginnings of the long-awaited popular rebellion. Lebedev, in an article which appeared in the first leaflet issued by Narodnaya Volya in the summer of 1881, described the pogroms as an 'awakening of the popular consciousness' and predicted that the time was approaching when the people would rise up against an enemy they clearly recognised. The 'victory of 1 March' had stiffened the spirit of the masses and, although the pogroms had not been incited by the revolutionaries, they were 'in essence and in time an echo' of the party's efforts.[23] Another contribution to the leaflet, written by a revolutionary of long standing now active in the party, Zhebunyov, and entitled 'From the Countryside', discussed the pogroms in greater detail. Zhebunyov claimed that the people had begun to suspect the operation of some benevolent external force and admitted that the peasants considered individuals from St Petersburg, whose arrival was eagerly awaited, to have launched the pogroms; but it did not seem to concern him that those who incited the violence were not revolutionary socialists but hooligans whose rampages had been encouraged and tolerated by reactionary dignitaries. Nor did Zhebunyov question the belief that the Jews themselves had provoked the violence. The Jews, he alleged, had thrown in their lot with the landowners and the *kulaks*, connived with the authorities, requested military and police protection and threatened to have peasants sent to Siberia. Their behaviour had been 'tactless in the highest degree'.[24]

Foremost among those Narodovoltsy who in the course of 1881 took the view that the pogroms were a prelude to a larger popular upheaval which would sweep away Tsar, government, police, armed forces, landowners and *kulaks* was Romanenko, son of a Bessarabian landowner and already familiar as a champion of remorseless terrorism. Having returned to Russia after the assassination of Alexander II, where he now became a member of the Executive Committee, Romanenko addressed to the Ukrainian people a venomous proclamation imbued with racial hatred and approving the supposed hostility of the masses towards the Jews.[25] Many copies of the proclamation were printed and distributed to various towns in which the party was active. And in the sixth number of *Narodnaya volya* Romanenko again took up the subject of popular unrest and the pogroms in a leading article and in a protracted 'internal review'. The people were beginning to rebel, declared Romanenko, although as yet rebellion was only sporadic, except in the south, where the discontent had begun to express itself in a 'mass revolutionary movement' to which local conditions had lent an 'anti-Jewish complexion'. This peculiarity of the southern disturbances Romanenko explained by invoking the widely held belief that the Jews had replaced the landowners as the principal local exploiters – a view borrowed from the pages of the reactionary paper, *Kiyevlyanin* (*The Kievan*).[26] Various aspects of the mob violence in the south afforded particular satisfaction to Romanenko. It was now clear, he thought, that the Russian people were not pusillanimous; on the contrary, clashes with the armed forces and the arrest of their fellows only inflamed their passions. The 'movement' had spread to the villages. A 'chance spark' would be sufficient to kindle the 'conflagration of a popular uprising' which would sweep Russia 'like a hurricane' and submerge the land in the sea of blood that had long fascinated Romanenko.[27]

It is true that in some radical quarters toleration and encouragement of the anti-Semitic violence was criticised. Kropotkin and Lavrov condemned Romanenko's proclamation,[28] for example. There seems to have been disagreement on the subject within the Executive Committee, too: Korba unequivocally condemned the proclamation (in her memoirs at least)[29] and Figner destroyed all copies of it which were delivered to Odessa.[30] Nevertheless, the temptation to accept Romanenko's interpretation of the pogroms, which was after all published prominently in the party's journal, must have been very strong, for it was an unpalatable fact that they were the only significant and widespread disturbances in the months following the assassination of Alexander II. Even leading Chernoperedeltsy dissuaded Akselrod from publishing a pamphlet in which he contested views such as those held by Romanenko, on the grounds that the revolutionaries should not alienate the peasantry.[31] How much more reluctant must the Narodovoltsy have been to condemn upheavals which might be seen as the fruits of terrorism and the pledge of future triumph if the old tactics were pursued.

THE ASCENDANCY OF 'JACOBINISM' IN THE EXECUTIVE COMMITTEE AND THE PARTY'S ORGANISATION IN THE ARMED FORCES

The weakness of Narodnaya Volya after 1 March is illustrated not only by this sanguine interpretation of the pogroms on the part of certain members of the party but also by the fact that the vacancies on its Executive Committee were now being filled either by individuals such as Lebedev and Martynov, whose qualifications for such eminence were dubious, or by revolutionaries such as Romanenko who had a record of disagreement with the old Executive Committee and had lived abroad during the most desperate phase of the terrorist campaign. Indeed, one of the new recruits to the Executive Committee, Stefanovich, had not only been in emigration until after the assassination of Alexander II, but had even belonged to the opposing revolutionary faction, Chornyy Peredel. Moreover, serious disagreement, which must have further weakened the leadership, evidently arose between Stefanovich and other members of the Executive Committee, for bitter accusations were subsequently made against him to the effect that he intended to undermine the party from within and to discredit terrorism, and that after his arrest he collaborated with the police and betrayed Bogdanovich, who was arrested in the spring of 1882.[32]

The dispute about the questionable sincerity of Stefanovich's allegiance to Narodnaya Volya was envenomed by references made in the course of it to a letter addressed by the Executive Committee to socialist émigrés in December 1881 and providing strong evidence that revolutionaries at the centre of the party were abandoning hopes of a democratic revolution. The letter, which is now reliably attributed to Tikhomirov,[33] unequivocally defined the party's ambition as the seizure of power in the near future. Tikhomirov argued that the ground for revolution had already been prepared and that it remained only to organise the *coup d'état* which would set the revolution in motion. Work among the masses was now pointless except in so far as it might promote the seizure of power. Great importance was attached to the role of the state. Political power had to be 'intelligently organised'. 'Revolution' could not be carried out until power rested 'in good hands'. And, despite his insistence that it was 'all the same' whether the intelligentsia or the unskilled working mass seized power, Tikhomirov now asserted that the masses, as long as they remained the 'slave of a thousand other conditions', would not be able to hold power themselves. Therefore, if the revolutionaries gained control of the political apparatus they would not relinquish it until they had 'put the people firmly on their feet'. There followed the usual assurances that the party would not make a 'permanent system' of this guardianship and that an Assembly of the Land would be convoked. Towards the end of the letter, no doubt anticipating the probable reaction of the émigrés to this *profession de foi*, Tikhomirov delivered himself of a few observations on political terminology. 'As for our Jacobinism,' he wrote apologetically, 'we don't know what to say.' Such foreign words caused so much trouble. The word 'Jacobin' was unpopular in Russia and for that reason the Narodovoltsy should not adopt the title, whatever its real meaning. Thus, even if they were 'Jacobins', the Narodovoltsy would not publicise the fact, for they might antagonise potential supporters and lay themselves open to the charge of 'despotism'.[34]

Former Narodovoltsy such as Figner and Korba, when they came to write their memoirs in the 1920s, did their utmost first to deny the existence of such a letter and then, when Deych published a copy of it, to represent it as a forgery on the grounds that its contents were implausible. Thus Korba argued – though not very sensibly – that Bogdanovich, Tellalov, Oshanina and Grachevsky, four of the most influential members of the Executive Committee by the beginning of 1882, were of such high moral calibre that they could not have been responsible for the composition of such a shameful epistle. Stefanovich, by contrast a man of low moral calibre, had written the letter himself, Korba alleged, in order to discredit the Executive Committee.[35] Nevertheless Korba, and Figner, must have known that the offensive letter was not an isolated example of the advocacy of seizure of power by the revolutionary minority after 1 March 1881, for at about the time that the émigrés received the letter early in 1881, nos. 8–9 of *Narodnaya volya* appeared in Russia, carrying an equally unambiguous leading article which defined the objective of the party as the 'carrying out of a *coup* by means of a conspiracy'. The party should concentrate its forces in the most important administrative centres and 'only among those elements' which were going to play an active role in the *coup* itself. The author of the article expressed the hope that the people themselves would be able to carry out the 'economic revolution' after the *coup* and that the temporary revolutionary government would have 'merely to sanction the economic equality won by the people' from their traditional oppressors and exploiters. But if events took a less favourable turn then the 'temporary revolutionary government' would itself implement the necessary economic changes.[36]

Taken in conjunction with Tikhomirov's letter, this article, which came to be regarded as the clearest statement of 'Jacobinism' by the Executive Committee of Narodnaya Volya,[37] may be seen as a further sign of the weakness of the party by the beginning of 1882: in the first place it represented a tacit acknowledgement that the revolutionaries stood on their own without the masses solidly behind them; and in the second place its publication showed that there were no longer enough, or sufficiently forceful, Narodovoltsy left at the centre of the party to preserve the ideals which the party had formerly cherished, for, as it happened, those few Narodovoltsy from the original Executive Committee who had survived the waves of arrests in 1880 and 1881 included precisely the individuals who had always leaned more strongly than the rest towards 'Jacobinism'. Tikhomirov, after all, in his capacity as editor of the journal of the Executive Committee, had been responsible for many of the statements – on the inertia of masses in particular and on the frailty of the Russian autocracy and the need to forestall the rise of the bourgeoisie – which linked the earliest Narodovoltsy most closely to Tkachov. Sergeyeva, Tikhomirov's wife, was also known for her Jacobin views, which, like Oshanina, she had acquired from Zaichnevsky in Oryol. As for Oshanina herself, a powerful personality much respected by her comrades, she was on home ground in Moscow, where the party now had its headquarters, and it is very probably her growing influence that accounts for the unashamedly Jacobin character of the leading article published in nos. 8–9 of *Narodnaya volya*. Oshanina may have been exaggerating when she declared in her memoirs that 'towards the end' all the members of the Executive Committee had become 'more or less' 'Jacobins';[38] but certainly in the absence of such inspiring leaders as Zhelyabov, Perovskaya and the other luminaries of the party in its first phase, she and Tikhomirov now enjoyed an unprecedented freedom to push the party in an authoritarian direction. And it was no doubt with this object in view that Tikhomirov was engaged at this time in forming within the Executive Committee a new 'alliance', a 'secret society', or, as it was ironically known by some, a 'council of generals'.[39] Very probably, too, it was the ascendancy of the Jacobins that lay behind the animosity towards Stefanovich, who as a former Chernoperedelets could have approved less than anyone of the direction Narodnaya Volya was now taking.

As the 'Jacobins' at the centre of Narodnaya Volya, who pinned their hopes on an armed insurrection, began to prevail, so the organisation in the armed forces was appropriately revived and given a more prominent role in the party's affairs. This development was assisted by several factors, particularly the mobility of the officers, posted to various corners of the Empire at short notice, the comparative inefficiency of the secret police in the remote garrison towns, and the slowness of the authorities to notice that revolutionary circles had begun to appear in the armed forces as well as in the higher educational institutions.

Towards the end of 1881 emissaries of the Executive Committee and the military centre of the party began to travel to garrison towns far from St Petersburg and Moscow in an attempt to organise local circles and incorporate them in the party's network. Groups sprang up in Tiflis, Odessa, Kiev, Minsk, Oryol, Orenburg, Pskov, Riga, Samara, Saratov and Vilna, and a circle led by Druzhinin in the Kronshtadt naval base, which had hitherto professed allegiance to Chornyy Peredel, also came over to the side of Narodnaya Volya .[40] A programme written for the military organisation and approved by the Executive Committee during the winter of 1881–2 reflected the importance now attached to work in the armed forces. An 'exclusively military' insurrection was envisaged with the 'seizure of supreme power' as the revolutionaries' objective.[41] Further extensive journeys were made by Rogachov (brother of the propagandist of the early

1870s) in the hope of strengthening the military organisation, early in 1882, and plans were also discussed for the compilation of the officers' own revolutionary journal.[42]

Despite the proud assertion of the Minister of the Interior, D. A. Tolstoy, in 1883, that not a single Guards officer had been arrested 'for Nihilism' and that those soldiers implicated in the activities of Narodnaya Volya belonged 'exclusively' to that class called 'Bourbons' (here used in the sense of 'upstarts') who were 'little better than *moujiks* in education and knowledge',[43] there is little doubt that attempts to subvert the armed forces disturbed the authorities more than any branch of revolutionary activity except terrorism. Their concern to stamp out the organisation in the forces is illustrated by the fact that death sentences passed on officers were more rarely commuted than those passed on civilians. And yet the very fact that Narodnaya Volya was compelled after 1 March to give a more central position in its ranks to the military organisation – which previously it had carefully isolated from other groups – serves again to show the extent of the depletion of the party's resources by this time. Moreover, a glance at some of the more or less extravagant and desperate plans being formulated by Butsevich, one of the prominent members of the military organisation, seems to provide further confirmation of the poverty of the party's strategy now that its major offensive had failed. The revolutionaries should not wait until whole garrisons were ready, Butsevich argued; a single company under strong leadership could render great assistance to the party by seizing the arsenal in the town in which it was stationed and handing the arms over to the people. Again, Butsevich suggested, the revolutionaries might disarm the entire Russian army while the soldiers attended the Easter service in church. About ten armed men could raid the arsenals, guarded only by a few Jews and Moslems, dismantle the rifles, put them in sacks, load them on a cart and dump them in the nearest river. Alternatively, the insurgents might capture the Kronshtadt fortress and launch an attack on St Petersburg. Or they might seize the Tsar, grand dukes and royal entourage during the May parade in St Petersburg and imprison them in Kronshtadt. Or, if an escape from the capital proved impossible, then they would have to kill the prisoners and themselves.[44]

Such severe blows soon began to fall on the party, however, that the Narodovoltsy had no chance to put the plans of the 'Jacobins' or of members of the military circles to the test. In February 1882 Lebedev, Martynov and Stefanovich were arrested in Moscow; Zlatopolsky was taken in April, the party's press was discovered, and soon afterwards

Butsevich, Grachevsky, Korba and others were arrested in St Petersburg. Tikhomirov and Sergeyeva escaped abroad and Oshanina followed them. Out of the Executive Committee of 1879–80 only one member remained active in Russia, Vera Figner, whose eloquence, beauty and distinguished revolutionary record made her a focal point for the party's remaining forces, first in Odessa and then in Kharkov until her own arrest in February 1883. One assassination was carried out during this period, in March 1882, when Strelnikov, an officer in the secret police, was shot in the face at point-blank range as he took his afternoon stroll in Odessa; another clandestine press was set up, plans were made to replenish the party's funds by robbing the treasury in Gori, and some work continued among the students in Kiev, Odessa and Kharkov. But, as she herself admitted, Figner was trying only to 'remake the likeness of what had been destroyed'.[45] The programme drawn up by her, while stressing the need for even greater security, reiterated former organisational principles and instead of recommending tactical innovations merely nominated more targets for the party's assassins.[46]

THE WORKERS' GROUPS OF NARODNAYA VOLYA IN ST PETERSBURG AND PROVINCIAL CITIES

The pre-eminence of Narodnaya Volya in the revolutionary movement at the beginning of the 1880s made it difficult to contemplate revolutionary activity in Russia under the banner of any other organisation. But as the old leaders were arrested and the terrorist campaign abated, more and more of the energy of the party's supporters came to be devoted to a form of activity, propaganda among the workers, for which Narodovolchestvo had no sound theoretical justification once the prospect of popular rebellion or insurrection supported by the masses had receded. In all probability force of circumstances helped the Narodovoltsy to allocate their resources in this way: propaganda in the factories was less demanding than a terrorist campaign and less fraught with danger. It also had certain advantages over the old practice of 'going to the people' in the countryside, for the facilities needed by the propagandist – a supply of literature and, ideally, a printing press on which to produce it – were easier to conceal in the town. Moreover, many workers were concentrated within a single factory or in the wretched hostels where they spent their short leisure, not scattered over a large area, and were consequently more accessible in large numbers to the propagandist than the peasant had been. There is no doubt, however, that the

Narodovoltsy found propaganda among the workers not merely convenient but also more rewarding than terrorism, for, however small the scale of such activity and however far the Narodovoltsy retreated from the main centres of political power, they still found some workers receptive to their message wherever large-scale industry was beginning to develop. It was as if exploitation in the factory broadened the outlook of the common people and strengthened their will to resist. Their misery seemed more obviously the product of human greed and an unjust social order than did the hardship of the peasant in the countryside, where natural disasters might plausibly be blamed for human suffering and where in any case the peasant persistently believed that he owned the land he tilled.

Even as the remnants of the Executive Committee of the party were being destroyed in 1881–2, students of St Petersburg University, Bodayev and Flyorov, who had known Zhelyabov and Perovskaya and had attended meetings of Narodnaya Volya's central student circle, were forming a new 'preparatory group' with a view to training propagandists for work in the factories of the capital and re-establishing and extending their connections there. Each propagandist was to be given at most three workers' circles and each circle would consist of only three to six members. The more advanced workers were drafted into a special circle for more intensive study of subjects such as political economy and the condition of the working class in Russia and abroad. Contact was maintained with teachers in the schools which provided elementary education for workers in the capital; sometimes workers from the circles would be sent to these schools, while teachers in the schools would in turn send promising pupils from their classes to the propagandists. Reading-material used in the circles covered a broad spectrum of socialist thought and included much imaginative literature, especially literature dealing with the life of the masses, such as the poetry of Nekrasov and the stories of Gleb Uspensky.[47] Thus thoroughness and a certain patience were now beginning to characterise the work of some members of Narodnaya Volya, as if these revolutionaries were preparing for a more protracted campaign than that envisaged by their predecessors up until a year before. Their main concern was now to win 'conscious' adherents in the working class; 'demagogical' methods they dismissed as unsuitable for the preparatory phase of revolutionary struggle. Indeed, so seriously did some Narodovoltsy now take the task of preparing cadres of 'conscious' workers that they were apparently beginning to look on propaganda in the factories as the be-all and end-all of revolutionary activity and to keep their distance from the party's other sympathisers lest implication in disorders such as student demonstrations jeopardise this activity. For these reasons Bodayev and Flyorov for a while dissociated themselves from the student movement in St Petersburg and operated independently of the party centre there. When they did formally affiliate their workers' group to the party early in 1883 they did so because they found others at the centre of the party who respected their evaluation of the usefulness of this branch of activity and who indeed saw it as one of the party's most 'serious and revolutionary' functions.[48]

In Kharkov, Kiev and Odessa, too, some Narodovoltsy were stepping up their activity in the factories and operating there with some success, as the authorities ruefully admitted.[49] Some of the party's members in these centres, it is true, still nourished characteristically violent ambitions. Goncharov in Kharkov and Levinsky in Kiev, for example, hoped to form 'battle detachments' among the workers, while pupils of a school in Kherson and students in Odessa discussed the perpetration of some act of terrorism in a factory with a view to dispelling the torpor which prevailed among some provincial workers.[50] But many Narodovoltsy in the southern cities, such as Bakh, a former Kiev University student and one of the party's leading itinerant organisers in 1883–4, now seemed prepared, like those in St Petersburg, to devote most of their attention to more patient propaganda among the workers, beginning by reading legal publications, gradually introducing social and political topics into their talks and only turning to illegal literature and discussion of the programme and activity of Narodnaya Volya when the group could be considered entirely trustworthy.[51]

Those Narodovoltsy who advocated propaganda in the factories found rather unexpected encouragement in some of the smaller towns to which their attention was turned as the party's forces were dispersed through the provinces. Conditions were particularly favourable for them in Rostov, an important port situated near the mouth of the Don, which by the beginning of the 1880s housed several foundries, mechanical engineering plants, tobacco factories and the main workshops of the Caucasian railway network. In the summer months large numbers of men would come into the town in search of seasonal employment in the docks loading grain. Even the *bosyaki*, drifting workers, a lumpenproletariat among whom it would have been difficult to build a stable organisation, had a certain use as bearers of the revolutionary message to other towns.[52] Militant feeling had been widespread, at least since 1879, when many workers had run amok in the town, ransacking several police stations following the arrest of one of their number.[53] And now after 1 March Narodnaya Volya inherited from

Chornyy Peredel a number of circles already in existence in Rostov in which they began to work systematically under the leadership of Peshekerov, younger brother of the network's founder.[54] The party was assisted in this work by the comparative freedom from police supervision in such provincial backwaters and also by the outstanding quality of local labour leaders such as Karpenko and Kudryashov. Late in 1883 the workers produced a journal, entitled *Rabochiy* (*The Worker*), the first Russian revolutionary publication consisting entirely of material supplied by the workers themselves. The journal opened with a 'letter' urging the soldiers no longer to defend the government; another contribution, *à propos* of the coronation of Alexander III, attempted to explode the belief that the ruler was benevolent towards his people, and other articles dealt with the concentration of capital, the introduction of new machinery into factories and the resultant redundancies, and the appalling conditions in which workers lived. Historical experience, one contributor argued, had shown that 'not a single "reformer", not a single "emancipator"', had improved the position of the workers. And yet united, organised and self-reliant, the workers would become an awesome and irresistible force.[55]

Another hitherto neglected town which proved in the 1880s to have worthwhile material for the revolutionaries was Yekaterinoslav, situated some 250 miles to the west and north of Rostov and incorporated in the railway network in 1884. The importance of the town for the revolutionary camp grew as the town's industry developed. Located between the rich coal deposits of the Donetsk Basin to the east and the iron-ore mines of Krivoy Rog to the west, Yekaterinoslav rapidly became a centre for the metal-working and metallurgical industries. Whereas at the beginning of the 1880s it accommodated only a few small foundries, by the end of the decade it housed several large workshops and plants. Narodnaya Volya had some sympathisers there among the pupils of one of the schools who in 1881 had tried to incite disorders, and under the supervision of the party, workers' circles began to develop in 1884–5.[56]

The shift to this more productive, if less glamorous, form of activity was by no means inconsistent with what might be termed the classical Narodovolchestvo of 1879–81. It will be recalled that leading members of the old Executive Committee, such as Zhelyabov and Perovskaya, had devoted much attention to the urban workers in 1880–1, when conditions seemed to demand it, and in any case it was axiomatic that the party should be flexible and constantly modify its tactics in the light of current needs and opportunities. There was nothing in Narodovolchestvo that precluded or discouraged activity among the masses so long as such activity seemed useful at the given moment; indeed, most Narodovoltsy, unlike Tkachov, had always been keen to return to such work. All the same, the early Narodovoltsy had not envisaged such heavy concentration on this form of activity and had not therefore added much to the traditional Populist view of the purpose of propaganda among the urban workers. Like the Chaykovtsy and the Zemlevoltsy before them, they had not drawn the sharp distinction between workers and peasants that their comparatively warm reception in the factories might have warranted. Indeed, they considered the workers in most industries and enterprises to be still peasants in a sense, since these workers had only recently come to the towns from the countryside and frequently returned to the villages for seasonal work, holidays or visits to their families. The workers were simply the members of the mass whose domicile and mentality made them most accessible to the intelligentsia and they were therefore the best carriers of the revolutionary message to the countryside, where the party was weak. Hence the eagerness of some Narodovoltsy, such as those in Odessa in 1880–1, for example, to win over to their side workers who had just moved into the town but were not permanently settled there.[57] The activity of Narodnaya Volya among the urban workers in 1883–4 might therefore have been effective and satisfying, but its ultimate purpose, as the prospects of revolutionary upheaval receded, could no longer have been so clear as before.

A further problem for Narodovoltsy who were devoting themselves to propaganda among the workers, apart from their lack of a strong and positive theoretical justification for this form of activity, was the need to reconcile themselves to the relatively *passive* role that their party was in fact beginning to play (in spite of the bluster of some of its members), for to a certain extent the party's propagandists were sacrificing the initiative that Narodnaya Volya had so boldly seized in 1879. Some aspects of their experience in the south, for example, suggest that far from giving history a push they were beginning to yield to history's barely perceptible processes. The existence and success of the workers' circle in Rostov, after all, clearly owed as much to the talents and labours of workers themselves as to the efforts of Narodovoltsy. Moreover, it was workers such as Karpenko, Kudryashov and one of the party's prominent organisers during the years 1883–4, Antonov, rather than members of the party from the ranks of the intelligentsia, who were mainly responsible for the development of the new circles in Yekaterinoslav. Nor could the party's propagandists be sure even that all the tenets of Narodovolchestvo would be accepted uncritically once firm contact was established with such independent workers as those in Rostov. Some workers, such as one Rudomyotov, did believe that terrorism was the only form of political struggle that the party could wage, but others altogether repudiated violence, even terrorism in its 'factory' and 'agrarian' forms.[58] Thus while Narodnaya Volya, as the most prestigious revolutionary party in Russia, undoubtedly enjoyed considerable authority in workers' circles, it was in all probability not able to exercise full control over all the circles in which it gained a following.

It could not have been easy for all revolutionaries who had been inspired by the terrorist campaign of their predecessors and who saw their party as providing dynamic leadership in the revolutionary movement to accept the more cautious and self-effacing work, much of it in remote provincial towns far from the centre of political power, to which many Narodovoltsy were now devoting themselves. And before long, in 1884, the need to take account of the new emphasis in the party's activity and to revive, in the new circumstances, the tradition of violence for which the party was famed, found reflection in – though it was not perhaps the only cause of – a controversy that broke out between the so-called 'old' and 'young' factions of the party.

THE DISPUTE BETWEEN THE 'OLD' AND 'YOUNG' NARODOVOLTSY IN 1884

The success of the workers' groups of Narodnaya Volya in 1882–3 was thrown into relief by the disarray of the party as a whole during those years. A tenuous unity was preserved only by means of the prolonged journeyings to the provincial centres by a number of revolutionaries who came to the fore after the collapse of the old Executive Committee, notably Antonov, Bakh, Ivanov and Ovchinnikov. St Petersburg had by now become, in the words of Ivanov, who returned there at the end of 1882 after escaping from Siberia, the 'most inconvenient place out of all the large cities' in which to attempt to establish a base for the party.[59] The 'centre' which existed there in 1883 exercised no formal control over the party's provincial groups.

To a large extent the responsibility for the desperate position in which the party now found itself rested with Degayev, the first major representative of that type so striking in the history of the Russian revolutionary movement, the traitor who contrived simultaneously to help build an organisation and to destroy it by collaboration with the police. Arrested late in 1882 as he was engaged in regrouping Narodnaya Volya's forces in the south, Degayev soon began to divulge to the police all he knew about the remnants of the party, in which he had by this time, owing to the rapid depopulation of its upper echelons, achieved some eminence. Information provided by Degayev helped the police to arrest Figner, to whom he presented himself in Kharkov early in 1883, claiming to have escaped from the police by throwing snuff in the face of his escort. On his return to St Petersburg Degayev continued to collude with the police, regularly meeting Sudeykin (a lieutenant-colonel in the gendarmerie with a more successful record than most in the struggle against the revolutionary movement), but he also set up another clandestine press and played an important part in discussions which took place in the capital in October 1883 concerning the reorganisation of the party centre. Degayev's activity in both his guises was shortly to be curtailed, however, for towards the middle of 1883 he seems to have been moved to go to Paris and to repent of his sins to the émigré leaders of the party and to have struck a bargain with them: his life would be spared if he would kill Sudeykin and then have no further involvement in the revolutionary movement. Thus in December 1883 at Degayev's lodgings in St Petersburg Sudeykin was shot in the back and clubbed to death, with considerable difficulty, by two Narodovoltsy summoned from Kiev for the purpose. Degayev was hastily spirited out of the country, reunited with his wife whom the émigrés had held in London pending his return, and allowed to emigrate to the United States, where he worked first as an unskilled labourer and later as a university teacher and professor of mathematics in South Dakota.[60]

The group of Narodovoltsy Degayev was helping to consolidate in St Petersburg towards the end of 1883 was to provide leaders both for a concerted and significant attempt to revive the party, which took place in 1884, and for the faction which in the same year entered into heated controversy with supporters of those émigrés with whom Degayev had recently re-established contact. Prominent among these 'young' Narodovoltsy, as the members of this faction came to be known, were Ovchinnikov (whose support could not have been very valuable: he was 'something of a dreamer', recalled one of his contemporaries);[61] members of the intelligentsia such as Karaulov and the Populist publicist Krivenko; and the leaders of the flourishing workers' group, Bodayev and Flyorov. The most notable representative of the 'young' faction, however, was Yakubovich, a regular contributor to the journal *Russkoye bogatstvo* (*Russian Wealth*), who was beginning to enjoy a certain prestige as a 'civic' poet. Yakubovich had already made a substantial contribution to the revolutionary movement by the time disagreement broke out between the factions in 1884, having in autumn 1883 created a 'Union of the Youth of Narodnaya Volya' with a view to supervising the party's work in the 'self-education' circles among the students of the capital, recruiting students into the party and providing an 'intellectual and practical revolutionary school' for the preparation of future activists. Yakubovich also hoped through the Union to discourage the student disorders in the higher educational institutions, which invariably resulted in numerous arrests and each year deprived the revolutionary camp of many of its most militant members.[62]

In opposition to Yakubovich and his supporters there stood the 'old' Narodovoltsy, Oshanina and Tikhomirov, the only members of the old Executive Committee still at large and retaining an active interest in the revolutionary movement, but both long since in Parisian exile. Close to these leaders, in whom supreme authority within the party was still vested, were other revolutionaries formerly active in the ranks of Narodnaya Volya in Russia, such as Chernyavskaya and Serebryakov, more recent refugees such as Salova and Sukhomlin and two new and distinguished allies of the party, Lavrov and Lopatin, the latter a revolutionary of long standing, well known and much respected in international socialist circles. Inside Russia the 'old' Narodovoltsy were supported by Bakh and Ivanov; by Stepurin, one of the prominent members of the party in St Petersburg; by Sabunayev, who also had a certain standing in the capital; and, as it transpired, by local groups in most of the provincial centres, including Moscow, Kharkov, Rostov, Kazan and even Yaroslavl, where the party had attracted several enthusiastic supporters in the law school.[63]

Early in 1884 the émigrés met in Paris to review their own role in the movement in the new conditions. They decided that the Executive Committee of the party should be located inside Russia, but that pending the proper revival of the party Oshanina and Tikhomirov should remain abroad in control of the journal, *Vestnik 'Narodnoy voli'* (*Herald of 'Narodnaya Volya'*), which had been set up in Geneva in 1883, and in charge of the addresses of the party's connections so that another wave of arrests in Russia should not preclude further reorganisation. It was agreed formally to dissolve the old Executive Committee and to transfer its powers to a new central group of seventeen people, to be headed by an 'administrative commission' consisting of Lopatin, Salova and Sukhomlin, all three of whom promptly set out for St Petersburg with the purpose of reuniting the party's groups inside Russia.

The choice of Lopatin as head of the 'administrative commission' had both its advantages and disadvantages. On the one hand, Lopatin enjoyed a reputation that was sure to earn him respect, and a love of active involvement in the struggle that fitted him for a difficult organisational task. Born in 1845 into a gentry family of quite ancient lineage, Lopatin was a man of considerable talents. He had a good command of English, French and German and undertook translations of works by Spencer and Taine as well as parts of Marx's *Capital*. Writers such as Turgenev and Gleb Uspensky held him in high regard,[64] Marx and Engels considered him their intimate friend. From his own student days in the 1860s Lopatin had always been close to the revolutionary camp, undiscriminatingly assisting various groups. In 1870, by now in emigration, he was elected a member of the General Council of the First Workingmen's International. But the life of an émigré never satisfied Lopatin and the thirst for practical activity repeatedly drove him back to Russia, where he helped Lavrov to escape from exile in Vologda and made an unsuccessful attempt to free Chernyshevsky from his Siberian captivity. On the occasions when he himself fell into the hands of the authorities Lopatin made audacious escapes; in 1883, for example, he galloped off on a stolen horse into the woods around Yakutsk and made his way several thousand miles across Siberia and back to St Petersburg before fleeing the country. On the other hand, though, Lopatin's talents and energies were combined with a disdain for the simplest rules of conspiracy, which was bound to endanger the organisation he was hoping to reunify. While carrying out his revolutionary mission in Moscow in 1884, for example, he insisted on using his own name, would freely visit his friends in society and spend nights at their houses, and would drive fellow revolutionaries to despair by taking meals in a student refectory, where there were always likely to be police agents. Other Narodovoltsy could therefore claim with justification that revolutionary work was an occupation which Lopatin pursued 'like an amateur actor', that in conspiratorial matters he was an 'absolute child'.[65] Equally damaging was an arrogance which infuriated those towards whom it was directed, not least the 'young' Narodovoltsy, whom Lopatin derisively dismissed as troublemakers.

For some time after Lopatin, accompanied by Salova, arrived in St Petersburg the 'young' Narodovoltsy remained recalcitrant. They were particularly angered by the overweening manner in which Lopatin conducted negotiations with them, and also by the fact that the new central group elected by the émigrés contained only one member, Ovchinnikov, who could be said to represent them. Soon Flyorov was appointed to the commission and Yakubovich became a *de facto* member as well, but antagonism between the two factions persisted. Envoys were despatched to the provinces by the 'young' Narodovoltsy in a fresh attempt to sway local groups and a proclamation was printed on a new press set up in Dorpat giving notice of the division of Narodnaya Volya into independent organisations and sketching the position of the 'young' faction. The need for unity remained acute, however, and before long Yakubovich had returned to St Petersburg for further negotiations. Agreement was finally reached and the reconciliation confirmed in a notice published in the tenth number of *Narodnaya volya*, which appeared in September 1884.[66] That is not to say that the reconciliation proved to be of much practical use, though, for Lopatin, who in a bout of feverish activity in the summer of 1884 had visited local groups in Moscow, Odessa, Rostov and Kharkov in the hope of reunifying the party's scattered forces,[67] was arrested in St Petersburg in October and found to be carrying a largely uncoded list of the names of the party's agents and contacts. Heartened by this windfall, the police again made numerous arrests in all the main centres of the party's activity. Yakubovich, who briefly assumed control after Lopatin's arrest, was himself taken in November, and Narodovolchestvo in St Petersburg went into an irreversible decline.

To a certain extent the conflict of 1884 must be seen as the result of an attempt on the part of the 'young' Narodovoltsy to come to terms with the experience of the party in Russia after 1 March and with the failure of the ambitions it had nourished in the first phase of its activity. The proposals of the 'young' Narodovoltsy on organisational matters reflect this concern to adapt the party to new conditions. They provided for some relaxation of the centralist principle that had always dominated the party's thinking on its organisation. Yakubovich's programme of the 'young' faction did envisage the survival of a central group and local central groups supervising the work of the party in their regions. But the 'central committee', as the new central group would be known, would be responsible only for the preservation of the party's ideological unity and the publication of its journal and would have diminished jurisdiction over the party's other groups. Its authority would be further reduced by a change in the method of recruitment to its units: rather than co-opting new members it would accept representatives elected by local central groups. The convocation of frequent conferences at which the 'central committee' would surrender its authority and submit its actions to the judgement of the delegates of local groups would also help to make the party's central authority more susceptible to, and representative of, the wishes and interests of the membership as a whole.[68]

On the purely practical level, these organisational proposals seemed to offer some protection from the sort of damage recently inflicted on the party by a traitor who had won the confidence of those at the centre. But they also seemed to respond to the needs of a party which was now devoting most of its energies not so much to more or less single-minded struggle with the autocracy as to propaganda in a large number of localities. Certainly the 'young' Narodovoltsy had much to say on the subject of propaganda among the workers. Yakubovich, in one of the testimonies he gave to the police in 1885 – and usually there is no reason to doubt the accuracy of such statements on matters of revolutionary theory and practice – declared that the 'workers' question' was the 'main cause' of the split of 1884.[69] In a later testimony he referred to the concern of the 'young' Narodovoltsy to broaden the party's base, to expand the network of local revolutionary groups and to win over the workers.[70] Similar concerns had been expressed in a resolution at the congress of the party in St Petersburg in October 1883 and affirmed in a programmatic statement of the 'young' party in May 1884.[71] In any case the 'young' faction drew most of its support from precisely those Narodovoltsy, the members of the workers' group of Bodayev and Flyorov, who had been carefully conducting their propaganda in the factories of St Petersburg and had been so anxious to safeguard that activity.

Moreover, in the hope of forging a closer link between the revolutionary intelligentsia and the popular masses, the 'young' Narodovoltsy began to express a preference for 'economic' terrorism as opposed to the 'political' terrorism with which the name of Narodnaya Volya had come to be associated. Already at the conference of 1883 it had been decided to wage 'agrarian' and 'factory' terror as alternatives to political terror directed at the autocracy and its officials.[72] The 'young' Narodovoltsy reasoned thus: if they were to move nearer to the masses they might often have to kill some official responsible for putting down a peasant revolt or some factory owner who called out the Cossacks to suppress a strike and pacify his workers, rather than liquidate a Sudeykin whom neither workers nor peasants knew and whom the authorities would soon replace with another of his kind. Thus, although the 'young' Narodovoltsy did approve of the killing of spies and traitors, in general they recommended acts of terrorism which were 'closer to the daily needs and interests of the working people'. Besides, once such 'economic' terrorism had helped the masses to understand the revolutionaries, political terrorism would also become more easily comprehensible to them.[73]

However, to draw attention to the undoubted concern of the 'young'

Narodovoltsy to safeguard and promote their propaganda among the factory workers is not a sufficient explanation of their dispute with the 'old' Narodovoltsy in 1884. The conflict was also indicative of the strains produced by the retreat of an organisation whose mission was active combat in Russia but whose leaders – or at least those who claimed ultimate authority in the party – now lived abroad. The Executive Committee no longer exemplified the heroic spirit of a party of action. The party's leaders had put themselves *hors de combat*. And yet they still made decisions, elected commissions and sent emissaries to Russia as if they retained the right to control the affairs of those who were more actively continuing the struggle. They seemed to have 'forgotten Russia and its needs'. Thus when Lopatin, Salova and Sukhomlin arrived in Russia early in 1884 they were seen by active Narodovoltsy in the capital as 'Varangians', alien rulers like the Scandinavians led by Ryurik who, according to the chronicles, had come to exact tribute from the Slav tribes at the dawn of Russian history.[74] Undoubtedly, this grievance was aggravated by several factors: by the unwillingness of the émigrés to review the platform of the party in the light of the latest developments; by the failure of the émigrés to disclose to the Narodovoltsy inside Russia all they knew of Degayev's treachery; and by the arrogance with which Lopatin treated them in the course of negotiations between the factions. Finally, personal animosities further exacerbated relations. 'All kinds of differences' arose, wrote a Muscovite Narodovolets of the time, 'at first on personal grounds' and in the form of rivalry between individuals who thought highly of themselves; but soon, 'according to the Russian custom', personal conflict developed into a matter of principle.[75]

A number of factors seem to provide confirmation that the basic cause of the disagreement between the 'old' and 'young' Narodovoltsy in 1884 lay in the vague unease of the 'young' faction at the party's current passivity rather than in deep dissatisfaction with the party's theoretical position. Firstly, it is indicative of the lack of clear divisions on theoretical matters that the author of an article intended for the tenth number of *Narodnaya volya* as an expression of the views of the 'young' Narodovoltsy was Stepurin, one of the St Petersburg revolutionaries ultimately sympathetic to the 'old' faction.[76] Secondly, the frequency with which Narodovoltsy who were engaged in the controversy changed their opinions also suggests a lack of profound theoretical differences. Yakubovich had at first heatedly opposed 'economic' terrorism. Flyorov soon sought a compromise with the 'old' Narodovoltsy.[77] Yakubovich himself accomplished a volte-face in the summer of 1884 and began to criticise the recalcitrant members of the workers' group, who refused to do likewise.[78] Olesinov, one of the propagandists in this group, continued to operate independently for a while but later became more 'compliant'.[79] Finally, and most importantly, the 'young' Narodovoltsy did not question the general validity of Narodovolchestvo. Yakubovich explicitly stated that he accepted the 'social and political' views of Narodnaya Volya even as the differences between the 'old' and 'young' factions were coming to a head. The theory of Narodnaya Volya was the 'only vital revolutionary theory for Russia at the given historical moment'.[80] The programme of the old Executive Committee remained the 'basis' for the activity of the 'young' faction.[81] Even in their thinking on the 'workers' question', in their discussion of the virtues of 'economic' terrorism, the 'young' Narodovoltsy seemed to be succumbing to the traditional appeal of violence for the party. In any case the old doctrine evidently continued to attract many other revolutionaries besides the 'young' Narodovoltsy inside Russia, such as Bakh and most of the members of the provincial groups who, in spite of their success in the factories, did not even waver in their support for the established leadership in 1884. Indeed, it was becoming increasingly doubtful whether it was possible to make substantially new developments in the tactics of Narodnaya Volya without altogether abandoning the spirit of the party in its first phase.

ORZHIKH'S ATTEMPT TO REBUILD THE PARTY IN 1885

The history of Narodnaya Volya after 1884 seems to underline the unalterability of the party's doctrine. Whenever leading Narodovoltsy were called upon to make major theoretical pronouncements or to look for an outlet for the frustration they inevitably experienced when working patiently in pursuit of long-term objectives, they consistently reverted to the aggressive 'heroic' stance of their predecessors and reaffirmed their basic assumptions.

With the collapse of Lopatin's organisation at the end of 1884 Narodnaya Volya as an organised entity ceased to exist. Those Narodovoltsy who had for the moment eluded the police, such as Bakh and Ivanov, had either gone into hiding inside Russia or had left the country. Nevertheless one further attempt to revive the party on a national scale was made, in 1885, by a young Jewish revolutionary, Orzhikh. Born in Odessa in 1864, Orzhikh, like so many of his contemporaries, fell in with revolutionaries while still at school. His father, a lawyer, prospered sufficiently to move with the family to

Tobolsk in the 1870s and thence to Tomsk, where Orzhikh met, among others, the leading Narodovolets Bogdanovich, took part in attempts to free prisoners on their way to Siberian exile, harboured revolutionaries seeking refuge from the police, and became adept in the necessary skills of the revolutionary, forging papers and sewing documents into the binding of books. Late in 1881 the family left Tomsk for Odessa to seek medical treatment for the mentally sick father and back in his native city Orzhikh entered the University, where he immediately began again to move in revolutionary circles. By the autumn of 1883 he had built a small group of his own in Odessa and the following summer went on behalf of this group to the Russo-Rumanian border to make arrangements with smugglers about the importation of 'illegal' literature, passing through Kiev on his return to consolidate connections there. While he had been away, however, most of the members of his group in Odessa had been arrested and he was now forced to take refuge, first in Yelizavetgrad, then in Kharkov, where he went 'illegal'. After a trip to Yekaterinoslav, where a workers' group led by Yasevich remained at large, Orzhikh returned to Kharkov and began to devote himself to the revival of Narodnaya Volya.[82] In this task he was assisted by V. G. Bogoraz, another young Jewish revolutionary, who was subsequently to receive some renown as a writer and scholar in the fields of ethnography, philology and folklore, and who in 1885, by the age of twenty, was already the erudite leader of a circle of Narodovoltsy in Taganrog, where he had attended the same *gimnaziya* as Chekhov.

It cannot be coincidental that the leaders of the new attempt to revive Narodnaya Volya – and several of the other revolutionaries at the centre of the organisation they built (for example, Kogan, Krol, Shekhter, Shternberg) – were Jews. That the Jewish involvement in Narodnaya Volya should suddenly become much more sharply apparent in 1885 is no doubt due in part to the increased official persecution of the Jews after the assassination of Alexander II and to the pogroms, which had been most widespread and virulent in precisely that area, the Ukraine, from which Jewish Narodovoltsy now emerged. But the new prominence of Jews in Narodnaya Volya is also undoubtedly a reflection of the fact that cities such as Kharkov, Kiev, Odessa and Yekaterinoslav, where there had long been a sizeable Jewish population, were now assuming greater importance for the revolutionary movement. St Petersburg had again ceased to serve as the focal point for Narodnaya Volya in 1885. Any revolutionary who contemplated reorganisation of the party there had to reckon with the comparative efficiency of the secret police in the capital and with the incurable inquisitiveness of the *dvorniki*, or concierges, who now made it difficult to live undetected for long as an 'illegal'.[83] In most of the southern towns, especially the smaller ones, on the other hand, officials still slumbered, stirring only when orders came from St Petersburg. Conditions for an organisation such as Narodnaya Volya were therefore much more favourable. And yet at the same time the insignificance and remoteness of the centres in which Narodovoltsy began to establish themselves under-lined again, and to an even greater extent than before, the frailty of the party and threw into perspective the *braggadocio* of its leaders. There is an absurd naïvety in Orzhikh's claim that he hoped to set up a 'base for broad revolutionary work' in Rostov and even more rustic neighbouring towns such as Novocherkassk and Taganrog,[84] which did not even have the advantage of an embryonic proletariat to commend them. Nor could he have realistically hoped to recruit very useful support in small coastal towns such as Simferopol and Sevastopol, which he also visited in the course of his protracted journeyings in the south.

In 1885 the new leaders of the party held a congress at Yekaterinoslav. They elected a new central group, discussed tactics and agreed to give priority to the publication of more illegal literature in the hope of showing the public that Narodnaya Volya was still in good health.[85] In October they succeeded in producing a further substantial issue of the party's journal (the last number ever to appear) and at the end of the year printed a pamphlet by Bogoraz, who had been elected to the centre at the recent congress. The revival of the party was short-lived, however: at the end of 1885 and the beginning of 1886 arrests in many towns again destroyed the organisation. And although a further stubborn attempt was made in 1886 to sustain the party in Kharkov, Moscow and Tula, where a new press functioned briefly under the direction of Bogoraz and Kogan, Narodnaya Volya had by this time been effectively crushed.

It is very clear from the views expressed in their copious publications and in their discussions at the congress in Yekaterinoslav that, in spite of the plight of the party by the middle of the 1880s, these new Narodovoltsy envisaged no substantial changes in the party's basic assumptions, strategy and tactics. Central to the argument of Bogoraz's pamphlet on the 'struggle of social forces in Russia', for example, were a familiar premiss – that the various 'social forces' were not the same as their Western European counterparts and stood in different relationships to one another – and the deduction that the strategy of Russian revolutionaries should be corre-spondingly different from those commended by Western socialists. The

Russian gentry, Bogoraz contended, had been reduced to political impotence, or rather it had never tasted of political power at all. Whereas in Western Europe the nobles had been strong enough to fight the monarchy and 'often even to triumph completely', in Russia the gentry had at an early date been subdued by the despotic tsars. Again, the bourgeoisie in the West differed greatly from that in Russia. The French bourgeoisie, for instance, had already been strong, self-confident and dissatisfied with the *ancien régime* by the time of the French revolution; it had been able to speak in the name of all the people, and it had attracted the best elements from other estates, including the ruling classes, with the result that the monarchy had been easily overthrown. In Russia, on the other hand, that section of the population that went by the name of 'bourgeoisie' was so weak and so dependent on the caprice of the autocrat that it could scarcely be seen as an independent 'estate'. Russian entrepreneurs might clamour for protective legislation, but they prospered only because the Russian govenment had begun to indulge itself, after the emancipation of the serfs, in the fancy that it could create wealth on a Western European scale if only it could create industry and a bourgeoisie according to a Western European pattern, too. Thus the Russian bourgeoisie was a 'monstrous' creature sustained 'exclusively' by the government and bound to disappear with it. As for the supreme power in Russia, the autocracy was a law unto itself with no foundations or support in the Russian social structure – Tikhomirov's 'colossus of iron on feet of clay' – the very existence of which would be put in jeopardy by the first strong blow inflicted on it. Certainly, this blow would have to be delivered quickly, as earlier Narodovoltsy had insisted, for it was quite possible that Russian society would yet develop along Western European lines (indeed, the government had already taken steps to bring about this development), and the road to capitalism, even if it did lead ultimately to socialism, as Marxists supposed, passed first through a 'very foul purgatory' which the Narodovoltsy of 1885 were no more prepared to countenance than their predecessors had been.[86] But if the autocratic régime *were* overthrown, then a 'gigantic' step would have been taken towards the healing of all social ills, for the autocracy, these Narodovoltsy still believed, was the source of all ailments in the Russian organism, a 'festering ulcer' which was undermining the nation's health as 'slowly and surely as rust corrodes iron'. And, precisely because the effects of the ulcer were so far-reaching, the prospects for a complete recovery, once it had been properly treated, seemed good.[87]

In their attitude towards terrorism, as well as in their views on the 'social forces' in Russia, the Narodovoltsy of 1885 resembled their predecessors. They harboured no doubts about the value of the tactic in principle or about the need to begin again to apply it systematically against the government. Shternberg, another of the Narodovoltsy elected to the centre at the congress at Yekaterinoslav, defended terrorism in a blusterous pamphlet and attempted to provide a serious theoretical basis for it, arguing that it was no longer an intuitive reaction to persecution, a means of revenge, or the 'unconscious protest of despair', but rather a *conscious and considered* revolutionary weapon. Certainly terrorism was not a universally appropriate means of struggle, Shternberg admitted. The Fenians in Ireland, for example, would not achieve radical results by its use because they were making attacks on a deeply entrenched system, English landowning; in other words, they were attempting to undermine the powerful 'economic interests of a whole category of people'. But in Russia, where terrorism was directed at a clearly defined and isolated target – the Tsar, the incarnation of all the evil in the realm, and the 'handful of pillars of despotism' who supported him – political violence was entirely appropriate. Indeed, it was the only feasible tactic, for although the party could count on the indifference of the masses towards the fate of the government, it could not expect them to initiate the revolution themselves. (The peasant, in particular, would endure almost any conditions, Shternberg admitted in terms reminiscent of Tikhomirov's articles of 1879 and 1880, rather than exchange them for a 'risky future'.)[88] Bogoraz, too, enumerated the assets of terrorism in his own pamphlet and in the pages of *Narodnaya volya*, arguing that it might bring the autocracy to the verge of ruin and even deal the fatal blow, that it had great 'moral significance' as a means of awakening society and the masses from their long slumber, that it would breathe courage into the most timid spirits, undermine the authority of the government and encourage the masses to wage a similar campaign on their own account.[89] Orzhikh also spoke in favour of terrorism as a possible means of overthrowing the autocracy in a firmly worded reply drafted to a letter from Tikhomirov in which the émigré counselled cautious reorganisation. If the party gave itself up to propaganda then the government would regain support and the revolutionaries would lose the sympathy of the public. Viewed in this light, each act of terrorism seemed a 'step forward'.[90] Indeed, early in 1885 Orzhikh was apparently contemplating the assassination of the Minister of the Interior, D. A. Tolstoy, and he even went to Novocherkassk to collect bombs for the purpose, although the attempt was never carried out and the bombs were prudently abandoned in a pond.[91]

In yet other respects as well the Narodovoltsy of 1885 were true to the spirit of Narodnaya Volya in its earlier phases. They were no less impetuous than their predecessors, fearing lest the oncoming wave of capitalism in Russia should submerge the instincts and institutions on which socialism might be built there. 'Faster, comrades! In close order let us rush into battle!' proclaimed some verses at the beginning of their journal.[92] Shternberg, too, urged a new revolutionary onslaught as soon as possible and reminded his readers at the end of his pamphlet that time was precious: 'any delay' was a 'step backwards' and ruinous for society, and bolstered the hopes of the government.[93] Again, like the founders of the party and the 'young' Narodovoltsy, they were eager to wage the struggle within Russia and rejected the interference of émigrés in their affairs: they even refused, for instance, to tell Tikhomirov exactly where their press was located.[94] They also attempted, just as their predecessors had done, to convince the public, and perhaps themselves, that the masses were ready to erupt 'like a terrible storm'; thus in an 'internal review' in nos. 11–12 of *Narodnaya volya* Bogoraz chronicled the manifestations of popular discontent.[95]

At the same time, however, these southern Narodovoltsy went further than most of their predecessors in their glorification of the revolutionary minority. Bogoraz, for example, described this minority in exalted terms, reminiscent of Chernyshevsky's passages on Rakhmetov in *What is to be done?*, as the 'salt of the earth', the 'most powerful and active force of progress', which contained in its ranks 'fighters' who were distinguished from 'other people' by the 'flame of divine fire' burning 'within their breasts'.[96] Bogoraz also seems, in spite of his account of unrest among the masses, to have placed little hope on the masses as a political force in the near future: even if they were given an opportunity to exercise political power, they might, he feared, quickly relinquish it. These extreme formulations of the potency of the intelligentsia, on the one hand, and the unreadiness of the people for an active role in the country's political life, on the other, encouraged a revival of the Jacobin strain which had come to the fore after the assassination of Alexander II when Tikhomirov and Oshanina had enjoyed their greatest authority in the party. Thus Bogoraz assigned to the intelligentsia not only the task of generating the revolutionary upheaval but also the responsibility for ensuring that the people did not accept a new pretender to the throne once the autocracy had been defeated. This responsibility the revolutionaries would fulfil by stepping into the political arena with their set of 'magical ideas'. 'Immediately, before the bewitching force of these ideas', all the trappings of tsarism would disperse, 'like smoke'. The people would accept the revolutionary intelligentsia as 'leader and chief'. Any social force, Bogoraz argued in justification of this reassertion of the 'Jacobin' tendency of Narodovolchestvo, should use the remnants of the political organisation of the defeated force for its own purposes upon its accession to power; that was to say, it should pour 'new wine into old skins'. At the end of his pamphlet Bogoraz again made the point unequivocally: should power fall into the hands of the revolutionaries, then they should not take the quixotic view that they had no right to 'usurp the popular sovereignty' and so surrender power 'prematurely' to the unorganised mass, but should first awaken and organise the revolutionary forces in the people. Only then could Narodnaya Volya transfer power to a popular assembly without 'apprehensions' about the future. Indeed, Bogoraz envisaged the possibility 'that the revolutionary party, taking advantage of the demoralisation of the government', might 'unexpectedly seize power into its own hands even before the outbreak of a general popular uprising'.[97] Shternberg's pamphlet had a similar Jacobin tinge. Given the unpreparedness of the masses, Shternberg argued, the objective of overthrowing the government would be achieved by means of a 'seizure of power' and the intelligentsia would be the people's 'leader' at the 'critical moment', empowered to express the people's aspirations.[98]

Once again, then, the Jacobin strain of Narodovolchestvo had emerged, and once again it was essentially a symptom of weakness and desperation, the last resort of a party as near to death as the Narodovoltsy themselves imagined the autocracy to be. It proved irresistible to new young converts fired with a messianic vision but hard pressed to sustain the party far from the centres of political power and without widespread popular support, just as it had to some surviving members of the old guard when they wearied of the unequal struggle in 1881–2. It was an ever-present potentiality in Narodovolchestvo. All the same, it was *only* a potentiality, not an inevitable development of Narodovolchestvo, which was still just as capable of inspiring either dedicated labours among the masses, as the events of 1883–4 had shown, or further examples of derring-do like that in which certain students in St Petersburg were to be involved in 1887.

A. I. ULYANOV AND THE PLOT TO KILL ALEXANDER III IN 1887

By 1886 the destruction of Narodnaya Volya as a formal party was more or less complete and those Narodovoltsy who had escaped arrest had fled abroad. Some workers' circles survived in St Petersburg but in general only isolated individuals and scattered groups remained in the northern capital. And yet, even after its organisation had collapsed, Narodnaya Volya continued to provide inspiration for students when they felt the need to carry their revolutionary sentiments beyond the numerous 'self-education' circles of the higher educational institutions and to take some decisive action against the repressive government.

A major catalyst in the generation of further support for terrorism was the response of the authorities themselves to a pilgrimage made by the students to Dobrolyubov's grave in the Volkovo cemetery in St Petersburg on 17 November 1886, the twenty-fifth anniversary of the death of the critic. After placing wreaths on Dobrolyubov's grave and giving a spirited rendering of the *vechnaya pamyat'* ('May his memory live for ever'), the students began to return towards the Kazan Cathedral, scene of the famous demonstration of 1876; but before they even reached Nevsky Prospect they were surrounded by Cossacks and detained for several hours in the icy conditions of a St Petersburg winter. They were released in small groups only as evening fell. Several arrests were made. The demonstration showed that there was still much material in the higher educational institutions of the capital for revolutionaries to exploit, even if parties capable of organising this material had temporarily been rendered inactive. More importantly, the official decision to call out the heavily armed and notoriously vicious Cossacks to confront peaceful demonstrators honouring the memory of a great publicist revealed the authorities at their most repressive and vindictive and seemed to many to confirm yet again the impossibility of voicing any unorthodox views under the existing régime.[99]

One university student who undoubtedly put this construction on the events of 17 November was A. I. Ulyanov. Although he is best remembered today as the elder brother of Vladimir Ilich (Lenin), nevertheless Aleksandr Ilich Ulyanov himself had the makings of a revolutionary leader. The eldest son of a respected school inspector resident in Simbirsk, a provincial town on the Volga to the south of Kazan, A. I. Ulyanov soon distinguished himself in the local *gimnaziya*, from which he graduated with a gold medal and an excellent testimonial in 1883. In the autumn of that year he entered the scientific faculty of St Petersburg University, where he seems at first to have devoted himself almost entirely to the pursuit of academic knowledge, initially in the field of chemistry and then zoology. At the end of 1885 he was awarded a gold medal for a paper he had written on the basis of his own research; a successful academic career seemed to lie before him.

During 1886, however, he evidently began to take a greater interest in social questions. More of his time was now taken up with the activities of an 'economic' self-education circle and the 'Scientific-Literary Society' of the University, a society founded in 1882 and gradually turned by radical students to their own use. In October 1886 Ulyanov was elected secretary of this society and the subject matter of the papers presented at its meetings underwent a change; purely or predominantly academic themes began to give way to more topical, overtly social and political ones.[100]

It was only after the 'Dobrolyubov' demonstration of November 1886, however, that Ulyanov began to lay plans for a more hazardous undertaking, the assassination of the Tsar. In September he was clearly not contemplating such a venture: in that month he moved into new lodgings with a friend from the 'economic' circle, Chebotaryov, whom he was later to exclude from his tsaricidal plans.[101] Another student at the centre of the St Petersburg student movement at the time recalls his surprise when he heard of the arrest of Ulyanov for complicity in a plot to kill the Tsar: he had not expected Ulyanov's revolutionary energies to express themselves so soon or in that form.[102] And it may be added that Ulyanov would have been acting out of character if, having conceived a plot to kill the Tsar before mid November 1886, he had then drawn attention to himself by participating so openly in the 'Dobrolyubov' demonstration, for all accounts portray him as exceptionally cautious and thorough. Evidently, then, it was his view of the behaviour of the authorities at the 'Dobrolyubov' demonstration that prompted Ulyanov to forsake peaceful activity for violence. Not that his reaction to the events of 17 November was exceptional: anger at the treatment meted out to the demonstrators was widespread. Many students began to talk of another act of terrorism, though the act itself, as a sign of retaliation against the authorities, probably seemed more important to them than the elimination of any specific individual, since some saw the town-governor as a worthy victim while others again named the Tsar himself on the grounds that he was more than anyone else to blame for all the evil in his realm.[103]

Together with other St Petersburg students who even without the evidence of the Dobrolyubov demonstration were already inclined towards terrorism, Ulyanov founded a 'terrorist faction' late in 1886. By February 1887 this 'faction' had crystallised under the leadership of Shevyryov, Lukashevich, Govorukhin and Ulyanov himself and when Shevyryov, chronically sick with consumption, left the capital for Yalta, Ulyanov assumed effective control. Osipanov (who had come to the capital from

Kazan in 1886 with the express purpose of shooting the Tsar even if he found no revolutionaries of like mind there), and two other students, Andreyushkin and Generalov, were chosen to throw the bombs which Ulyanov and Lukashevich were preparing and which were to be concealed in book covers so that the prospective assassins would be able to stroll up and down Nevsky Prospect without arousing suspicion. Three other students were to act as signallers, patrolling Nevsky Prospect in anticipation of the emergence of the Tsar from the Winter Palace. On 25 February plans were finalised and the next day the signallers and bomb-throwers went out onto Nevsky Prospect, but the Tsar failed to oblige them with an appearance either on that day or two days later, when they were again at their stations. Finally, when the conspirators emerged for a third time, on 1 March – the sixth anniversary of the assassination of Alexander II – they were all arrested. The police had recently decoded an intercepted letter bound for Kharkov, in which Andreyushkin had foolishly advertised his passion for terrorism. Andreyushkin had been followed round St Petersburg and his contacts noted. All the same, the police do not seem at first to have realised exactly what they had stumbled upon, for Osipanov was still in possession of his bomb, concealed in the book cover, when he arrived at the police station. (It failed to explode when he dashed it on the floor in the hope of killing himself and his captors.) Even after the arrest of the bomb-throwers and signallers the police might not have apprehended Ulyanov, had not one of the signallers divulged all he knew of the plot. Ulyanov was arrested, Shevyryov was tracked down in the Crimea and the whole 'terrorist faction' (with the exception of Govorukhin, who had escaped abroad) and another student, Novorussky, who had not even belonged to it, were put on trial in April. Ulyanov's honesty, the dignity with which he conducted himself at the trial and his manifest willingness to accentuate his own guilt in order that other defendants might receive lighter sentences bore witness to a character of great integrity and high moral awareness and made a great impression even on his prosecutors. Having been sentenced to death, he declined to appeal to the Tsar for clemency, on the grounds that as he had intended to take the life of another it would be unworthy now to plead for his own, and together with Osipanov, Generalov, Andreyushkin and Shevyryov he was hanged in the Shlisselburg fortress on 8 May.

It is not surprising that some of those deeply involved in the St Petersburg student movement of the time and close to the conspiracy subsequently took pains to refute the charge, made shortly after these events by old Narodovoltsy in emigration, that it was indignation at the effrontery of the government rather than any coherent revolutionary programme that had prompted the 'terrorist faction' to attempt to assassinate Alexander III.[104] Such a charge amounted to an accusation of aimlessness and the memoirists tried to rebut it by insisting that the terrorists' plot 'followed from a definite plan'.[105] And yet there seems little doubt that on this occasion the émigrés were right: the conspirators for the most part advocated terrorism in terms that were extreme and undiscriminating. Shevyryov, according to Govorukhin, 'could not be a convinced socialist, since he did not concern himself with socialist issues and nowhere did he speak of them. The programmatic issues which excited the entire revolutionary youth did not exist for him.' It was 'all the same' to him 'what programme a person adhered to, so long as he agreed to aid terrorism'.[106] Generalov, like Shevyryov, was poorly versed in socialist theory, and set himself only one task, to throw bombs.[107] Andreyushkin, too, was a man of action rather than a theoretician and spoke of terrorism with a blind reverence: 'I am not going to list the merits and advantages of red terror,' he wrote to his friend in Kharkov, 'for I shan't finish until the end of the century, because it's my hobby-horse'. It was quite feasible, Andreyushkin believed, to wage a campaign of the 'most merciless terror' which would shatter the prevailing calm.[108]

Naturally, men such as these found their inspiration in Narodnaya Volya. Andreyushkin and Osipanov both professed allegiance to that party in their testimonies to the police.[109] Andreyushkin and Generalov shouted 'Long live Narodnaya Volya' from the scaffold.[110] And Lukashevich later claimed that he had been prevented from joining Narodnaya Volya only by the fact that the party as such no longer existed in Russia in 1886–7.[111] More indicative of the continuing attraction of Narodnaya Volya, however, is the fact that even a student such as Ulyanov should associate himself with that party when he grew impatient with painstaking self-education in student circles and sought some more energetic pursuit. In character Ulyanov was most unlike his fellow conspirators, and to the end he retained, as they did not, an interest in his studies and in theoretical matters. Moreover, in several important respects he was already beginning to reject some of the assumptions on which Narodovolchestvo was based. He had studied the first volume of Marx's *Capital* in the summer vacation of 1886 and was apparently already critical of the prevailing faith in the peasant commune as a source of Russia's social regeneration.[112] In the programme he wrote for the 'terrorist faction' and in which he tried to give a satisfactory explanation of terrorism, there were clear traces of the socialism of Marx and Engels. Ulyanov suggested, for example, that a socialist order would necessarily emerge from a capitalist one. True, this 'law' did not preclude a more direct transition to socialism if particularly favourable conditions obtained in the 'customs of the people, the character of the intelligentsia and the government'. But it did describe the 'historical inevitability' with which each country approached a socialist order if its development took place 'without the conscious participation' of any social group. Again, the unorganised peasantry lacked a 'clear consciousness of its political needs' and could only lend 'unconscious support' to political struggle. It was the working class that was the 'natural bearer of socialist ideas', the social group 'most capable of political consciousness'. Workers should constitute the 'nucleus of the socialist party, its most active part' and the main resources of the revolutionaries should be devoted to propaganda and organisation in the factories. Ulyanov also omitted the term 'Populists' from the opening sentence of his programme, which was otherwise identical with that of the programme of the old Executive Committee. And yet, while conceding all these points to Marxian socialists, Ulyanov also reiterated the traditional belief that the autocracy had no foundation in the Russian social structure and that the bourgeoisie was weak, and on this basis inferred that the revolutionary intelligentsia – the 'vanguard in political struggle' – could begin to operate 'without preliminary class organisation'. Indeed, organisational and propagandistic work were 'almost impossible' under the existing régime. Therefore the 'struggle for free institutions' was a necessary phase in the revolutionary campaign in Russia. Terrorism was a temporary expedient, the capacity of which to win the freedoms desired seemed to Ulyanov to be beyond doubt. Not surprisingly, in view of the coincidence of these beliefs with those customarily upheld by Narodovoltsy, Ulyanov designated the new St Petersburg group the 'terrorist faction of the party Narodnaya Volya'.[113]

Thus whatever the extent of the admiration of Ulyanov – and of many others – for Marxism by the beginning of 1887, it was still the tradition of Narodnaya Volya that inspired students from the moment they began to contemplate practical as opposed to purely theoretical activity. Only 'exceptionally theoretically disposed minds' could yet abandon that tradition in favour of the apparently more bookish Marxism.[114] And in so far as it was Narodovolchestvo that inspired Aleksandr Ulyanov, it was Narodovolchestvo in its classical form, free of any Jacobin tinge. The thoughtful student who was finally driven to violent protest by a sense of moral outrage, who resolved to sacrifice himself in the struggle for free institutions, who considered it unworthy to plead for his own life to a ruler whose life he himself had intended to take and who spent the last hours before his execution reading the poetry of Heine – Aleksandr Ulyanov answered not the description of the Machiavellian conspirator determined to impose his will on others but that of the chivalrous hero who had long since occupied a central place in the Populist outlook.

ATTEMPTS TO REVIVE NARODNAYA VOLYA IN 1888–90

The history of Narodnaya Volya in the 1880s would be incomplete without the mention of yet two more attempts to reorganise sympathisers of the party in Russia at the very end of the decade. The first was led by a young Jewish woman, Ginsburg, from the autumn of 1888. Conceding that Narodnaya Volya had lost some of its appeal, Ginsburg proposed to recruit surviving Narodovoltsy for a new organisation which would set itself more modest ambitions than those of the old party. It no longer seemed possible to destroy the prevailing order; only to struggle for the political freedoms that would facilitate the building of an organisation among the workers and peasants. In Kharkov Ginsburg found her cousin, Stoyanovsky, and another local student, Freyfeld, who were trying to build a new group of Narodovoltsy and who apparently remained faithful to the tradition of Narodnaya Volya, inasmuch as they were still contemplating terrorist action against the autocracy. (Indeed, they were manufacturing bombs for this purpose and greatly regretted that they had been unprepared when the Tsar stayed in Kharkov in autumn 1888 following the interruption of his journey from the south by a railway accident at Borki.) In St Petersburg Ginsburg had talks with some student leaders and won the support of some radical members of the intelligentsia, including the Jewish poet, Minsky. Conditions were everywhere unfavourable, however, and in any case events soon took a disastrous turn. Early in 1889 a Polish revolutionary, Dembo, blew himself up in a secluded spot outside Zurich, where he had been experimenting with a new type of explosive, and before he died in hospital provided the Swiss authorities with sufficient information about his activities to prompt an investigation into plots being hatched by Slav revolutionaries on Swiss soil. The ubiquitous Russian police contrived to uncover evidence linking Dembo and his accomplices with Ginsburg and Narodovoltsy in Russia. Another wave of arrests, including that of Ginsburg, followed shortly.[115]

The second attempt to create a new pan-Russian revolutionary organisation was begun in 1889 by a number of students – led by Kacharovsky,
Belyayev and Foynitsky – whom Ginsburg had found in St Petersburg
during her brief stay there. A programme drafted by Kacharovsky
reiterated the basic tenets laid down a decade before in the programme of
the Executive Committee and unimaginatively recommended that
Narodovoltsy continue to wage terror with a view to winning freedom of
speech and forcing the convocation of a popular assembly. Ambitious
journeys were made round European Russia in the course of 1889:
Kacharovsky went to the Crimea, and Foynitsky to Vilna, Minsk, Kharkov,
Simferopol and Odessa. Meanwhile Belyayev visited Yaroslavl, Kostroma,
Voronezh and Ryazan and, together with Sabunayev, who had recently
escaped from Siberian exile and was attempting to revive Narodnaya Volya
from the periphery, travelled down the Volga to Kazan, Simbirsk, Saratov
and Astrakhan. In September a congress was held in Kazan at which further
plans for reorganisation were discussed. It seems that by the beginning of
1890 the St Petersburg students were flirting with Social Democracy and
that they were proposing to oust from their organisation the Narodovolets,
Sabunayev, but arrests prevented any such development. Sabunayev
remained at large for a while, directing operations from Kostroma,
despatching agents to Vladimir and Vologda, and making plans for the
establishment of a press in Voronezh. In December 1890, however, the
police arrested him, too, and soon they apprehended his agents, who were
languishing in the various provincial backwaters to which Narodnaya
Volya was by now confined.[116]

CHAPTER THREE

❈ 'POPULISTS', 'MILITARISTS', 'CONSPIRATORS' AND OTHER GROUPS IN THE 1880s

RUSSIAN CULTURE IN THE 1880S

The failure of Populism either to stir the masses in the mid 1870s or to achieve any useful results through terrorism at the end of the decade and at the beginning of the 1880s combined with the hardening of the government's conservatism to produce a general sense of despondency and pessimism in the radical intelligentsia in the 1880s. The Narodovoltsy of the 1880s, it is true, continued to find inspiration in the heroic example of their predecessors and were borne along by their enthusiasm for acts of terrorism, even if they were no longer in a position to perpetrate such acts. Other revolutionaries and their sympathisers, though, were deeply affected by the prevailing gloom and their more patient activity and modest ambitions need to be seen against the general cultural background.

As it happened, the onset of crisis in the revolutionary movement and the implementation of more blatantly reactionary official policies coincided with the end of the golden age of classical Russian literature. Nekrasov had died in 1877, Dostoyevsky early in 1881. Tolstoy, after the completion of *Anna Karenina* in 1877, entered an artistically unproductive phase; and Turgenev, who in his late years was much fêted by the young generation as a courageous opponent of autocracy, died in 1883. A sense of loss and even senescence therefore combined with the consciousness of the collapse of utopian dreams and with official policy to demoralise the intelligentsia. Nekrasov's poem, 'Knight for an Hour', written many years before in a state of deep melancholy, now took on a new significance, for it seemed to give most eloquent expression to the current mood. The poet's recollection of youthful hopes is marred by a mocking voice which insistently tells him:

> You are not yet in the grave, you still live on,
> But for the cause you have now long since been dead;
> Noble impulses you are destined to feel,
> But nothing are you fated to accomplish.

It was a time when the living 'lurked in tombs', wrote Saltykov-Shchedrin, and the dead rose from their graves, and the atmosphere of the cemetery came to prevail.[1] Mikhaylovsky gave expression to the general feeling when he wrote that Fate had beaten him down, that he now lived for nothing.[2] The all-consuming desire to serve others at all costs now yielded to a concern to pursue selfish interests and insulate oneself from the misfortunes which a harsh reality could inflict. Students in the higher educational institutions began to think not of abandoning their courses in order to go to the people in a spirit of self-sacrifice or to devote their lives to revolutionary struggle, but rather of completing their courses and then living 'within the law'.[3] The great expectations of the previous decade were replaced by a preoccupation with trivia. Many devoted themselves to 'small deeds', legally permissible attempts to bring about minor temporary or local amelioration rather than sudden and universal regeneration.[4] This atmosphere, unprecedented in the history of the Russian intelligentsia, is captured in much of the work of Chekhov, whose talent emerges in the course of this decade. The 'man of the 80s' – once characterised as 'neither hot nor cold', like Don Quixote or Hamlet, but 'merely warm'[5] – finds his most typical expression in Ivanov, the eponymous central character of Chekhov's first major play, first performed in 1887 and reworked in the course of the next two years. Ivanov, a man of thirty-five, clearly belongs to the same generation as the Chaykovtsy; but now the hopes of that generation have been dashed and its youthful promise is unfulfilled. Ivanov is 'prematurely exhausted', 'shattered, broken without faith or love or aim in life', 'disillusioned, crushed by his own pathetic efforts', 'bitterly ashamed of himself, sneering at his own feebleness'. The play ends, logically, with his suicide.[6]

Many men of Ivanov's generation – and not only those who saw ahead intolerable years of imprisonment or penal servitude – chose the same way out of despair as Chekhov's character. Others, like Gleb Uspensky, perhaps unable to bear the collapse of ideals by which they had lived, suffered mental breakdown from which they would not recover. (Tkachov, in emigration, was afflicted by the same fate in 1882, and died in a Paris mental hospital in 1886 (NS).) Some who had once been active revolutionaries abandoned the underground and renounced their past. Tikhomirov, having explained his apostasy in a pamphlet written in 1888, received royal permission to return to Russia and embarked on a new journalistic career in defence of the autocracy he had recently tried to destroy.[7] Yet others sought refuge from an unacceptable reality in a conscious aestheticism; such apostles of art for art's sake as Baudelaire and Flaubert, who had never previously fared well in Russia beside strident social critics such as Byron, Dickens and Victor Hugo, now began to enjoy popularity.[8] Finally, many sought comfort in the pacifist interpretation of Christ's teaching offered by Tolstoy, who in such tracts as *Confession* (completed in 1882) and *My Faith* (1884) insisted that the 'pivotal idea' of the sermon on the mount was Jesus' admonition to his followers that they 'resist not evil' by force, that instead of answering wrong with vengeful violence they turn the other cheek.[9] Naturally, Tolstoyanism was vigorously resisted by publicists such as Mikhaylovsky and Shelgunov,[10] who feared that it would impede a revolutionary movement generated at least in part by hatred of the autocracy. All the same, these teachings gained such currency that one revolutionary group of the period found it expedient to print some of Tolstoy's tracts on its clandestine press in order to help to finance other printing ventures,[11] and there is no doubt that Tolstoyanism, like so many other tendencies in the intellectual life of the 1880s, did indeed serve to paralyse political opposition in Russia and to check the momentum that revolutionaries had recently achieved there.

At the same time, the resilience of the old theoretical premises of Populism made it very difficult for socialists to explore new paths to revolution. Many writers and publicists, far from being dispirited by the failure of the 'going to the people' in 1874, had continued in the second half of the 1870s to voice admiration of the common people and the commune. Engelgardt, whose letters 'From the Country' were published in *Otechestvennyye zapiski* and who enjoyed great popularity towards the end of the 1870s, portrayed the peasants as more honest and hard-working and less dissipated than the upper classes.[12] Zlatovratsky, also a contributor to *Otechestvennyye zapiski*, attributed Russia's ills to the failure of the intelligentsia to observe the customs of the common people, and in his major cycle, *Foundations* (1878–83), portrayed the peasant as robust and capable of resisting the encroachment of a different civilisation on the idyllic rural order. Mikhaylovsky continued to belabour the detractors of the commune[13] (on which several more monographs were published in the second half of the 1870s).[14] Other publicists, such as Chervinsky and Kablits (who wrote under the pseudonym Yuzov), elaborated a legal brand of Populism which uncritically extolled the collective principles supposed to be embodied in the Russian village community and treated the emotions of the masses as the legitimate moving force of history.[15] Finally, at the beginning of the 1880s, the view that Russia was following a path of development distinct from that taken by the major Western European nations was reasserted, with apparent academic authority, by respected economists such as Danielson (who wrote under the pseudonym Nikolay -on), Vorontsov and Yuzhakov.

Danielson, it is true, did acknowledge that capitalism, assisted by governmental protection, had been making progress in Russia since the emancipation of the serfs in 1861. In a treatise on the 'Capitalisation of Agricultural Income', which was first published in 1880, he tried to demonstrate that Russia's economy was being transformed into a monetary (that is to say, capitalist) one by the new force of credit. In spite of the intentions of the statesmen who had framed the terms of the emancipation, all economic activity in the post-reform period had in Danielson's view assisted this process. More and more producers were being expropriated and leaving the land, and individual utilisation of the land was replacing the communal system. Nevertheless, Danielson clearly considered it possible abruptly to halt the development of this tendency. In order to prevent a recurrence of the impending economic crisis – which he held to be a natural consequence of Russia's post-reform development – Danielson insisted that Russia should leave the capitalist path and revert to the course of development which he believed that the emancipation edict had been designed to promote, namely improvement of the efficiency of labourers who themselves owned the means of production.[16]

Vorontsov, in his influential work, *The Fate of Capitalism in Russia*, which was published in 1882, not only recommended that Russia be guided along a distinctive path of economic development but even denied that capitalism was likely to flourish there. Whereas Western European economic life seemed to Vorontsov easy to characterise, the Russian economy, on the other hand, revealed a bewilderingly complex pattern of modes of production in which capitalism was only one constituent. Admittedly, there was evidence of the growth of phenomena associated with capitalism, for example the rapid extension of the railway network, the exploitation of female and child labour, and, Vorontsov added, bankruptcies and bank robberies. But the appearance of these phenomena Vorontsov regarded as indications that Russia was 'playing at capitalism' rather than proof that she was adopting it in earnest. Russian capitalism was an 'imitation', a 'transplantation' of an alien growth, and conditions, Vorontsov argued, were unfavourable for its further development. There was neither the necessary external market nor sufficient domestic consumer demand to stimulate competition. The immensity of the country made communications too difficult. Even climatic conditions, in Vorontsov's view, were unpropitious: the long, harsh winters necessitated excessive expenditure on the provision of adequate buildings, lighting and heating for an enterprise and on wages high enough to enable workers to acquire suitable food and clothing. Therefore, not only would capitalism fail to embrace all areas of production; it would not even prevail in a significant proportion of them and would certainly never attain the hold on the economy which it had in the West. Not that it was to Russia's disadvantage that capitalism had been still-born there, for other modes of production might also lead to prosperity. Thus Vorontsov proposed that the government grant the free use of the land to the peasants, reiterating the belief that Russia was fortunate to have preserved the commune and the co-operative spirit it fostered and again kindling the hope that Russia might play a unique historical role as a model for an egalitarian society.[17]

Yuzhakov, in a long article on the 'Forms of Agricultural Production in Russia' which was published in *Otechestvennyye zapiski* in 1882, gave further support to the view that Russian economic development was not directly comparable to that of Western Europe. Using statistical information which was incomplete and rather randomly chosen, Yuzhakov examined the types of agricultural production found in Russia and contended that, although there were regional differences, the capitalist form did not exist anywhere in any significant degree. Indeed, less than 11% of the land currently suitable for agricultural use in Russia, Yuzhakov claimed, was utilised according to a capitalist system. Capitalism nestled 'on the outskirts, nowhere achieving predominance'. Nor did it seem to Yuzhakov to have a future; on the contrary, he predicted its decline. The conditions necessary for its development – the availability of capital and a proletariat – did not exist and were not likely to exist in the near future. The attempt to implant it had been premature and fruitless.[18]

The writings of these Populist economists represented serious scholarly attempts to characterise Russia's economy some twenty years after the abolition of serfdom. They did not serve as a medium for virulent criticism of the régime and therefore lacked the revolutionary significance of Chernyshevsky's earlier excursions into similar territory. Nevertheless, the questions to which Danielson, Vorontsov, Yuzhakov and others addressed themselves were by no means of purely academic significance to their contemporaries, for on the answers given to these questions entire revolutionary strategies rested. If it could indeed be proved that capitalism was developing in Russia, then Russian revolutionaries might legitimately infer that they should adopt means of struggle similar to those employed by Western European socialists. Those, on the other hand, who continued to accept the view that Russian economic development was subject to its own laws – and the proponents of this view were in a vast majority throughout the 1880s – could still insist that Russian revolutionaries were bound to persevere with a distinctive strategy of their own.

'MILITARISTS' AND STUDENT GROUPS IN MOSCOW AND ST PETERSBURG

Throughout the 1880s faith in the acceptability and usefulness of terrorism tended to unite as well as to inspire all revolutionaries who considered themselves Narodovoltsy. Those groups of revolutionaries, on the other hand, who did not consider terrorism to be of crucial importance in their programme of activity for the foreseeable future generally lacked the degree of organisation which Narodovoltsy succeeded in bringing to their party in the early years of its existence and at least strove to bring to it even in the later years when it became scattered through the provinces. Personal contacts among these less militant revolutionaries in various cities continued to flourish, it is true, thanks partly to the government's policy of banishing its opponents from major cities to remoter regions where, it was thought, they might pose less of a threat to the régime. But cohesion and sense of purpose were greatly reduced, after the formation of Narodnaya Volya, among all who were not members of that party. Not surprisingly, therefore, the numerous groups which existed in Russia outside the ranks of Narodnaya Volya in the 1880s were characterised, firstly, by extreme lack of clarity in theoretical matters and, secondly, by resignation to very prolonged activity with no prospect of significant early success. Many courses of action were countenanced but the contours of each theory and even the dividing lines between different groups were blurred, precisely because there was general agreement outside Narodnaya Volya that a long period of cautious preparatory activity would be necessary before any militant action could again be taken. If these groups were bedevilled by theoretical confusion and a sense of impotence, however, they did nevertheless lay some solid foundations, for since the authorities viewed attempts to assassinate the Tsar as the gravest threat to their security, such groups attracted comparatively little official attention. They consequently survived for longer than groups of Narodóvoltsy and those members of them who were arrested were not removed so decisively from the revolutionary stage.

Imprecision in theory and patience in practice were especially characteristic of revolutionary circles in Moscow, where the grip of Narodnaya Volya on the movement had in any case never been so strong as in St Petersburg. Three overlapping groups existed in the city in the first half of the 1880s. Firstly, from among the numerous disaffected students of the various *zemlyachestva*, Yanovich, a Lithuanian student of the Petrovsko-Razumovskaya Academy, attempted in 1883 to organise a General Students' Union with branches in all the higher educational institutions of the city. Under the auspices of this union students discussed social questions in their so-called self-education circles, set up libraries stocked with illegal publications, organised a protest when the government ordered the closure of *Otechestvennyye zapiski* in 1884 and compiled an address signed by several hundred students to the journal's editor, Saltykov-Shchedrin.[19] Secondly, a student of the University, Raspopin, began at roughly the same time to assemble around himself a group of students who designated themselves 'militarists' and who saw their main objective as the organisation of a conspiracy in the armed forces and the overthrow of the autocracy. Russian autocrats themselves, the militarists argued, had come to power in this way in the eighteenth century. The Decembrists, too, had planned a *coup d'état*, and, although their attempt had failed, their method still seemed to the militarists to commend itself in Russian conditions. The militarists did not discount the possibility that non-military groups might overthrow the autocracy, nor did they object in principle to the use of tactics such as the perpetration of acts of terrorism or the incitement of demonstrations among students and even workers (to whom in fact they sent propagandists). But their primary objective was the building of a strong organisation, a 'revolutionary "fist"', as they described it, in the armed forces.[20] Thirdly, there appeared a 'Society of Translators and Publishers', founded and directed by the militarists themselves and reflecting their view that the creation of the strike force they envisaged would require many years of careful preparation. Before a *coup* could be staged it would be necessary to lay firm theoretical foundations among the radical students with whom the initiative currently lay; this preparation would take the form of assiduous study of socialist writings and in order to make such writings more widely available the students of the society set about translating and hectographing works by English, French and German writers on economic, historical and philosophical subjects. Their most ambitious venture was the compilation of a substantial illegal journal, *Sotsialisticheskoye znaniye (Socialist Knowledge)*, the first number of which appeared early in 1884. The activities of the 'translators and publishers' were financed by donations from a wealthy sympathiser, by collections made at student meetings and by the proceeds of the more lucrative literature they issued, such as Tolstoy's pacifist pamphlets. The society was short-lived, however; arrests, many facilitated by the testimonies of one of the students, undermined the whole militarist network in 1884 and an attempt to reorganise the group foundered in the spring of 1885.[21]

The shades of socialist opinion tolerated by the students in these groups were very diverse. For some of them Marxist writings evidently held a strong appeal. Marx's *Wage Labour and Capital, Wages, Price and Profit* and *The Civil War in France*, Engels' *The Housing Question* and Plekhanov's *Socialism and Political Struggle* were among the first texts issued by the Society of Translators and Publishers, and chapters from Engels' book, *The Condition of the Working Class in England*, and his pamphlet, *Socialism: Utopian and Scientific*, appeared in translation in the first number of *Sotsialisticheskoye znaniye*. Contact with Engels himself was established by Yevgeniya Paprits, an opera singer sympathetic to the Muscovite group, who requested from him a list of Marx's and his own less known articles and also mentioned in her letter that she herself was translating Marx's *Outlines of a Critique of Political Economy*.[22] Contact existed, too, between the translators and the by now Marxist émigrés of the 'Emancipation of Labour' group in Switzerland. Plekhanov's pamphlet, *Socialism and Political Struggle*, reached them promptly; the 'Library of Modern Socialism' series which the émigrés began to publish in 1883 was highly praised by the Muscovite students, who expressed the hope that more support would be forthcoming for this 'enormously useful venture'; and at the beginning of 1884 Akselrod's 'Letter to Comrades', which welcomed the appearance of support for Social Democracy inside Russia, was lithographed and circulated by them.[23] Moreover, Raspopin, towards the middle of the decade, was already rejecting the well-worn Populist view that society was not following the same course of development in Russia as in Western Europe, where a socialist order might logically be born of a capitalist one. In an article published in 1887 he was to apply the Marxist methodology to an examination of the rural class relations existing in Russia.[24] His studies later earned him the approval of the young Lenin, who, in his own far-reaching analysis of the character of Russia's economy, cited statistics used by Raspopin and referred the reader in several places to Raspopin's treatment of aspects of the evolution of the rural economy in the direction of capitalism.[25]

In spite of the Marxist leanings which all this evidence seems to indicate, however, the Muscovite translators and publishers did encourage study of other streams of socialist thought and did contemplate courses of action and allegiances which would have been unpalatable to orthodox Marxists. They produced in addition to works of 'scientific socialism' Russian versions of writings by Lassalle and Louis Blanc and even some Populist literature. They also planned to issue more works by Blanc and some by Dühring, whose views were the object of one of Engels' critical tracts.[26] Moreover, even Raspopin advocated seizure of power by the armed forces – not a strategy that followed from complete acceptance of Marxist doctrine – and the journal, *Sotsialisticheskoye znaniye*, through which the translators hoped to acquaint the intelligentsia with 'scientific socialism', bore the stamp, in coded form, not of any social democratic or proletarian party but of a 'Department of the Military–Conspiratorial Organisation'.[27] Nor, finally, were the Moscow groups entirely and unanimously unsympathetic to Narodnaya Volya. Talks were begun between the militarists and the Executive Committee of that party, represented by Sabunayev.[28] Yanovich in particular showed a predilection for terrorism which prompted the Social Democratic émigrés to associate him with Narodnaya Volya, and he is even said in one source to have become a 'follower' of that party in 1883–4.[29] Not that the Muscovite students ultimately took up a position any closer to Narodnaya Volya than to any other faction of the time: their talks with the Narodovoltsy were broken off after several meetings, no agreement having been reached, and the bitterness with which Tikhomirov refers to Akselrod's letter to them suggests that he did not cherish the connection.[30] Even Yanovich is not accepted by former Narodovoltsy as their own. Vera Figner, describing the political disputes which took place among the prisoners of the Shlisselburg fortress, recalls him as one of a number who would 'declare that they were Social Democrats although they still adhered to the tactics of Narodnaya Volya'.[31]

Developments similar to those in Moscow took place in St Petersburg in the 1880s as the fortunes of Narodnaya Volya declined there. In 1882–3 there were already certain revolutionaries in the northern capital, for example, who were beginning, like the Muscovite 'militarists' – though independently of them, it seems – to advocate seizure of power by the armed forces with a view to the eventual installation of their own nominee on the Russian throne in place of the Tsar. Headed by a writer, Sazonov, these revolutionaries designated themselves *Nemisty*, a word derived from the Latin *nemo* (nobody), in the hope of dissociating themselves from all other revolutionary groups.[32] And after the collapse of Lopatin's attempt to reunite Narodnaya Volya in 1884 'militarism' assumed more serious proportions in St Petersburg. A fairly extensive network of circles which was built among the cadets of the military colleges of the city by students and soldiers contained a strong militarist element, inspired by Chizhevsky and Dushevsky, cadets of the Mikhaylovskoye Artillery College, and by Yastrebov, a former student of Kazan University, who had come to St Petersburg with the specific object of conducting propaganda among the armed forces. Like their counterparts in Moscow, these militarists drew attention to the crucial role played by the army in all power struggles in Russian history, and to the fact that movements which had lacked the support of the army, such as the great peasant rebellions of Russian history and the recent struggle of the terrorists with the government, had proved ineffectual. The task of the movement was therefore to revolutionise the soldiers, with work among other sections of the population seeming comparatively futile (although there was an element in the military circles, led by N. N. Shelgunov, son of the celebrated publicist and the organiser of circles in the Kronshtadt naval school, which tried to give a broader character to its activity and split from the militarists over this issue early in 1886). Like their Muscovite counterparts, these St Petersburg militarists regarded revolution in Russia as a distant prospect and set themselves in the short term narrow and unambitious tasks. Their circles, which met in great secrecy, did not yet even embrace soldiers in the ranks; it was hoped that their support would be won later by popular officers.[33]

As in Moscow, the student movement in the civilian higher educational institutions also began to revive in St Petersburg in the middle of the decade. There were several manifestations of student discontent besides the pilgrimage to Dobrolyubov's grave in November 1886. A demonstration attended by about four hundred people, most of them students, marked the twenty-fifth anniversary of the emancipation of the serfs on 19 February and wreaths were placed on the graves of Dobrolyubov, Turgenev and other writers in the Volkovo cemetery.[34] Students also attempted to whistle down a production of a play by Prince Meshchersky, who had attacked the historian Semevsky, a popular figure in the radical camp, in the pages of his journal *Grazhdanin* (*The Citizen*).[35] More important, a fresh attempt was made towards the end of 1885 to harness student dissatisfaction by uniting the various *zemlyachestva* and setting up a council – one of the members of which was A. I. Ulyanov – to govern their corporate affairs.[36] Most important of all, self-education circles began to proliferate again and to take on a more serious character. A number of these circles now specialised in one particular subject: there was, for example, an 'ethical' circle, a 'historical' circle, and an 'economic' one, to which Ulyanov also belonged, which, under the guidance of the head of the statistics office of the St Petersburg *zemstvo*, Gizetti, studied the work of major political economists from Adam Smith, Ricardo and Malthus to Marx.[37] A large number of these self-education circles, it is true, were ephemeral, appearing and disappearing 'like soap bubbles',[38] but in several of them membership was fairly constant. In any case many students did receive in circles they frequented only briefly their initial revolutionary training, for the attention of participants invariably turned before long to 'illegal' works, and discussions, being free and therefore illicit, soon acquired a political tone. All the same, these circles, for all their application and potential hostility, posed a much less immediate threat to the authorities than the Narodovoltsy had done. It was becoming clear that unless the energies of the régime's opponents were concentrated by Narodnaya Volya those opponents resigned themselves to preparation for a distant future, lost sight of a common programme and tended rather undiscriminatingly to examine numerous different shades of socialist opinion. They were, as an envoy of the 'Emancipation of Labour' group colourfully described the Moscow students of 1883–4, a 'flock without a shepherd', a 'mash that would stick in the throat of the Devil himself'![39]

STUDENT GROUPS IN KHARKOV

Whereas in Moscow and St Petersburg some revolutionaries began in the 1880s to pay increasing attention to the works of Western socialists and to the armed forces and even to the urban workers as groups among whom it would be useful to conduct their propaganda, in the provincial centres, surrounded by the vastness of rural Russia, traditional Populist beliefs understandably prevailed for longer. Variations continued to be heard on the themes of Chernoperedelchestvo; indeed, it was mainly to the tradition of Chornyy Peredel that the term 'Populist' came in the 1880s to refer. Nevertheless, 'Populism' in this narrow sense was subject to the same stresses as revolutionary socialism in Moscow and St Petersburg once it became clear that the movement of the 1870s had brought no social improvements. Revolutionaries in the provinces fell into disarray as Narodnaya Volya declined, just as they did in the capitals. They, too, speculated as to which course should now be taken, showed confusion in theoretical matters and tended to resign themselves to what they called 'small deeds' for the foreseeable future.

One of the provincial cities in which Chernoperedelchestvo proved particularly resilient was Kharkov, where a 'Populist' faction began to grow in 1881 under the leadership of Bunin, elder brother of the celebrated writer, who had been expelled from Moscow University for his part in disorders there, Balabukha, Merkhalev, and Bekaryukov, son of a rich landowner of Kharkov province, who was to play a prominent role in 'Populist' circles throughout the decade.[40] Balabukha, Merkhalev and Bekaryukov were themselves to be expelled from Kharkov University after disorders there in 1882, but Bunin continued to provide leadership during 1883. In a pamphlet, the very title of which – *A Few Words on the Past of Russian Socialism and the Tasks of the Intelligentsia* – seems to underline the relative ponderousness of Chernoperedelchestvo, Bunin explained the strategy of the group. The revolutionaries should persevere with their work among the masses in order to break down the barriers separating them from the people and to win the people's sympathies. They should not attempt to organise uprisings, or to wage 'factory' and 'agrarian' terrorism until the intelligentsia and the masses understood one another. Bunin's pamphlet was moderate in tone by comparison with the excited writings of the Narodovoltsy and in general reflected the feeling that the uncompromising demands and great expectations of Narodnaya Volya had been unrealistic. Political terrorism had after all failed to disorganise the authorities and stir the masses.[41]

Bunin's pamphlet was printed on a press belonging to a group of students led by Iordan and Manucharov and including others, Makarenko and Zaboluyev, who in 1881 had been members of the 'Southern Social Society', an organisation of students from the University and the Veterinary Institute and pupils from the technical high school who had distributed literature among the peasantry in the surrounding countryside.[42] Two proclamations printed by this group also illustrate the persistence of the old attitudes of the 1870s. The first, written in Ukrainian early in 1883 and issued in the name of 'Socialist-Populists', was of unashamedly Bakuninist orientation, inviting the peasants to seize the land in a bloody uprising. (An attempt was also made to exploit Ukrainian anti-Semitic feelings.) The second, written in Russian in April of the same year and addressed 'to the Russian people', sought to undermine popular faith in the Tsar, urged the masses to take over the land and the factories, and proclaimed the old slogan 'Land and Freedom'.[43] These views must have been held with less certainty than before, though, for the group was at the same time receiving literature issued by the Society of Translators and Publishers in Moscow and brought to Kharkov by Zaboluyev (now a student in the Petrovsko-Razumovskaya Academy). They also printed an announcement about the foundation of the 'Library of Modern Socialism' by the émigré Marxists and even maintained amicable relations with local Narodovoltsy such as Makarevsky, who worked for Iordan's 'Populist' circle when he found on his return to Kharkov that the circle of Narodovoltsy to which he had previously belonged had ceased to meet during his absence from the city.[44] On Manucharov, moreover, the police found a proclamation drafted by Narodovoltsy after their killing of an informer; while on the Narodovolets Goncharov they found a copy of a 'Populist' programme written in Bunin's hand which recommended the recruitment of professional men such as doctors, lawyers, teachers and *zemstvo* officials, who could conduct propaganda in the countryside, but which also recognised the programme of Narodnaya Volya as authoritative in theoretical matters and, in spite of what Bunin had written in his pamphlet, acknowledged the need for 'factory' and 'agrarian' terrorism.[45]

Arrests undermined the group of Iordan and Manucharov, but other 'Populists' continued the work they had begun. A circle led by Shelepenko, Dzyubenko and Mazurenko, which had arisen independently among the students of the local agricultural college in 1883–4, persevered in the summer of 1884 with the familiar tactic of going to the countryside to help the peasants with their work and to read revolutionary pamphlets to them during their hours of leisure. Shelepenko also started to organise elementary lessons for the peasants, assigning to members of the circle the job of teacher in various villages. Sensing their isolation and immaturity in theoretical matters, however, these 'Populists' soon sought contact with like-minded students in other higher educational institutions in the city and in 1885 located and merged with a group consisting of students at the University and the Veterinary Institute, a former pupil of the ecclesiastical academy, Grabovsky (subsequently well known as a Ukrainian poet and translator of Russian literary works into Ukrainian), and a number of other revolutionaries long since active in various centres, including Merkhalev, recently returned from Odessa, and Balabukha, back from Kazan.[46] Like their contemporaries in other cities, these 'Populists' found it necessary to re-examine some of their theoretical assumptions, but their conclusions were no more decisive than those reached elsewhere. They admired the selfless exploits of the Narodovoltsy, as did all revolutionaries of their generation, but they doubted whether it was possible to shake the autocracy or win concessions from it by the use of terrorism. Still less did they approve of plans to seize political power. Rather, they claimed to share the views of Plekhanov, whose writings they studied, but to Plekhanov's proposition that the Russian régime could be brought down at the decisive moment by the workers they added the clause 'and by the peasants too'.[47] In practice their main achievement was the setting-up of a hectograph in the woods outside Kharkov, on which they printed an edition of Schäffle's work, *The Quintessence of Socialism*, a story by Saltykov-Shchedrin, a programme written by the group's leaders, a pamphlet relating to the twenty-fifth anniversary of the emancipation of the serfs and three proclamations on the same subject. These proclamations were posted on walls in Kharkov and copies sent to villages in several provinces, but arrests promptly followed the appearance of this literature and it is an indication of the timidity of the group that the hectograph and the store of incriminating documents printed on it were hastily buried in the forest refuge.[48]

STUDENT CIRCLES IN KAZAN AND THE NETWORK OF FOKIN AND BEKARYUKOV

Nowhere did the principal tenets of Chernoperedelchestvo remain more popular or mingle more freely with other tendencies than in Kazan. While in Russia as a whole the epigones of Chornyy Peredel disappeared, here they survived.[49] To some extent this resilience was a product of the decline of the movement elsewhere, for many of the students expelled from higher educational institutions in other cities resumed their studies in one of the institutions in Kazan – the Veterinary Institute, the Ecclesiastical Academy, the teachers' training college, or the prestigious University, opened in 1804, through which many celebrated men of culture (for example, S. T. Aksakov, the composer Balakirev, and L. N. Tolstoy) had already passed. But above all it was the character of the city itself which determined the nature of the revolutionary circles it harboured. Situated at the southward turn of the Volga about 450 miles east of Moscow, Kazan was not incorporated in Russia's railway network until the 1880s. It was consequently isolated and backward and had as yet no large-scale industry. Contact with urban workers was therefore bound to be limited, even granted a predisposition on the part of the intelligentsia to establish such connections. Narodovoltsy who had abandoned the peasantry would find more material in St Petersburg and in the rapidly growing cities of the Ukraine if they still wished to work among the masses, whereas Chernoperedeltsy and their successors, who wished to continue to work in the countryside, regarded Kazan as an excellent base from which to despatch propagandists to the villages and sectarian communities of the Volga region. Moreover, the local authorities in a city such as Kazan were much less obtrusive and much less obviously persecutory than the authorities in the capitals and even other major provincial centres, such as Kharkov and Odessa. 'Government terror', as the revolutionaries described the persecution they received at the hands of the authorities, was not much practised in Kazan; the 'local satrap', a colonel in the secret police, 'slumbered in comparative peace'.[50] There were therefore no local officials who seemed to revolutionaries to merit assassination as Strelnikov and Sudeykin had done, and attention could still be concentrated, in theory at least, on the masses towards whom most revolutionaries of the 1870s had originally gravitated.

In the early 1870s, it is true, the students of Kazan had given little hope to revolutionary sympathisers of any complexion. According to the account of one activist who entered the University in 1875, academic interests above all absorbed the students at that time. The leisure pursuits which were in vogue, such as drinking and uprooting lampposts, were decidedly unrevolutionary. Two circles professing allegiance to Zemlya i Volya did develop during the second half of the 1870s, however, and the predilection for work among the masses   or at least the tendency to recommend it – which was to remain fundamental to Chernoperedelchestvo soon began to manifest itself. The members of these circles considered themselves in the main to be followers of Lavrov and resolved, like those who had gone to the people a few years before, to acquire extensive knowledge and to master some craft by which they might support themselves among the masses. Several made attempts to conduct propaganda among the peasants of the region and by 1877–8 there were connections with workers in the Alafuzov plant in the city itself.[51]

As for Narodnaya Volya, the party was not entirely without support in

Kazan: agents of the Executive Committee made visits to the city and a local committee seems to have been formed;[52] after the assassination of Alexander II some students issued a proclamation in the name of that party; and members of a circle of Narodovoltsy went off to some nearby islands in order, in the spirit of their party, to learn to shoot.[53] Even in its heyday, however, Narodnaya Volya was unable to pin any great hopes on Kazan. It had no strong organisation there, as Vera Figner admitted, and the authorities clearly attached little importance to the activities of its local members.[54] Nor did its position improve after the assassination of Alexander II, even though the nomadic organisers of the party did not neglect Kazan any more than their predecessors had done. Bakh, for example, complained that he had failed to mould the revolutionary sympathisers he had found there into an organised unit and explained his failure by suggesting that the students who came to Kazan after expulsion from the educational institutions in other cities devoted themselves mainly to the task of completing their studies.[55] Contacts in Kazan mentioned in the papers of Lopatin also proved disappointing from the point of view of Narodnaya Volya.[56]

It did not follow from this evidence of lack of support for Narodnaya Volya in Kazan, however, that the revolutionary movement in general was in decline there in the early 1880s. Bakh's regretful conclusion to that effect probably only reflected his personal disappointment at the frailty of his own party in the city. It accorded neither with the rumours he himself had heard, which indicated that there were many revolutionaries there,[57] nor with the concern of the authorities, who, reviewing their investigations into the activity of revolutionary groups in 1885, noted that the city had become one of the main centres of political agitation in Russia.[58] There were indeed numerous revolutionary sympathisers there, but they tended to fall into two overlapping categories, neither of which contained many advocates of the view that the strategy of Narodnaya Volya should be pursued in the near future.

The first category, consisting largely of survivors from the circles of the second half of the 1870s – such as Golubev, Kvashnina, Pechorkin and Vershinina – reiterated the slogan of Chornyy Peredel: 'Everything for the people and through the people'. Attributing the collapse of Narodnaya Volya to its failure to establish contacts among the masses and anxious to ensure that they themselves did not make the same mistakes, these revolutionaries persevered with tactics associated with Chornyy Peredel. In the autumn of 1883 they sent copies of a leaflet addressed 'to the Russian people' to the villages of numerous provinces in the Russian heartland; and they themselves made occasional sorties into the countryside to conduct propaganda, in all probability collaborating for this purpose with a statistical commission sent by the Kazan provincial *zemstvo* to collect data on the peasantry in one of the neighbouring districts.[59]

The second category of revolutionaries in Kazan in the early 1880s consisted largely of recent arrivals such as Charushnikov, Fokin, Bekaryukov and Balabukha, many of them expelled from the higher educational institutions of other cities, who now devoted themselves almost exclusively to meticulous work in student self-education circles. During the academic year 1883–4 the leaders of these circles, guided mainly by Fokin, began to form a nucleus which itself served initially as only a self-education circle but which after Fokin's departure, on completion of his studies, began, under the direction of Bekaryukov in particular, to supervise the construction of a more serious and tightly organised network on the foundations already laid. In the course of this work the newly arrived students mixed freely with the older revolutionaries sympathetic to Chornyy Peredel and displayed a patience, thoroughness and caution no less incompatible than the attitudes of those revolutionaries with the spirit of Narodnaya Volya. At the meetings of the self-education circles the writings of various thinkers would be studied so carefully that only a few pages would be read at each sitting. A syllabus was drawn up which included the history of revolutionary movements in the West, the current state of affairs in Russia and political economy and which each new circle was expected to cover in the first year of its existence. Studies were guided by a systematic reading catalogue widely circulated in Kazan and elsewhere and known as the 'Chelyabinsk index', which had been compiled by Golubev in collaboration with pupils of a *gimnaziya* in Troitsk, where he had once taught, and which had been printed on a legally owned press in Chelyabinsk by the simple ruse of making it identical in outward appearance with the authorised catalogue of a local public library. Most of the material used in the circles in Kazan was legally available and 'illegal' literature was introduced only 'at the end of the course'. Revolutionary activity beyond the confines of the self-education circles was not even discussed in the early stages, or at least only in very general terms. Finally, an atmosphere of great secrecy surrounded the network: Fokin and Bekaryukov were known as conspirators who believed that the 'methods and modes of work in the revolutionary underground' had to be reviewed and a new type of organisation built if the propagandists they were preparing were to be effectively protected from the authorities. So strictly were the rules relating to security observed that the network established by Fokin and Bekaryukov in Kazan survived intact for almost a decade, during which time about twenty revolutionaries probably passed through its nucleus.[60]

From the theoretical point of view the revolutionaries prominent in this network of circles in Kazan seem to have displayed that lack of discrimination, even that bewildering diversity of opinion, which were as characteristic as patience, thoroughness and caution among most groups not aligned to Narodnaya Volya towards the middle of the 1880s. The nucleus in Kazan was certainly 'Populist', affirmed one memoirist,[61] meaning that it was faithful to the traditions of Zemlya i Volya, as Fokin himself confirmed.[62] Bekaryukov, too, is described elsewhere as being close to the position of that party and as seeing propaganda among the peasants as the main eventual task of the revolutionaries being prepared in the self-education circles. On the other hand, Fokin is described by a revolutionary who knew him after he had left Kazan as favourably disposed towards Narodnaya Volya in general and towards the views of Zhelyabov in particular.[63] Another member of the nucleus, Milovsky (also known under the pen name Yeleonsky), tells us that the centre was composed of remnants of a southern group of Narodovoltsy, had a 'touch of Chernoperedelchestvo' and was influenced primarily by the ideas of Lavrov![64] Still other shades of opinion were represented. Another member of the nucleus, Kudryavtsev, was said to endorse militarist ideas and to believe that revolutionaries should try to attain senior rank in the army and then direct a seizure of power.[65] Another, Baramzin, was a future Social Democrat,[66] and yet another, Chekin, already considered himself a 'Marxist', though that term, too, like the term 'Populist', was often very loosely used in the 1880s to denote one who was not a member or supporter of Narodnaya Volya.[67]

Thus with the disintegration of a dynamic revolutionary theory providing a key to the course of action to be taken in the immediate future, definition of theoretical alignment had become very unimportant to the revolutionaries in Kazan. The impassioned debates about the destiny of Russia, attended by the motley crowd of students at the house of Derenkov – owner of the bakery in which Peshkov, the future writer Gorky, lived and worked[68] – could not have been very divisive. Numerous theories were discussed: supporters of Narodnaya Volya were free to put forward their belief that the 'basic issue' remained the 'seizure of power' by the heroic revolutionary minority, while the more numerous 'Populists' placed emphasis on the 'economic' rather than the 'political' aspects of the revolution they desired.[69] But theoretical preferences now had no practical implications outside the nocturnal meetings at which they were expressed, for there was no longer any immediate prospect of translating them into action which might quickly bear fruit.

THE STUDENT MOVEMENT AND THE DISTURBANCES IN KAZAN IN 1887

The end of the year 1887 was marked by one of those series of disturbances which had been breaking out among the students of Russia's higher educational institutions with some regularity for the previous twenty-five years. From the point of view of the authorities these disturbances represented an intractable problem. On the one hand, of course, post-reform Russia required technological expertise if it was to function effectively as a major European power, and access to higher education was granted to an increasing, though still small, number of the nation's youth. On the other hand, many students, especially those from less privileged backgrounds, were quickly alienated by the rigorous discipline and pedantic attitudes that often prevailed in the institutions they attended. They soon turned away from what they saw as official learning and sought the key to a more just society in the radical writings which circulated freely in self-education circles within the educational institutions. Moreover, the study of scientific subjects, which might have an eventual practical application of use to the state, tended in fact to encourage in students an outlook antithetical to the religion and emotional veneration of autocrat and motherland to which the established order appealed for legitimacy. Such subjects also attracted in the main students motivated by a desire to pursue some vocation, such as medicine, which might be of practical benefit to the lower classes – an ambition that was itself radical and potentially subversive in the conditions of the time. It is not surprising, therefore, that higher educational institutions were at this period the seedbeds of political discontent and the main source of new recruits for revolutionary groups; nor that student disturbances were common not only in the universities in St Petersburg, Moscow, Kiev, Kharkov and Odessa, as well as Kazan, but also in such scientific institutions as the Medical-Surgical Academy, the Technological Institutes in Kharkov and Kazan and the Petrovsko-Razumovskaya Technological Academy in Moscow.

The frequent involvement in the disturbances of students of provincial universities and technical institutions, and the preponderance in these disturbances of students from certain faculties within the universities, provide an indication of the social composition of the milieu from which the revolutionary movement was drawing the bulk of its recruits at this period. Count Witte, who was a student at the University of Odessa at the end of the 1860s, tells us in his memoirs that the atmosphere there was particularly turbulent because the university, being new (it had been opened in 1865), attracted primarily the sons of merchants, *meshchane*, clergymen and peasants, that was to say the children of the *raznochintsy* rather than the scions of aristocratic lines, who gravitated towards the older universities of St Petersburg and Moscow.[70] It was from precisely these backgrounds that the students came who in the 1880s transformed the University of Kazan into a major source of disquiet for the authorities. Of the 916 students of all years registered in Kazan University at the beginning of the academic year 1887–8 (the institutions with which we are dealing were small by modern standards), only 99 were classified as of 'gentry' origin; of the remainder, 189 came from the families of *meshchane* and guildsmen, 101 were the sons of clergymen, 92 the sons of merchants and 'honorary' citizens, 71 the children of peasants and 24 from Cossack families.[71] It is significant, too, that when disorders broke out in Moscow University in 1887 the majority of the participants in them were students of those faculties, law and medicine, where *raznochintsy* were most numerous, making up some 45% of the total.[72] The technical institutions attracted an even higher proportion of *raznochintsy* than the provincial universities, not least because the socially less privileged children who at the secondary level had been pupils at the *Realschulen*, or technical schools, where the curriculum in any case had a scientific orientation, did not have the opportunity, until 1888, to go to university (to which only the pupils of *gimnazii* were permitted to apply). That is not to say, of course, that children from gentry families did not play a very significant role in the revolutionary movement of the 1880s or mingle freely in radical circles with members of other social classes – the student movement was certainly not narrowly representative of any single social stratum – but *raznochintsy* did predominate in it, and their prominence is a reliable pointer as to the social composition of the revolutionary movement as a whole during the 1880s.

As far as the revolutionaries themselves were concerned, the regular disturbances in the higher educational institutions were not to be welcomed without reservation, for they usually resulted in numerous arrests and the expulsion and removal to another region of some of the most rebellious individuals. (It was for this reason that Yakubovich had discouraged participation in student disorders.) On the other hand, the transfer of student leaders to other institutions – many succeeded in gaining readmission to higher educational institutions in this way – did assist the propagation of the revolutionary message in the provinces. Moreover, the authorities themselves also helped, by their habitually extreme reactions to the disturbances, to foster the discontent that had given rise to them. Demonstrations 'such as in any other country would be but slightly punished as mere ebullitions of youth', remarked a phlegmatic English observer in 1883, were in Russia 'magnified into political risings' both by the populace and the police, who were quick to make arrests at the slightest provocation.[73] Thus disturbances which had a purely local and academic origin frequently assumed a wider significance as a result of the bluster and vindictiveness with which the authorities responded to them. Their outbreak and their repercussions therefore tended ultimately to assist the revolutionary cause more than they harmed it, by radicalising the students who took part in them.

The new discontent among the students in St Petersburg had found expression in the demonstrations of 1886, particularly the Dobrolyubov demonstration, and in the terrorist plot which had followed in its wake at the beginning of 1887. In response to this plot the authorities in turn made attempts – which were to prove counterproductive – to quell the growing student unrest. The rector of St Petersburg University, on hearing of the plot, addressed a note to the Minister of Education, Delyanov, in which he urged that more rigorous checks be carried out on the background of applicants to higher educational institutions and that the lives, work and contacts of students be more closely supervised. His note referred in particular to his own university, which he wanted to make 'worthy of the favour of the monarch', but it set a general tone. On 18 June Delyanov issued a circular, which immediately became notorious, directing the *gimnazii* (from which pupils could proceed to a university education) to accept 'only those children whose guardians can guarantee the proper domestic supervision and the necessary accommodations for scholarly pursuits'. Fees were raised by forty roubles a year in the hope of excluding the 'children of coachmen, footmen, cooks, laundresses, small shopkeepers and other similar people'. Heads of secondary schools were instructed to supply detailed information on the views of their pupils, and on the material circumstances and social background of their parents, to the higher educational institutions to which the pupils were applying. The universities meanwhile were deprived of their cherished autonomy and placed under the direction of the Minister of Education. Professors were henceforth to be appointed not internally but by the political authorities, and some eminent academics who had incurred official displeasure, such as Kovalevsky, Professor of Law at Moscow University, were dismissed. Students were required to wear uniform, the courses available to women were drastically reduced, and attempts made to reduce the status of the natural and social sciences.[74]

In Kazan, as in other provincial centres, the student movement took a more militant turn in 1887 as a result of the recent reinvigoration of the movement in St Petersburg, where Kazan students had many personal contacts. Students exiled from St Petersburg for their part in the Dobrolyubov demonstration resumed their activities in Kazan under the leadership of Galkina (whose circle included one Sakharova, once a friend of Perovskaya's) and kept in touch with circles in the capital and with members of the 'terrorist faction' who were plotting to kill Alexander III. Osipanov, one of those hanged for his part in this plot, had been active in student circles in Kazan from the early 1880s and still had many acquaintances there, such as Zhenzhurist and other students who had disrupted the University's speech day in November 1886. Andreyushkin was also known from his school days in Yekaterinodar by students in Kazan such as Vygornitsky of the Veterinary Institute. Former class-mates of Aleksandr Ulyanov's came to the fore as leaders of the Simbirsk *zemlyachestvo*. It is not surprising in view of these connections that news of the failure of the plot to kill the Tsar in March 1887 reached Kazan quickly in the form of a coded telegram and that copies of proclamations issued by St Petersburg students were distributed there. After the execution of the former aquaintances of Kazan students involved in the terrorist plot feelings again ran high and several students, including Zhenzhurist, were expelled. There remained in Kazan, though, individuals such as Galkina (whose influence on the volatile student youth the police very much feared) and students such as Vygornitsky, Podbelsky (a former pupil of the Troitsk *gimnaziya* and brother of a Narodovolets prominent among the St Petersburg students at the beginning of the decade) and Motovilov, who was evidently well known to Bekaryukov and the conspirators since they maintained contact with him when he left Kazan and settled in Rostov.[75]

Towards the end of 1887 the movement in Kazan, as elsewhere, again gathered momentum, this time as a result of the unpopularity of the measures taken by the government to suppress it. Late in November serious disorders had broken out in Moscow University, where a student had publicly hit the inspector. The disturbances found an echo first in Kharkov and Odessa, then, on 4 December, in Kazan, where, as the University authorities had been warned in advance, students had been planning to hold a meeting 'of a not very peaceable character'. In the mid morning a crowd of shouting, whistling students surged down the corridor, pushing to one side the inspector who tried to bar their way, and ran up the staircase and into the assembly hall, where a clamorous meeting began. The inspector, when he reappeared and ordered the students to disperse, was attacked and withdrew. The crowd, probably about 150 to 200 strong, was shortly joined by another throng which had just come from the Veterinary Institute, where the students had presented their own petition to the director. In due course the rector of the University appeared amid the uproar and entered into talks with the students which lasted for some three hours. He was presented with the students' demands, which covered not only matters affecting themselves – such as the right to hold meetings to discuss their corporate affairs – but also some grievances of a more general political nature, such as the social restrictions on access to higher education; indeed, one of the petitions drawn up by the students opened with a transparently political statement about the 'impossibility of all the conditions in which Russian life in general and student life in particular' had been placed. It was not, of course, in the power of the rector to accede to any of the students' demands and no concessions had been gained by the students when in the late afternoon they finally agreed to disperse after the rector had assured them that they would not be molested as they made their way home. Arrests began that night. The higher powers in St Petersburg were infuriated by the flight of the inspector, the rector's parley with the students and his assurances that they would have a safe passage home, and stern action was soon taken against the ringleaders. Some forty-five students from the University and a substantial number from the Veterinary Institute were expelled and both institutions, like the universities in Moscow, Kharkov, Odessa and St Petersburg, were temporarily closed.[76]

V. I. ULYANOV (LENIN) AND HIS ROLE IN THE STUDENT MOVEMENT IN 1887

The demonstration of 4 December 1887 in Kazan is of particular interest in the history of the Russian revolutionary movement in the 1880s not only inasmuch as it reveals the continuing, if ill-directed, discontent among the student youth in the city, but also because it marks the appearance in the movement of V. I. Ulyanov, younger brother of the executed terrorist and the future Lenin.

As the brother of a man convicted of plotting to kill the Tsar, V. I. Ulyanov had found the doors of the University of St Petersburg closed to him. (It is possible that in any case his mother was happy to have him placed in a provincial university on the grounds that the risk of her second son, too, becoming involved in dangerous political conspiracies was smaller there than in the capital.) Vladimir's academic record at school, like that of Aleksandr before him, had been outstanding – he was awarded a gold medal after his final examinations (as Aleksandr had been) and his conduct had been exemplary. Thus with the help of a generous testimonal from the headmaster of his *gimnaziya* in Simbirsk[77] – who happened to be Kerensky, father of the man whose provisional government the Bolsheviks under Lenin's leadership were to overthrow in 1917 – Ulyanov did succeed in gaining admission to the University of Kazan. Here he enrolled in the autumn of 1887 as a student in the law faculty. Ulyanov's choice of subject was unexpected and disappointed Kerensky in particular, who believed his most gifted pupil had the makings of a classical scholar. It is conventional to explain Ulyanov's decision by reference to the memoirs of a cousin, Veretennikov, who tells us that Ulyanov considered it a time in which one should study the 'sciences of law and political economy'.[78] It is equally probable, of course, that Ulyanov already appreciated the advantages of the relative financial security which a career in the legal profession might afford. Nor is Veretennikov's explanation of Ulyanov's choice of subject borne out by Ulyanov's timetable in his first term, for with the exception of several periods devoted to theology his lectures dealt exclusively with the history of Roman and Russian law. And in any case in the second half of the term Ulyanov's attendance left much to be desired.[79] All the same, the choice of subject did not rule out the possibility of earnest participation in student circles, for a course in law was generally considered by the students to allow more time than most other courses for extra-curricular pursuits, whatever they might be: it was felt that the annual examinations in the law faculty could be passed on the basis of a few weeks' cramming.

It is true that since he was the brother of a recently convicted terrorist the new student, Vladimir Ulyanov, was watched by the authorities with particular attention. It would be wrong to infer, however, that his pursuit of contacts in radical student circles was less energetic than it is made to seem by this special official vigilance. Once in the University he had easy access to revolutionary circles through the Simbirsk *zemlyachestvo*, in which there were doubtless students who not only remembered him from their days in the *gimnaziya* but had also known and respected his elder brother. He was initiated into the preparations for the demonstration of 4 December and observed by an informer some days before the demonstration to be behaving furtively, spending time in the smoking room in conversation 'with the most suspicious students';[80] he was in the forefront of the demonstration itself and was expelled for his part in it. More significant than his introduction to the *zemlyachestvo* and his participation in the demonstration, however, was his involvement, since the early part of the term, with a circle which the police considered to be of an 'extremely harmful orientation'. One member of this circle was Motovilov, a student of the Veterinary Institute who had been prominent in student circles in the city for some time. Another was Andreyushkin's friend, Vygornitsky. But the circle also included A. Skvortsov, a student who had enrolled in autumn 1887 at the Veterinary Institute, and his class-mate from the Taganrog *gimnaziya*, L. Bogoraz, brother of the man who had led the attempt to revive Narodnaya Volya in 1885–6. As a pupil expelled from his school, Bogoraz failed to gain admission to a higher educational institution in Kazan, but he remained in the city all the same. These students kept in touch with events in student circles in St Petersburg through another friend from Taganrog, Zelenenko, who was a student at the University in the capital, where he moved in the same circles as Kacharovsky. Another former companion of Bogoraz and Skvortsov from the Taganrog *gimnaziya*, Kondoyanaki, was now in Paris, where he was in touch with leading Narodovoltsy in emigration. The police in Kazan pondered a possible connection between Bogoraz's circle and Galkina and noted the frequency of Bogoraz's visits to Ulyanov.[81]

These scraps of evidence on Lenin's earliest involvement and associations in the revolutionary movement do allow one to form some impression of the nature of his political affiliations in autumn 1887 at the time of his revolutionary baptism. But before attempting to evaluate them it is as well to be aware that the subsequent eminence of Lenin and the existence of conflicting interpretations of the régime he eventually helped to establish in Russia serve to make discussion of even his earliest revolutionary aspirations exceptionally controversial. Several of the questions relating to his views and activity in 1887, for example, assume a contentiousness which hinders dispassionate examination of the evidence. To what extent, for instance, was Vladimir Ulyanov familiar with his elder brother's views at the time of Aleksandr's arrest, trial and execution? To what extent did he endorse Aleksandr's views? Most importantly, to which doctrine did he give his earliest political allegiance, Narodovolchestvo or Marxism? And in any case how clear were his views? To these questions others have to be added as soon as one comes to consider Vladimir Ulyanov's period of exile at Kokushkino in 1888, following his expulsion from the University in 1887, and his second stay in Kazan from the autumn of 1888 to the spring of 1889. What was the extent and nature of the influence of Chernyshevsky on him? When did he first become properly acquainted with Marxist thought, and how quickly and thoroughly did he assimilate it? The differing answers given to these questions are inextricably connected with larger divergent interpretations of Lenin's political thought, which – to state them in their simplest and most extreme variants – postulate, on the one hand, that a clear and unequivocal Marxist orthodoxy may be traced back to Lenin's earliest revolutionary strivings; and, on the other hand, that Lenin developed an early sympathy for authoritarian socialism which continued to colour his thought even after he had absorbed Marxist doctrines.

The first viewpoint, according to which Lenin from the very beginning commended an essentially Marxist strategy for the Russian revolutionary movement, finds expression to a greater or lesser extent in most Soviet work on his early years. By the time Aleksandr Ulyanov was executed, so it is assumed, Vladimir's views on the best course for the Russian revolutionary intelligentsia were sufficiently clearly defined for him to be able to pronounce judgement on his brother's participation in the terrorist plot to assassinate Alexander III. 'No,' Vladimir is reported by his younger sister, Mariya, to have said on hearing of his brother's execution, 'we shall not take that path. That is not the path that should be taken.'[82] The authenticity of these words is accepted more or less uncritically by the Soviet scholars who have made the closest study of Lenin's activity at this period. Thus Nafigov deftly gives the impression that it was in 1887 that V. I. Ulyanov 'became convinced once and for all' that it was necessary to take a path different from the one his elder brother had chosen.[83] Even Polevoy, who has written the most meticulous account of the early history of Russian Social Democracy, faithfully affirms that in 1887 Ulyanov already took a critical attitude towards the Populist theory of 'peasant socialism' and that he understood the need for 'another path'.[84] Shcheprov tells us explicitly that the student demonstration of December 1887 in Kazan was led by 'Marxists such as V. I. Lenin'.[85] Official Soviet biographies have persistently reiterated the assumption that V. Ulyanov did indeed develop a precocious hostility to

Populism and have added a further embellishment to the effect that while still at school he was introduced by his elder brother – who was himself 'on the verge of renouncing the Narodnaya Volya and adopting Marxism' – to the 'traditions of revolutionary democracy and Marxist literature'.[86]

However, the only evidence on which this case for V. Ulyanov's early acceptance of Marxism rests (Mariya's recollection of Vladimir's profession of faith in May 1887) is valueless, for not only were the words attributed to Vladimir written down some forty years after the event, but also Mariya, at the time of their supposed utterance, was not yet ten years of age. Even when she comes to speak of a slightly later period in their lives, the years 1889–93, she confesses that she was then 'still quite a child'.[87] We have to weigh Mariya's testimony, moreover, against other evidence which makes it seem very unlikely that Vladimir had either the inclination or the capacity to criticise Aleksandr's views in May 1887. In the first place, he appears to have been much influenced by Aleksandr and guided by his tastes and opinions. As a child he imitated his brother to such an extent – so we are told by the elder sister, Anna, a much more reliable witness – that the other children began to laugh at him. Aleksandr, a figure of great intellectual and moral authority in the Ulyanov family – as indeed he was outside it – evidently commanded a greater respect from Vladimir than could their mother when she was left in charge of the household after the death of the father early in 1886.[88] In many respects, it is true, the brothers were very different from one another: Aleksandr, scholarly and considerate towards others, had a quiet and unassuming charm, while Vladimir, boisterous and self-assertive, even overbearing, was as likely to hurt or offend as to please. All the same, Vladimir's reverence for Aleksandr, strengthened now by an awareness of hitherto unsuspected depths in the elder brother's character, would in all probability have suppressed any inclination on Vladimir's part to pass judgement on his brother's actions, and confidence in Aleksandr's decisions would in any case have blunted his capacity to do so. In the second place, Vladimir is said quite explicitly by Anna to have had no definite political views before his brother's execution, only a vague adolescent opposition to authority. And, although the official version of Lenin's biography has it that Vladimir began to study the first volume of Marx's *Capital* when Aleksandr brought it home with him from St Petersburg in the summer of 1885 and again in 1886,[89] Anna maintains that even during the summer of 1886, when the two brothers shared a room, Vladimir showed no interest in the book. Instead, he spent his time reading and rereading Turgenev.[90]

Nor is it arguable even that Vladimir's earliest revolutionary endeavours represented a radical departure from the example set by Aleksandr. Rather the opposite would seem to be the case: that they constituted an attempt to follow that example. It is sometimes pointed out, it is true, that Vladimir was in fact ignorant of his brother's ideas; Trotsky maintains, for instance, that 'Aleksandr introduced no member of his family into his inner world, and least of all Vladimir' and that there 'can be no question . . . of Aleksandr's having any direct political influence' on his younger brother.[91] And, admittedly, Vladimir is said himself to have told a close associate in 1893 that for him, as for the whole family, the participation of Aleksandr in the terrorist plot 'came as a complete surprise'.[92] However, the inference should not be drawn from this evidence of Vladimir's ignorance of Aleksandr's plans that Aleksandr's influence on Vladimir's revolutionary activity could only have been negligible, for we know that in June 1887 Vladimir had an oppportunity to find out in some detail about his brother's last days and the views he had expressed in court from Aleksandr's former friend, Chebotaryov, whom Vladimir questioned very closely.[93] And in any case it is not necessary to establish that Vladimir was apprised of all the niceties of Aleksandr's thinking in order to be able to assert that the elder brother had indicated a path which the younger brother might in the first instance choose to take. No explanation was needed to make Aleksandr's action perfectly comprehensible to Vladimir; Aleksandr had resorted to the by now time-honoured violence which to many seemed the only form of effective protest possible in the circumstances. His heroic death was a source of inspiration to Vladimir, as the self-sacrifice of Narodovoltsy in general had been to a whole revolutionary generation; his blood, as Anna put it rhetorically, 'lit up the path of the brother Vladimir who was following him with the glow of the revolutionary blaze'.[94]

Such recollections as there are of Vladimir's attitude to the demonstration of 4 December 1887 in Kazan University tend to confirm his early faithfulness to the example his brother had set. There are the memoirs of one of the students detained by the police together with V. I. Ulyanov shortly after the demonstration. After indulging in the usual practice of singing a few revolutionary songs, during which Vladimir remained silent, one of the students thought of asking his comrades, in turn, what they intended to do after their release from detention and their expulsion from the University. Most were evidently caught unawares and their answers revealed uncertainty behind a façade of recklessness. When Ulyanov's turn came, he reflected for a moment and replied to the effect that his elder brother had blazed a trail for him.[95] There is also the celebrated story of Ulyanov's remark to the police officer who was acompanying him to prison after his arrest following the demonstration. '"Why are you up in arms, young man", the policeman asked. "You're up against a wall, you know." "Yes, a wall," Lenin is said to have replied, "and a rotten one – give it a shove and it'll fall over"'[96] – a sentiment reminiscent of the view of the autocracy as a colossus on 'feet of clay' traditionally invoked by Narodnaya Volya as a justification for terrorism.

These pieces of evidence, belonging as they do to the realm of anecdotal recollection, are of course inconclusive (though they are still more substantial than any information which might serve to refute them). More reliable, however, as an indicator of Vladimir Ulyanov's political mood in the autumn of 1887 is his well-documented involvement in the circle of Bogoraz, Skvortsov and Motovilov. Ulyanov's association with this circle is clearly a source of some embarrassment to Soviet historians. Polevoy altogether omits to mention it. Volin makes the circle sound innocuous by describing it as a circle for 'political self-education'.[97] Nafigov – who in a book of some two hundred pages on the subject of Lenin's 'first step' in the revolutionary movement between 1887 and 1889 devotes only about one and a half pages to the circle – produces no previously unpublished material on the circle, even though his study as a whole is based on painstaking research in local archives. He passes in silence over the fact that Bogoraz, whose pre-eminence in the circle he questions, was the brother of the celebrated Narodovolets and describes the members of the circle as linked with the 'Populist' movement,[98] a classification which further blurs their relationship with Narodovolchestvo. And yet it is only to a preference for Narodovolchestvo that all these connections can reasonably be held to point. The circle consisted almost entirely of young men who were either related to, or close friends of, known advocates of terrorism who had been arrested within the previous eight or nine months. And their contact in St Petersburg, Zelenenko, believed terrorism to be the 'only suitable method of struggle with the prevailing order'.[99]

Some Western historians proceed directly from the assumption that Vladimir Ulyanov's earliest revolutionary associates were inspired by the terrorist tradition of Narodnaya Volya to the conclusion that they were 'Jacobins'. Richard Pipes, for example, states that during the first phase of his intellectual evolution 'Lenin sympathised with the Jacobin wing of the People's Will. He believed that the revolution would derive its force from the peasant masses and its leadership from a conspiratorial group employing terror and aiming at a power seizure.' And again: there is 'no doubt that Lenin spent the first five or six years of his revolutionary career in the very midst of the most extreme Jacobin elements of the People's Will'.[100] The same basic position is adopted by Theen, who claims that the 'formative period of [Lenin's] revolutionary development clearly stood under the influence of Chernyshevsky and the Jacobin ideas of Narodnaya Volya'. Theen intends on the basis of this proposition to demonstrate that, while Lenin began later to 'think of revolution in Marxist terms and categories, he remained a Jacobin by disposition and temperament'.[101] Even Harding, who attempts to clear the young Lenin of the charge of Jacobinism, agrees that he 'spent the early years of his life in close contact with known and notorious Jacobins or Blanquists, or to render it in Russian Narodovoltsy'.[102]

It must be admitted that the *prima facie* case for the view that Lenin harboured an early sympathy for Jacobinism is strengthened by the paucity of the archive material relating to Lenin's early revolutionary activity which has been published in the Soviet Union. Moreover, Lenin himself later gave the years 1892–3 as the date at which his revolutionary activity began,[103] as if – it is argued – attempting to conceal earlier connections which might in the Soviet period invite obloquy. We may add one further piece of information which the exponents of the 'Jacobin' interpretation of Lenin's early activity have not themselves deployed. Bogoraz's elder brother was, after all, the author of the pamphlet, *The Struggle of Social Forces in Russia*, published at the beginning of 1886, in which it was boldly suggested that the intelligentsia, the 'salt of the earth', might seize power and bring to bear their 'magical ideas' if the masses proved too politically immature to implement revolutionary change themselves. Nor, as we have seen, was Bogoraz the only leader of the party in 1885–6 in whose thinking the Jacobin element of Narodovolchestvo was pronounced.

There is, however, no more firm evidence for the view that Vladimir Ulyanov was from the beginning a 'Jacobin' than there is for the view that he was from the beginning a 'Marxist'. This interpretation of his early allegiance depends to a large extent on the indiscriminate and unwarranted use of the terms 'Jacobin' and 'Narodovolets' as if they were synonymous – a confusion which may owe something to the polemical passages directed at Tikhomirov by Plekhanov in *Our Differences*.[104] Narodovolchestvo, however, was not inevitably equated by contemporaries with Jacobinism. Much more commonly, as its history during the 1880s shows, it was associated with the actions of the party's terrorists, with active, heroic, self-sacrificial struggle, clamorous protest against a stifling régime. That Vladimir

Ulyanov's earliest close associates were enthusiastic advocates of terrorism and thus inspired by Narodnaya Volya does not entitle us immediately to impute to them an authoritarian socialism. (Nor indeed does the activity of Motovilov or Bogoraz himself in the period immediately following their association with V. I. Ulyanov in Kazan reflect any Jacobin sympathies.) It seems most probable that – in 1887 at any rate – it was the destructive aspects of Narodovolchestvo which appealed most to Vladimir Ulyanov rather than any constructive role it might postulate for the revolutionary intelligentsia during a period of dictatorship. For the moment Vladimir and his associates were motivated by a rather blind desire, aggravated by the loss of people close to them, to strike in however crude a way at the prevailing order. Their boldness was undoubted and the experience of the student demonstration – in which Skvortsov, Motovilov and Vygornitsky, as well as Ulyanov, all played a leading part – was stimulating. But it was not the protest of conscious revolutionaries with clearly defined views, 'Marxist' or 'Jacobin', only an expression of the bitterness and frustration for which Narodnaya Volya had long since provided the best outlet.

THE SYMPOSIUM *THE SOCIAL QUESTION* COMPILED BY 'POPULISTS' IN KAZAN

While many students in various cities were spending their energy in the vociferous but in the final analysis rather aimless demonstrations of 1887, the 'Populists' in Kazan continued to act more cautiously and consequently remained unaffected by the arrests and the punishments which these forms of protest invariably entailed. Many of these 'Populists', however, were clearly beginning to feel the need to re-examine some of the more important issues confronting socialists in Russia and to clarify plans for future activity, or at least to initiate fresh debate. With these ends in view, a group of the experienced 'Populists', led by Charushnikov and including Pechorkin and Vershinina, withdrew from other revolutionary groupings in which their security might be threatened, obtained some printing equipment and installed it in a small house purchased specially for the purpose on the outskirts of Kazan, and set about compiling a collection of articles under the general title *The Social Question*.[105] The symposium included contributions from the writer, Korolenko, and the statistician, Annensky (who was married, incidentally, to Tkachov's sister), as well as a lengthy preamble 'from the publishers' in which the views of the Kazan 'Populists' themselves were set down.

Annensky's article, entitled 'Socialism and Populism', very clearly reflected the dilemma facing Populists, who had now to concede that they had failed, after fifteen years in the attempt, to stir the masses, but who still clung to the dream of a peasant revolution. Populism in its old form, Annensky admitted, had had its day; it would have to enter a 'new *critical* stage' if it were to survive at all. Annensky acknowledged too that the existence of capitalism in Russia could no longer be denied. Moreover, although 'capitalist industry' did not yet in Annensky's view determine the 'general tone and complexion' of the nation's economy, capitalism was a '*growing*' phenomenon. The question inevitably arose, therefore, as to whether Russia already stood at the beginning of that process of which the leading nations of Western Europe represented the end result. The Old Populism had emphatically rejected this notion, but a new stream of thought – Annensky had in mind Social Democracy – had endorsed it and foresaw the disintegration of the commune under pressure from capitalism. Annensky then proceeded to summarise the Social Democratic schema, with its prediction that socialism would emerge from the capitalist method of production and with the corollary of that prediction, that revolutionaries should devote themselves to the organisation of a party in the ranks of the proletariat.

Although Annensky had himself marshalled strong arguments against the old Populism, however, his instinctive opposition to Social Democracy, with its neglect of the peasantry, compelled him to seek ways of sustaining it. The criticisms which could be levelled at Populism, he argued, cast doubt only on the form which Populism had taken in its first phase; they did not invalidate the 'principle' of Populism, the 'essence of the Populist idea'. Populism would be undermined completely only if one considered its fundamental tenet to be belief in the possibility of building socialism on the foundation of the commune and if one insisted, moreover, that socialism be built in such a near future that all the vicissitudes of the period preceding the revolution need hardly be taken into account. But for Annensky the fundamental component of Populism was not so much this sociological belief as a moral concern for the suffering masses, the vast majority of whom happened in Russia to be peasants. The needy had to be succoured; they could not simply be put to one side by the intelligentsia, albeit temporarily, when another revolutionary strategy seemed to commend itself. And how much longer the masses would have to suffer if revolutionaries accepted the Social Democratic schema! The attainment of the goal at the end of the Marxist path would require the 'hard, long and dogged work of many generations', for Russian capitalism, Annensky warned, still stood 'at the bottom of its line of ascent', and, even if it could be proved that it would advance without encountering obstacles, what an immense period it would take all the same to reach its apogee, the point at which its antithesis would begin to undermine it. Had not Marx himself described how it had taken English capitalism three centuries to conquer the historical stage, and was it not clear that merciless vandalism had attended its victory? And how long would the next phase require, how long would it be before the expropriators were expropriated? What sense was there, then, in the Russia of the 1880s, in abandoning the peasant mass until it had been recooked 'in the factory cauldron' and in squandering all resources on the proletariat?

Thus Annensky tried to argue that even if the course described by Marx in his analysis of the economic development of Western Europe was indeed applicable to Russia, too, nevertheless it was immoral and futile to begin at that time to formulate plans for the implementation of proletarian socialism. Annensky was not going to help to drive the wheel of history if it crushed those social groups which tried to turn it back, especially since in Russia those groups included millions of the peasants beloved of the Populists. Like any other generation the peasants had a right to a share of the general happiness of mankind, even if their striving for that share tended to delay the ultimate resolution of social antagonisms. Any 'real programme of social activity', moreover, had to be based on the 'actual interests' of living generations. Populists were therefore bound to continue to concentrate their attention on the peasantry and to try to win for them a life as full and satisfying as possible at that particular stage of social development. Indeed, this 'Populist' programme, Annensky suggested, was essentially the same everywhere; it merely took different forms according to the level of development reached by a given society. In the West it found expression in workers' socialism, but in Russia it was the interests of the peasant mass that were bound to preoccupy the intelligentsia. That was not to say that the interests of the proletariat should be ignored even in Russia, of course, but the urban workers could not claim more attention than any other section of the populace because they were not yet, and for a long time to come would not be, the main element of the oppressed mass.[106]

Like Annensky, the 'publishers', too, 'men of the 80s' as they called themselves, frankly acknowledged the predicament in which they now found themselves. It was difficult in the present conditions to prepare and organise conscious socialists in the countryside, and yet if no socialists were found around whom a conscious party might be built the revolutionary programme would remain a dead letter. The propagandists, then, had either to 'burn their boats' or to turn back and review the path they had taken. Some had given up all hope, others had buried themselves in books, seeking an exit from the impasse. Like Annensky too, the 'publishers' had devoted much attention to the Social Democratic writings now emanating from Switzerland. In particular, they expressed an interest in Plekhanov's description of the commune as a decaying product of primitive agrarian communism which would give way to small private ownership within an ultimately capitalist economy. But, again like Annensky, the 'publishers', as latter-day followers of Chornyy Peredel, had reservations about the Social Democratic schema. In their case, however, it was not so much compassion for the peasant masses as continued belief, albeit in a rather novel form, in the distinctiveness of Russia's historical development that underpinned their arguments. The fact that Russia was currently passing through a phase of development through which the civilised peoples of the West had passed long before did not seem to the 'publishers' to make it inevitable that Russian development would henceforth continue to follow the pattern described by the 'cultural–historical schema' applicable to the West, for the international conditions in which Russia found herself at the time of her entry into the phase of a commodity economy were not identical with those conditions which had obtained when the Western European countries had themselves entered that phase. Russian history therefore still had a certain individuality for these 'publishers', but its distinctiveness lay not in any 'popular spirit' peculiar to the Russian masses, nor in the existence of economic institutions peculiarly Russian, but rather in the 'particular historical atmosphere' in which Russia was developing – in her international position and its domestic consequences. No other country that had attained a high level of industrial development had grown up in such an atmosphere or occupied a comparable position. In an age of rapidly expanding contacts between states, underdeveloped countries, or countries 'at the tail-end of civilisation' as the 'publishers' humbly put it, would initially be much influenced by the social structure and intellectual life of the 'pioneers' of civilisation. Thus, while conceding that the Russian commune would not of its own accord become the basic economic unit of a future communist society, the 'publishers' baulked at the conclusion Plekhanov drew on the basis of this premiss that capitalism was beginning in Russia to take the course it had already taken in Western Europe. They also rejected the corollary of this conclusion – that the revolutionaries must now place their hopes mainly on the proletariat. Instead of accepting these beliefs, they put another 'unsolved question': what were those forces which 'irresistibly' drew Russia along a path down which the 'history of the peoples of the West' had not yet gone? Only when an answer to this question had been found, the 'publishers' argued, could a *categorical* answer be given to the question as to the mission of the proletariat in Russian history.[107]

The Kazan 'Populists', then, were no longer denying that capitalism was developing in Russia, or that that cherished institution, the commune, was disintegrating under its impact. And yet, as socialists motivated primarily by humanitarian concern for the sufferings of the masses around them rather than by adherence to the intellectually appealing Marxist doctrine, they were bound still to concentrate their attention on the peasantry rather than on the proletariat. Moreover, dwelling as they did in the heart of a vast, overwhelmingly rural country, they were in any case understandably sceptical about the revolutionary significance of the urban workers. Thus, with its stifled admission of past failures and its attempt all the same to sustain Populism in some form for a little longer, the symposium of the Kazan 'Populists' eloquently attests to the dilemma and confusion of revolutionaries in Russia in the late 1880s. The fact that the symposium included Akselrod's article, "The Transitional Moment for Our Party', written nearly ten years before for the Bakuninist émigré journal, *Obshchina* (*The Commune*),[108] serves, like the indecisiveness of the articles by Annensky and the 'publishers', and like even the weakness of the very title of the symposium, to underline the fact that Populism was bereft of challenging ideas and was running out of momentum.

The Social Question was printed in more than two hundred copies at the end of 1887 and the beginning of 1888 and by the spring was ready for distribution. Its initial reception, in Kharkov and Moscow, was cool. Late in 1888, while members of the printers' circle continued to seek an answer in the writings of Marx, Engels and Plekhanov to the theoretical problems they had raised, Charushnikov departed for Nizhniy Novgorod, Moscow and St Petersburg; but the news he brought back was discouraging. Social Democracy, which was making progress in the revolutionary intelligentsia, had a theoretical source of its own without a Populist literature. The 'peasant question' had ceased to be crucial in the minds of the revolutionaries interviewed by Charushnikov.[109]

One further attempt was made to resolve the difficulties which the 'Populists' faced: members of the printers' circle prepared reports on the results of propaganda in the countryside. No conclusions were reached, however, which could serve as a basis for further activity. The 'Populists' had come to a critical point. On the one hand, they felt that they should establish closer contact with the peasantry; on the other, the apparent shortcomings of their theoretical premisses pointed to the need for further study. They agreed to go their separate ways in search of the right path, and in autumn 1889, as if in admission of defeat, they dismantled their press which had been set up with such affection and guarded so closely, and unceremoniously jettisoned it in the River Kazanka. Even those 'Populists' who had previously denounced the practice of settling in the villages in some official capacity and trying slowly to educate the people were now forced to resort to such *kul'turtregerstvo*, as this practice was known, if they were to remain active. Some emulated Charushnikov, who returned to the countryside from which the Zemlevoltsy had withdrawn a decade before.[110]

FOKIN'S CIRCLES IN KIEV IN THE SECOND HALF OF THE 1880s

Networks of circles similar to that which existed in Kazan in the mid 1880s were established by Fokin and Bekaryukov when they moved to other cities. In Kiev, where Fokin resumed his studies in 1884, a network was set up in the city's higher educational institutions which is said to have embraced at the height of its influence as many as twenty-five circles, organised at various levels. At the highest level was a nucleus, consisting of the most trustworthy members of the organisation and invested with dictatorial powers. This nucleus, to which new members were co-opted, was envisaged as the 'core' of a future revolutionary party. At the second level of the network were circles which accepted the political and revolutionary position of the secret society. Here the programme of the organisation, its tactics and immediate objectives were formulated. At the third level new recruits were trained, but even here political study was thorough and systematic. Experienced propagandists, using carefully compiled catalogues, supervised the work of the circles, and well-stocked collections of books, containing works on socio-economic and political subjects, were available to newly recruited sympathisers. The most promising members of these circles were eventually drafted into the circles of the second level.

Great secrecy surrounded the activities of circles at all levels of this network. Much time and money were spent finding and procuring premises where the circles could meet (gatherings at the homes of members of the society were not permitted). Members were strictly forbidden to keep 'illegal' literature in their homes or to establish contact with the passing epigones of Narodnaya Volya, who often proved to be under police surveillance and thus compromised all whom they visited. Even the initiated members of the organisation did not know the names of many of their fellows. The rules of secret societies such as the Masons, the Carbonari and the Decembrists were carefully studied. (The conspirators were particularly critical of the *buntari* of the 1870s, whom they considered to have recklessly neglected the need for discipline and hierarchical organisation.) And if the secrecy in which the Fokintsy, as these conspirators were known, shrouded their network earned them a certain notoriety among their contemporaries, nevertheless the effectiveness of the arrangements they made to ensure their security was indisputable. The network survived until the beginning of the 1890s and when the police finally did become aware of its existence it was disbanded and its members dispersed.

Whereas in Kazan the student circles to which Fokin and Bekaryukov applied their new 'method' of organisation were of a vague but perhaps predominantly Populist complexion, in Kiev the circles organised by Fokin seem to have contained a larger element of former Narodovoltsy. But, as in Kazan, former or even surviving theoretical allegiances were of little importance since no activity outside the network itself was contemplated in the near future. Indeed, not only was terrorism regarded as inadmissible, on the grounds that it was sure to jeopardise the security of the network's nucleus, but even work among the masses was discouraged and any individuals who remained there were advised to withdraw. For the 1880s, or what remained of them, were to be used for a 'gathering of forces' for battle in another historical epoch. Before the mobilisation of workers and peasants could be undertaken the movement would have to go through an 'organisational–educational phase', during which a 'sound *organisational base*' could be created '*in the towns*' and a centre capable of sustaining a prolonged underground campaign built among the senior students of the higher educational institutions from whom the Fokintsy expected the revolutionary initiative eventually to come. Only upon completion of this work would the revolutionaries move into a 'systematically offensive phase', during which they might again contemplate the formation of a fighting organisation for attack on the central political apparatus. Finally, the contest would enter a 'synthetic phase', during which the large, highly organised conspiratorial party would apply every possible means of struggle with the object of seizing power. The conspirators would then conduct agitation on a large scale and disseminate propaganda to all sections of the population. Their organisation would no longer consist of only a few members of the intelligentsia, but would take the form of a genuinely democratic party drawn from the ranks of the proletariat and the soldiers, that was to say the young peasants stationed in the garrisons. But this 'powerful, organised social force', as the Fokintsy envisaged it, would challenge the prevailing order only 'in the more or less distant future'. 'Conspiracy' culminating in an armed uprising and seizure of power was not an ambition about to be fulfilled, but a very remote prospect.[111]

BEKARYUKOV AND WORKERS' CIRCLES IN KHARKOV AND ROSTOV

While Fokin was building this network in Kiev, Bekaryukov assumed leadership of the 'Populist' faction in Kharkov, to which he had returned from Kazan in 1886 on his graduation from the medical faculty of the University. Here he began with characteristic thoroughness and caution to supervise the studies of circles which had existed among the workers in the city since the early 1880s and with which propagandists of numerous organisations had had contact at one time or another. In the later stages of this work Bekaryukov may have been assisted by two other able young propagandists who appeared in the city in 1888 – Perazich, a medical student, and Melnikov, one of those members of the educated class who had 'gone to the people' and now lived among them doing the same work and dwelling in the same conditions. It is also possible that the police exaggerated Bekaryukov's influence on the workers' group – as he was by now a qualified doctor (that is to say, a man of professional status) he was likely to impress the authorities more than other propagandists whom they apprehended. All the same, his role in the group seems to have been important. It was under his leadership, the police reported in April 1888, that workers' circles which had previously served merely as a 'testing ground' for propagandists from the intelligentsia had recently begun to assume a more serious character. Early in 1888 a new workers' centre was elected and relations between the workers and the revolutionaries from the intelligentsia were formalised. The workers' centre was obliged to render material assistance to the propagandists out of a fund into which workers paid 3% of their monthly wages. Plans made by the workers for more serious new ventures would have to be approved in a 'commission' consisting of two members of the workers' centre and one member of the group from the intelligentsia. Propagandists for their part visited the workers' circles regularly to give lessons in arithmetic, history and geography, as well as instruction for the more advanced workers in political economy. Occasional open-air meetings were held outside the city, one of which coincided with May Day.[112]

In character and ambition these circles in Kharkov were as typical of their period as those in Kazan and Kiev. The workers' centre included nominal supporters of both Chornyy Peredel and Narodnaya Volya, or rather 'new Populists' and 'new Narodovoltsy', as the members described themselves if they had to define their sympathies.[113] On the subject of terrorism, which still provoked the most lively debate, the workers generally clung to the views of the propagandist from whom they had first heard the revolutionary message. Thus Kondratenko, a *protégé* of the Narodovolets Pankratov, defended political terrorism, while nearly all the other members of the workers' centre, who had initially been exposed to the influence of Chernoperedeltsy, vigorously denounced it.[114] Good relations were not impaired by such controversy, however, and factional distinction probably in any case meant less to the workers than to the student propagandists who competed for their support.[115] Among the latter there now evidently prevailed a caution unacceptable to the few Narodovoltsy who lingered in Kharkov, but which was nevertheless consistent with Bekaryukov's belief that a socialist society would not be constructed in the near future. Bekaryukov did concede, in a programme written for the organisation in Kharkov, that terrorism as a means of 'self-defence' against spies and individuals who threatened the society of revolutionary circles was useful 'at any time', but emphasised that groups like his were not in a position to take the initiative in armed struggle with the authorities. Support for any groups which did engage in such struggle, moreover, was possible only so long as it did not divert the 'Populists' from their main task of winning support among the workers and peasants.[116]

A group of similar complexion, with which the Kharkov workers' centre soon established contact, arose independently in 1888 in Rostov, where L. Bogoraz and Motovilov renewed their activity after their departure from Kazan. Helped by another exile from Kazan, Boldyrev, and by Melnikov when he arrived from Kharkov, Bogoraz and Motovilov built their workers' group on the remnants of the workers' circles that had existed in the city throughout the 1880s. Like the group in Kharkov, their group, too, had at its disposal contributions from the workers – used in this case to purchase reading material – and contained several workers who were soon independent enough to go their own way. Also like the Kharkov circles, the group in Rostov was envisaged, according to the testimony of a police informer, as only a 'preparatory school for future revolutionaries', a function which accorded better with the plans of the Kazan conspirators than with those of the epigones of Narodnaya Volya. Again, because of the fact that it did not anticipate success for very many years, this group, too, had at present no 'special orientation'. Bogoraz, Motovilov and Boldyrev are all said to have read Marx's writings and to have tried to convey something of their spirit to their workers' circles – though without much success – but they could hardly be called Marxists on the basis of that evidence. The police described them as 'Populists', while a wishful Kharkov Narodovolets even classified them as representatives of his own party. Theoretical vagueness seems even to have been welcomed, at least by Motovilov, who feared that if propaganda were conducted in accordance with a single revolutionary programme circles would become too uniform in tone and too conspicuous.[117]

Perhaps in the final analysis, however, such groups as those of Bekaryukov in Kharkov and Bogoraz and Motovilov in Rostov had some usefulness in spite of the fact that their caution and theoretical confusion rendered them ineffectual as revolutionary organisations in their own time. In the first place, their practical experience was beginning to prove to them, as it had to the Narodovoltsy throughout the decade, that the most rewarding form of activity was propaganda among the urban workers. (The point was still not confirmed by Populist doctrine, which repeatedly turned the attention of the propagandists back to the countryside.) And, in the second place, such groups simply tended to remain active for longer than others, since the authorities considered them comparatively innocuous. Bekaryukov's activities, for example, had long since been known to the police; his name had appeared in surveys of investigations into political offences in the Empire as far back as 1884 in connection with such matters as possession of statistical tables on arrests and political trials and of lists of books on social, political and historical subjects.[118] But these offences were mere peccadilloes, and it seems even that the police believed that the survival of revolutionaries such as Bekaryukov might burden rather than help the revolutionary cause by paralysing the movement and discouraging its terrorist wing. Thus they allowed the Kharkov group to exist until they had discovered all its ramifications, the prosecution in the Kharkov court dismissed the workers' centre as a rather harmless organisation and those convicted were given relatively light sentences – in the majority of cases a mere eight months' imprisonment.[119]

CHAPTER FOUR

✣ THE BEGINNINGS OF RUSSIAN SOCIAL DEMOCRACY

ATTITUDES TO MARX AND ENGELS IN RUSSIA BEFORE THE 1880S

While for Populists of all complexions the prospect of revolution receded after the assassination of Alexander II and their notions as to how revolution might come about in Russia seemed increasingly untenable, there began to appear a few groups which found fresh inspiration in the works of Western socialists, particularly, though not exclusively, those of Marx and Engels. The first revolutionaries seriously to examine the possibility of applying Western Social Democratic theory to Russian conditions were émigré Populists, whose dwindling hope that revolution might be carried out from below was undoubtedly revived by the emphasis placed in that theory on the revolutionary potential of the urban masses. Inside Russia the growth, concentration and increasing discontent of these masses, combined with the relatively favourable impression they made on propagandists who worked among them, lent plausibility to claims that Social Democracy might have a revolutionary significance even in such a backward country. At first, it is true, groups which may more or less accurately be described as Social Democratic in character were not only few, small and isolated, but also sometimes rather difficult to distinguish from other groups of Populist or indeterminate complexion. Moreover, like most revolutionary groups of the time, they devoted themselves for the most part to activity that was so cautious and thorough that their role was often almost as much pedagogical as revolutionary. Nevertheless, their significance was very considerable, for they at least demonstrated the possibility of an alternative to Populism and laid foundations for a new movement which was to develop with great vigour from the early 1890s.

Marx and Engels were not of course unknown to Russian intellectuals before the 1880s. On the contrary, many Russians had corresponded with them or even been personally acquainted with them for periods since the 1840s, and some of their writings had been studied, translated into Russian and highly praised. In 1846–7 Marx had corresponded with Annenkov; indeed, it was in a long letter to the Russian that he outlined those reactions to one of Proudhon's works that were to be embodied in his famous tract, *The Poverty of Philosophy*.[1] In 1850 a Russian émigré, N. I. Sazonov, had written to Marx stating his support for 'all the essential points' contained in *The Communist Manifesto*.[2] Tkachov, in an article published in 1865, had made an approving reference to Marx's economic determinism.[3] In 1869 the first Russian edition of *The Communist Manifesto*, translated by Bakunin, had been published, and in 1872 Danielson completed the Russian translation, begun in 1870 by Lopatin, of the first volume of Marx's *Capital*. Russians formed their own section of the First Workingmen's International.[4] In 1870 A. A. Sleptsov, representing the editorial board of the journal *Znaniye* (*Knowledge*), warmly endorsed Marx's views and invited him to contribute to the journal.[5] Lavrov, who was personally acquainted with Marx and Engels, claimed in his autobiographical sketch that he had been a 'pupil' of Marx's in the field of economics ever since he had become acquainted with Marx's theory, and a clear understanding of that theory was expected of the ideal propagandist described by Lavrov in *Vperyod!*[6] Mikhaylovsky, in his contribution to a polemic which took place in the Russian press in the late 1870s on the subject of the first volume of *Capital*, defended Marx from the attack of a liberal economist, Zhukovsky, acknowledged him as an authority in political economy and praised his rare logical power and great erudition.[7] Another participant in that polemic, Ziber, a professor of political economy and statistics, sympathetically explained Marx's theories to the Russian public in a number of articles published in the legal press.[8] Finally, the Executive Committee of Narodnaya Volya addressed a letter to Marx in the autumn of 1880, in which it was declared that the Russian radical intelligentsia had received Marx's works with enthusiasm, that *Capital* was now considered essential reading for thinking people and that Marx's name was bound to be 'inextricably linked with the internal struggle in Russia'.[9]

Generally speaking, the popularity enjoyed by Marx among the Russian intelligentsia was due quite simply to the fact that he was one of the most authoritative European socialists of his day. Not only did his writings surpass in volume and solidity the output of any contemporary revolutionary socialist, but he had also been the leading organiser of the First Workingmen's International. However, if the quality and spirit of Marx's writings and his energy in promoting the socialist cause made a deep impression on Russians, nevertheless the essential difference of his revolutionary strategy from that of other Western socialists was not always very clearly appreciated, or at least not much emphasised, by Russians. We learn from a letter written by Lopatin in 1878, for instance, of a group of Russian socialists who were planning to produce a collection of quite incompatible works – by Proudhon, Marx and Dühring – on the grounds that all three thinkers were extreme opponents of the existing orders and that the writings of all three were equally obnoxious to the Russian authorities![10] More importantly, those who expressed an interest in the theories of Marx and Engels did not necessarily feel that they were relevant and useful to Russia, where conditions were very different from those obtaining in the more highly industrialised Western societies about which Marx and Engels had been writing. Russian revolutionaries were therefore understandably loath to commend a strategy based on those theories. Thus, while on the one hand they praised Marx and Engels and endorsed their ideas to a considerable extent, on the other hand Tkachov, Lavrov and Mikhaylovsky all indicated a path to revolution based on the view that Russia was a distinct historical entity. And Danielson while continuing to labour over the translation of *Capital* – he completed the second volume in 1885 – was prominent among those who sustained that view in the 1880s.

It was not until some revolutionaries were prepared to concede the failure of Populism, in both its phases (propagandistic and terroristic), that Marxism came to be viewed in a new light in Russia – as a doctrine from which Russian as well as Western European revolutionaries might draw some useful practical conclusions. But once the failure of Populism had been acknowledged, certain conceptions central to Marxist doctrine and vividly elaborated in the works of Marx and Engels must have seemed very palatable. In the first place, Marxism provided a view of history which, when compared with the voluntarist schema of Populist thinkers, tended to reduce the capacity and therefore the responsibility of the individual to effect social change or accelerate social development. In a period when 'heroes' could be seen to have failed in their quest to transform society and when the individual was coming to resign himself to relatively patient and anonymous preparatory activity, the revolutionary could draw some comfort from a doctrine which, while yet socialistic, assured him that life determined consciousness and that men made their history not just as they pleased but under circumstances inherited from their past and outside their control.[11] In the second place, whereas Populism supplied no historical laws which guaranteed the triumph of socialism, Marxism did seem to yield a promise of its eventual success. The unfolding of the class struggles to which various economic systems gave rise, the growth of 'misery, oppression, slavery, degradation, exploitation' as capital accumulated in the hands of fewer magnates, the corresponding development of a spirit of revolt among the working class and the increasing discipline and unity of that class, and the eventual downfall of the bourgeoisie – the 'expropriation' of the 'expropriators' – when the existing relations of property were no longer compatible with the new productive forces[12] – these processes seemed in Marx's and Engels' account of them to have an inevitability which provided a firmer hope than Populism had been capable of furnishing that socialism might indeed be attainable in Russia, provided only that Russia had set out on the same historical path as the more advanced Western European nations. In the third place, Marx and Engels, in depicting the proletariat as the main revolutionary force of modern society, were pinning their hopes on that very section of the masses in which the propaganda of Russian socialists had been best received. The Russian proletariat might as yet be small, admittedly; but if with the development of modern industry a proletariat inevitably grew in size, absorbed elements from other disintegrating classes, became concentrated in larger masses, acquired political experience and increasingly sensed and made use of its strength, then in backward Russia, too, the urban workers might constitute the only 'really revolutionary class'[13] once the pace of industrial development quickened there. Finally, Marx's and Engels' view of the peasantry as a reactionary group and their denunciation of the 'idiocy of rural life'[14] even provided an explanation for the failure of the Populists' activity in the countryside and reinforced the tendency of Russian revolutionaries, which was already established in practice, to concentrate their attention on the towns.

MARX'S AND ENGELS' VIEWS ON POPULISM

With the manifest failure of Populism, then, Marxism – like other Western forms of socialism – was bound to be viewed by some Russian revolutionaries in a new light. It is not surprising, therefore, that attempts were soon made to discover whether Russian economic and social conditions were not after all sufficiently similar to those in Western Europe to warrant the consideration, for use in Russia, of a revolutionary strategy based on this alien brand of socialism. Before examining the attempts of the first Russian Marxists to demonstrate the applicability of Marxist doctrine in Russia, however, it is worth noting that Marx and Engels themselves did not consistently claim that their analysis of the recent history of capitalism had a universal relevance. Still less did they argue that Russian revolutionaries should bear in mind that analysis when framing their strategy. On the contrary, they made several statements which afforded some comfort to the Populists, whose views the early Russian Marxists set out to refute.

On occasion, it is true, Marx and Engels did make statements which seemed to imply that the laws they had formulated, describing the progress of Western civilisation towards socialism, were infrangible and universally valid. Engels, for example, replying in 1875, in a very condescending tone, to Tkachov's 'open letter' to him, poured scorn on the idea that Russia might proceed to a form of socialism based on the commune and the *artel'* without passing through a capitalist stage of economic development. The development of society's productive forces in the hands of the bourgeoisie and the existence of a proletariat were prerequisites of socialist revolution, Engels argued. In any case, communal landowning in Russia was decaying. Engels did concede that the commune might conceivably be transformed into a higher social form, but only in the unlikely eventuality that it survived intact until proletarian revolution in Western Europe could create conditions favourable for that transformation.[15]

It is probable that at the heart of these objections to Populist doctrine lay Marx's and Engels' dislike of the chauvinistic belief that the Russian people had some more or less unique socialist character and therefore stood closer to socialism than the workers of the West. Both Marx and Engels emphasised that communal property-holding was an institution to be found at least among all the European peoples in the early stages of their social development, and Engels, in his polemic with Tkachov, declared in addition that there was 'nothing exclusively Russian or Slavonic' about the *artel'*.[16] It is also possible that Engels was more inclined than Marx to emphasise the necessitarian implications of Marxist doctrine and to insist on a more universal application of that doctrine's laws.[17] More importantly, the views of Marx and Engels on the strategy of Russian revolutionaries may have been modified by Marx's acquaintance with Chernyshevsky's thought, which was devoid of those notions to be found in the writings of Herzen, Bakunin and Tkachov about the innate communism of the Russian people. Chernyshevsky's work, Marx wrote in 1870, did great credit to Russia and showed that it, too, was beginning to 'participate in the general movement' of the nineteenth century. A considerable number of Chernyshevsky's works were known to Marx and those on the subject of Russia's rural economy in particular he regarded as excellent. It was largely his interest in Chernyshevsky's writings, and in the questions about the economic development of Russia which Chernyshevsky raised, that prompted Marx to embark on his study of the Russian language.[18]

The development of Marx's sympathy for the Populist movement is clearly discernible in a long letter which in November 1877 he addressed, but in fact did not send, to the editorial board of *Otechestvennyye zapiski à propos* of Mikhaylovsky's contribution to the Russian debate about the first volume of *Capital*. Mikhaylovsky had referred to a criticism which Marx had made of Herzen, to the effect that Herzen had used the commune as an argument to prove that, as Marx now put it, 'old, rotten Europe' was to be 'regenerated by the triumph of Pan-Slavism'. This criticism, Marx argues, might have been true or it might have been false, but it could not in any circumstances serve as a key to his views on Populism. Marx reminds Mikhaylovsky that in the afterword to the second German edition of *Capital* he had spoken of the 'great Russian scholar and critic', Chernyshevsky, who 'in his wonderful articles' had discussed the question as to whether the commune should be destroyed, as liberal economists wished, in order that Russia's transition to a capitalist order should be effected, or whether Russia might avoid the ills of capitalist society by, as Marx put it, 'developing its own historical data'. Chernyshevsky had chosen the latter possibility, and Mikhaylovsky had as much reason to suppose that Marx shared Chernyshevsky's view as to suppose that he rejected it. Indeed, Marx now gave clear support to Chernyshevsky's view, support based, he claimed, on long study of official and other publications; if Russia continued to proceed along the path which it had followed since 1861 (that is to say the path of capitalist development) then it would miss the best opportunity which history had ever presented to any people, and would experience 'all the fatal mishaps' of a capitalist order. Marx then summarised his views on the course by which the capitalist order in Western Europe had emerged from the feudal one, but emphasised that one was not entitled to draw from those views any inflexible conclusions about Russia's development. If Russia was tending to become a capitalist nation on the model of the nations of Western Europe – and in recent years it had taken pains to move in that direction – then it would not reach its goal without transforming a considerable number of its peasants into proletarians; and thereupon, already being 'in the lap of a capitalist order', it would be subject, like other peoples, to the 'inexorable laws' governing such orders. But Marx had not intended, as Mikhaylovsky had supposed, that his historical sketch of the growth of capitalism in Western Europe should be turned into a 'historico-philosophical theory about a universal course' along which all peoples were inevitably doomed to pass on their way to socialism, irrespective of the historical circumstances in which they found themselves.[19]

At the end of the 1870s and the beginning of the 1880s the apparently increased likelihood of revolution in Russia gave Marx, and now Engels, too, further encouragement to exempt that country from the immediate jurisdiction of the socio-economic laws supposedly governing the development of Western Europe. In the first place, Marx was heartened by Russian reverses in the war of 1877–8 with Turkey, which he saw as a *'new turning point* in European history'. Russia had long been standing on the threshold of an upheaval and the 'gallant Turks', by inflicting severe defeats which discredited the Russian army and government, had hastened the explosion by years.[20] And in the second place, Marx and Engels shared the general optimism aroused in revolutionary circles by the terrorist campaign of Narodnaya Volya. On the whole, it is true, they were critical of the use of terrorism by revolutionaries. In 1850, for example, they had written contemptuously of those 'alchemists of the revolution' who put their faith in 'inventions' such as 'incendiary bombs, destructive devices of magic effect', which were expected to bring about 'revolutionary miracles'.[21] But in the case of Narodnaya Volya they were evidently prepared to make an exception. Thus Engels, replying to a Russian correspondent in July 1880 – that is to say, after two major attempts by Narodnaya Volya to assassinate Alexander II – expressed his and Marx's interest in the movement in Russia, a country which had produced a 'revolutionary party possessing an unprecedented energy and capacity for self-sacrifice'.[22] In April the following year Marx expressed unqualified admiration for the terrorists in a letter to his daughter, Jenny:

They are sterling people through and through, *sans pose mélodramatique*, simple, businesslike, heroic . . . The Petersburg Executive Committee . . . is far removed from the schoolboy way in which Most and other childish whimperers preach tyrannicide as a 'theory' and 'panacea' . . . on the contrary they try to teach Europe that their *modus operandi* is a specifically Russian and historically inevitable method about which there is no more reason to moralise – for or against – than there is about the earthquake in Chios.[23]

This admiration is pointed up by Marx's evident disdain for Chornyy Peredel, the 'so-called party of propaganda as opposed to the terrorists who risk their lives'. In order to carry on propaganda in Russia, Marx wrote scornfully, the Chernoperedeltsy had moved voluntarily to Geneva![24] Again, writing after the assassination of Alexander II, Marx and Engels even suggested confidently that the tsaricide would ultimately lead to the establishment of a Russian commune comparable to the Parisian.[25] Later, in 1882, after the publication of their preface to the second Russian edition of *The Communist Manifesto*, they declared themselves proud to be among the collaborators of Narodnaya Volya.[26]

This unqualified admiration of Narodnaya Volya and the belief that that party's efforts might bring success no doubt helped to strengthen Marx's resolve to concede to Russia the right to take its own distinctive path to socialism. Thus, when in February 1881 he was sent an enquiry by Vera Zasulich about the possibility of socialist development in Russia on the basis of the commune, Marx replied unambiguously in terms which no Populist could have found offensive. Quoting from *Capital*, he asserted that the 'historical inevitability' of the process of the expropriation of those who worked the land was confined to the countries of Western Europe in which it had already begun. As for the 'viability' of the Russian commune, the research Marx had carried out on the subject led him to believe that the commune would prove to be the 'fulcrum of the social regeneration of Russia', though in order that it should function as such, pernicious influences on it would have to be eliminated and 'normal conditions' provided for its 'free development'.[27] A similar acknowledgement of the distinctiveness of Russia was made publicly in the preface which Marx and Engels wrote to the second Russian edition of *The Communist Manifesto*, translated by Vera Zasulich and published in Geneva in 1882. Here Marx and Engels again spoke with reverence of the progress made by Russian revolutionaries since the days of 1848–9 when the European princes and even the European bourgeoisie had found their 'only salvation from the proletariat . . . in Russian intervention', and the Tsar had been proclaimed the 'chief of European reaction'. Now, thanks to the efforts of Narodnaya Volya, the Tsar was a 'prisoner of war of the revolution', immured in Gatchina, and Russia was the 'vanguard of revolutionary action in Europe'. Conditions in Russia were obviously very different from those in the

Western European states which Marx and Engels had had in mind when formulating their revolutionary strategy. *The Communist Manifesto* had been written with the object of proclaiming the 'inevitably impending dissolution of modern bourgeois property', but in Russia, alongside the 'rapidly developing capitalist swindle and bourgeois landed property', more than half the land was owned in common by peasants. The question therefore arose as to whether the commune, which, 'though greatly undermined', was nevertheless still a form of the 'primeval common ownership of land', could 'pass directly to the higher form of communist common ownership'. Or would it have to pass first 'through the same process of dissolution' as constituted the 'historical evolution of the West'? Marx and Engels were inclined to accept the first possibility, or at least they did not reject it. If the Russian revolution became the 'signal for a proletarian revolution in the West', so that both revolutions complemented one another, then the present Russian institution of common landownership might serve as the 'starting point for a communist development'.[28]

Marx's and Engels' reasons for allowing of the possibility that socialism might be built in Russia not on the ruins of bourgeois society but on the peasant commune may have been various. They may genuinely have been convinced by Populist arguments such as those put forward by Chernyshevsky concerning the possibility of an autochthonous development. They may indeed have considered that the Narodovoltsy had a chance of toppling the Russian autocracy, which they detested, and that the ruling classes elsewhere would collapse as a consequence. Or they may simply have been fearful lest they might discourage revolutionaries who were widely considered heroic and who were fighting against overwhelming odds. But, whatever their motives, their pronouncements on the Russian revolutionary movement in the late 1870s and early 1880s – and particularly their public statement in the preface to the second Russian edition of *The Communist Manifesto* – made the task of the first Russian Marxists, irrespective of the merits of their case for applying Marxism as a revolutionary doctrine in Russia, seem even more forbidding.

PLEKHANOV AND THE 'EMANCIPATION OF LABOUR' GROUP

It is ironical that the first Russians to argue in favour of the use of Marxism as a revolutionary doctrine in their country were those very revolutionaries whom Marx had so disparagingly compared to the Narodovoltsy, namely the émigré Chernoperedeltsy Plekhanov, Akselrod, Deych and Zasulich.

On his arrival in the West in 1880 the acknowledged leader of this group, Plekhanov, had applied himself to an intensive study of the writings of Marx and Engels, which now seemed to him to hold a key to the solution of the problems confronting Russian revolutionaries. By the end of 1881 he had come to the critical conclusion that all paths of development other than the capitalist path were closed to Russia, and accepted the corollary that in Russian history there were 'no *essential* differences from the history of Western Europe'.[29] By the spring of 1882 he was looking on the 'scientific socialism' of Marx and Engels as the only doctrine with which to analyse the present economic, social and political conditions in Russia, and in a letter to Lavrov he expressed intolerance of other shades of socialist thought.[30] Admittedly, negotiations between Plekhanov's group and the Narodovoltsy did take place in spite of Plekhanov's leaning away from Populism in the direction of Social Democracy. At the beginning of 1881 Plekhanov proposed the reunification of the two factions on the basis of a programme that would both urge the creation of an organisation among the masses – an objective dear to the Chernoperedeltsy – and incorporate the demand for political freedom, to which the Narodovoltsy attached such importance.[31] And for some time the Chernoperedeltsy vacillated between, on the one hand, disapproval of the method of struggle chosen by the Narodovoltsy and, on the other hand, admiration of their heroism combined with approval – which, as revolutionaries close to a Marxist position, they could now give – of the 'political' nature of their struggle with the autocracy. Furthermore, negotiations continued, albeit uneasily, over co-operation on the proposed émigré publication, *Vestnik* '*Narodnoy voli*'. But eventually theoretical differences were to prove insuperable, particularly after the unequivocal endorsement of 'Jacobinism' by the surviving members of the Executive Committee of Narodnaya Volya in the early part of 1882. In the summer of 1883 the break was finally made, with some acrimony, and in September of that year Plekhanov and his supporters formally established a new faction, for which the name the 'Emancipation of Labour' group was chosen, and announced their intention to found a 'Library of Modern Socialism' under the auspices of which they would publish their works. With money provided by Ignatov, a wealthy sympathiser, they obtained a press and set about printing works of a Marxist orientation with the twofold purpose of systematically attacking Populist beliefs and laying the theoretical foundations for a new revolutionary strategy.[32]

These purposes were most fully achieved in Plekhanov's two major works of the period, *Socialism and Political Struggle* and *Our Differences*. Large portions of both these works were devoted to exhaustive, sometimes verbose and personally insulting polemic with the advocates of the various Populist strategies and tactics who had held sway over the previous decade. Tikhomirov bore the brunt of Plekhanov's criticisms, partly because he was the main surviving member of the old Executive Committee of Narodnaya Volya, currently the most influential faction in the Populist camp, but mainly because he also seemed to Plekhanov to endorse the views of Tkachov and therefore represented the 'Jacobin' or 'Blanquist' element of the party. In fact, criticism of the 'Blanquism' with which the leading Populist faction had now become associated was an important element in Plekhanov's argument and reflected the hope which these early Russian Marxists evidently preserved from their own Populist phase that the revolution might still be carried out from below – a hope nourished by Marx himself, who had after all insisted in his preamble to the General Rules of the First International that the emancipation of the working classes should be accomplished by the working classes themselves.[33]

A more important element of these early theoretical works, however, was criticism of the assumption, on which Populism in all its forms rested, that Russia was not necessarily subject to the laws of development governing the more advanced societies of the West. For the first time in the history of Russian revolutionary thought, Plekhanov made a well-substantiated attempt to prove that Russian development was indeed similar to that of the West and that Russian revolutionaries should therefore seek in the works of Western socialist thinkers material which was not only of academic interest but also of practical value to them. Marx's philosophy of history had the same validity, he argued, whether it was applied to the modern civilisation of Western Europe or to ancient Greece and Rome, India or Egypt; it embraced the 'whole cultural history of mankind'. Nor did the historical peculiarities of a country exempt it from the operation of such general sociological laws as Marx had discovered. Societies could not leap over certain phases in their development or abolish them by means of decrees, although, admittedly, an understanding of the laws of historical development might help them to shorten a phase or alleviate its attendant pains.[34]

The crucial question in any discussion of the nature of Russia's development was whether Russia, on the way to socialism, was bound like the Western nations to 'pass through the "school" of capitalism', and it was to this question – which the 'vast majority' of Russian revolutionaries had until very recently answered in the negative – that Plekhanov devoted most

attention in his voluminous tract, *Our Differences*. Plekhanov did not find
Russian capitalism to be the weak or still-born growth that Tikhomirov,
following Vorontsov, considered it. He dismissed the beliefs, which he
took to be fundamental to Tikhomirov's position, that the number of
Russian industrial workers was very limited (800,000 out of a population of
100,000,000) and that this relatively small number was not increasing but
static. These figures, Plekhanov contended, were unreliable, having been
poorly gathered at various times, and did not include all categories of
workers or workers in all parts of the Empire. The bourgeoisie, moreover,
had an interest in concealing the true extent of its enterprises, since it feared
taxation and other attempts to reduce its capital. Nor did such figures take
into account the workers in cottage industries, of whom there were already,
according to Plekhanov, several millions, and who were by now losing all
vestiges of independence. Weaving, for example, was being slowly but
inexorably transformed from a cottage industry into a large-scale form of
production. Workers in former cottage industries might not yet be 'united'
by capital, but they were undoubtedly '*enslaved*' by it. They already
constituted an 'irregular army' at the disposal of the bourgeoisie and would
in due course inevitably become a 'regular force'. Turning to agriculture,
which was almost everywhere the most backward branch of production,
Plekhanov found, even in the Russian countryside, plentiful indications
that capitalism was taking root. Under its impact the village community was
splitting into two strata: one which gradually accumulated all the land
formerly belonging to the commune; the other which went onto the labour-
market. Measures such as the granting of small-scale land credit, far from
strengthening the order dear to the Populists, in fact served further to
undermine the commune. Even from the agricultural point of view
communal landowning was deficient. All the principles of the contemporary economy, Plekhanov asserted in a devastating dismissal of the
decaying institution on which the Populists had pinned their faith, were
irreconcilably inimical to the commune. Plekhanov's answer, then, to the
question as to the destiny of capitalism in Russia was blunt and clear.
Capitalism was proceeding on its way, ousting independent producers from
their unstable positions, driving landless peasants off the land and creating
an army of workers in precisely the same way as it had in the West. Its
mainstream was not yet large in Russia, but its volume was increasing and
its great enlargement indubitable.[35]

The application of the Marxist schema to Russia, the conclusion that
Russia was following the same path of development as Western Europe,

carried several important implications to which Plekhanov drew attention. Firstly, it legitimised the decision, which in practice revolutionaries had already taken, to transfer attention from the peasantry to the proletariat. In *Socialism and Political Struggle* Plekhanov was already speaking apologetically about the quiescence of the peasantry and in *Our Differences* bluntly described the peasant as 'conservative in general and in his attitude to the land in particular'. If the peasantry was to become a significant revolutionary force, then it would only be as a result of the influence of the urban working class. The proletariat, which was being bred by capitalism, on the other hand, had a broader outlook than the peasantry, was more capable of conscious political action and more receptive to socialist propaganda. It was the 'political antipodes' of the peasantry, 'revolutionary' where the other was 'reactionary', the natural leader of all the exploited classes in Russia, and the revolutionaries should assist its development by organising a political party in its ranks.[36]

A second implication of Plekhanov's acceptance of the view that capitalism was developing in Russia and would continue to do so concerned the period of time likely to elapse before the outbreak of revolution. Marx had emphasised that no social order 'ever perishes before all the productive forces for which there is room in it have developed' and that the 'new, higher relations of production never appear before the material conditions of their existence have matured in the womb of the old society itself'.[37] In Russia, however, capitalism had not yet brought social antagonisms to the point at which Marx had observed them in the West and there could therefore be no question, if Marx's theories were rigidly applied, of imminent socialist revolution there. Thus the date of the revolution, which Populists had been accustomed, in the 1870s at any rate, to regard as impending, would be considerably postponed. Plekhanov admitted that he did not believe Russia would have socialist government in the near future, for the 'objective social conditions of production' had not yet sufficiently matured.[38] (All the same, Plekhanov did adduce certain arguments, rather reminiscent of Populist statements on the advantages of backwardness, in order to make this postponement palatable. Capitalism, he argued, would not take so long to flower in Russia as it had in the West, since it could benefit from the Western experience. Nor, having flowered, would it flourish for so long, since the socialist movement which would destroy it had begun at a much earlier stage in its growth.)[39]

The third implication of Plekhanov's adoption of Marxism concerned the nature of the activity which the socialists should undertake while they were waiting for the conditions necessary for successful revolution to mature. They would have to pursue two tasks simultaneously, on the one hand encouraging the workers to co-operate with the bourgeoisie in the struggle against their common enemy, the autocracy, and, on the other hand, cultivating the workers' consciousness of their own particular interests as a class hostile to the bourgeoisie. Plekhanov invoked the 'fine example of the German communists', who had fought just such a dual campaign.[40] The first task, quite abhorrent to Populists inasmuch as it involved co-operation with the bourgeoisie, must have seemed easier to Plekhanov now that he was living in the comparatively free and relaxed conditions of Western Europe, where the advantages of political freedom for the revolutionary in bourgeois society were clearly apparent.[41] The second task, in so far as it required the cultivation of the class consciousness of the proletariat, was considered no less 'political' in nature than terrorist attacks on the autocracy, for 'every class struggle', Marx and Engels had written in *The Communist Manifesto*, was a 'political struggle'.[42] Thus, while praising Narodnaya Volya for having inaugurated a period of conscious political struggle in the history of the Russian revolutionary movement, the first Russian Marxists gave the concept a new dimension.

In spite of the solidity of Plekhanov's attempts to popularise Marxism in Russia, the 'Emancipation of Labour' group enjoyed very little early success. The numerous letters and the emissary sent to Russia by the group in the early stages of its existence won it little firm support. The arrest of Deych in Germany in 1884 and his extradition to Russia proved a particularly severe setback since it was he, the group's most capable organiser, who had the task of establishing and maintaining connections with Russia. Contact was established with the Blagoyev group in St Petersburg, but after the collapse of that group in 1886 the émigrés had little further communication with Russian activists until the 1890s. In any case, the insistence of Plekhanov in particular on the need for ideological purity while the new doctrine was being promoted militated against the generation of a mass movement at this stage.[43]

Inside Russia the isolated groups and individuals sympathetic to the émigré Marxists were still overshadowed in the 1880s by the Populists and Plekhanov's works subjected to their gibes.[44] The continued prestige of Narodnaya Volya made it necessary for Plekhanov and his followers to concede that there was a 'need for terrorist struggle against absolute government' in the first draft of their programme.[45] And apparently even the name 'Emancipation of Labour' group was chosen in preference to some title containing an allusion to Social Democracy lest the group should excite the animosity of circles inside Russia which were still suspicious of this Western stream of socialist thought.[46] For some time the group also incurred the disapproval of Western European socialists who considered the Narodovoltsy capable of administering a *coup de grâce* to the tsarist régime. Even Engels' attitude towards them was still ambivalent in the middle of the decade. He continued to speak warmly of the Narodovoltsy and assured Zasulich that Russia might have a unique revolutionary destiny. Since the assassination of Alexander II, he affirmed, the country had been like a mine which needed only to have its fuse lit. Russia in 1881 had been one of those 'exceptional cases' when a 'handful of people' could '*make* revolution', or, 'in other words, make an entire system collapse with one small push'.[47] Not until the beginning of the 1890s, when it could clearly be seen that the Narodovoltsy had failed to accomplish their objectives, and also when Plekhanov's stature as a Marxist theoretician had come to be more widely recognised, did the prestige of the 'Emancipation of Labour' group begin to grow. Then the full extent of the achievement of these early Marxists became apparent: they had created an atmosphere in which Marxian ideas could begin to gain acceptance among Russian revolutionaries.[48]

THE BLAGOYEVTSY

Inside Russia acceptance of the orthodox Marxist ideas propounded by the members of the 'Emancipation of Labour' group was neither directly attributable to the influence of the émigrés nor clear-cut. Indeed, the first group in Russia to take a significant step in the direction of Social Democracy, the Blagoyev group, was formed quite independently of the émigrés, and the views of its members were much more eclectic than the accounts of some Soviet historians, anxious to discern early signs of the ascendancy of Marxism within Russia, would lead us initially to believe.

The members of this group referred to themselves as the 'Party of Russian Social Democrats', but are now more widely known as the Blagoyevtsy after the main founder of the group, Blagoyev, a Bulgarian student who subsequently achieved prominence in the socialist movement in his own country. Exuding energy and vitality and fired with a patriotism that led him to join the insurgents fighting against the Turks in Bulgaria in 1876, Blagoyev inevitably brings to mind Turgenev's earlier 'positive hero', Insarov. At the age of twenty Blagoyev came to Russia and entered a seminary in Odessa, which he soon abandoned for a *Realschule*, whence he proceeded in 1880 to the University of St Petersburg. Here he was hospitably received by the Russian students and quickly drawn into their circles and revolutionary activity.[49] During the winter of 1883–4 a group began to form around him which consisted mainly of other University students (Borodin and Kharitonov, formerly a pupil of the Troitsk *gimnaziya*), students of the Technological Institute (Arshaulov, Gerasimov and Shatko) and the Forestry Institute (Kugushev) and a rather older man, Latyshev, a doctor who had previously frequented circles of Chernoperedeltsy in St Petersburg. The Blagoyevtsy applied themselves above all to the task of conducting propaganda in workers' circles, probably about fifteen in all, which were scattered quite widely through the industrial regions of the capital and which consisted for the most part of metal workers and printing workers. The group's propaganda in these circles was based on a very detailed programme which contained instructions for the propagandist, recommendations for reading for workers at different levels of development, suggestions for material for lectures, and an exhaustive list of books. A small library of illegal books was kept for use in the workers' circles. Suitable texts were duplicated, first on a hectograph and subsequently on three presses which the group set up in succession in St Petersburg between 1884 and 1886. On the second of these presses the Blagoyevtsy printed among other things their own paper, *Rabochiy* (*The Worker*), two numbers of which were run off, probably in two or three hundred copies each. Some idea of the scale of the group's activity can be gained from Kharitonov's admission that this small circulation was determined not by technical, typographical considerations, but by fear of not finding a larger demand. There were no contacts in other cities and, as it was, the group was counting on the distribution of *Rabochiy* in student circles and among émigrés.[50] The Blagoyevtsy established connections with the 'Emancipation of Labour' group and corresponded with the émigrés, and in 1886 received from them a shipment of the socialist literature then being issued in Switzerland.[51] As in the case of all revolutionary groups operating in the 1880s, however, the Blagoyevtsy were hampered by the constant need to maintain secrecy and by the arrest of members of the group, which began in 1884 with the capture of Kugushev, whose address had been found among the papers taken from Lopatin. Blagoyev himself was arrested early in 1885 and deported to Bulgaria, and in December that year and January 1886 further arrests severely damaged the group, although some of its members did operate until the beginning of 1887.[52]

In certain respects the views of the Blagoyevtsy represented a significant step away from Populism in the direction of Social Democracy, a step which they were encouraged to take by the increasing electoral successes of the German Social Democrats,[53] who in 1884 secured 9.7% of the vote and 24 seats in the Reichstag (as opposed to 7.6% of the vote and 9 seats in 1878 and 6.1% of the vote and 12 seats in 1881). In the first place, of course, the name by which the Blagoyevtsy designated themselves – 'Party of Russian Social Democrats' – indicated a shift of allegiance. Nor should the boldness of this shift be underestimated, for not only did Populist premisses remain virtually unchallenged inside Russia in 1884–5, but a departure from them in favour of émigrés who had abandoned the battlefield for a Swiss refuge seemed at this time almost a betrayal of revolutionaries who had laid down their lives for the cause. In the second place, the Blagoyevtsy looked on propaganda among the urban workers as their main function. They assured the émigrés of the 'Emancipation of Labour' group – with whom they believed they had 'very much in common' – that they would concentrate on the 'political education' of these workers, who were the 'most suitable element' for the socialist propagandist;[54] all their other activities – the establishment of the press, the duplication of socialist literature, even the production of their paper – were designed to support this basic function. In the third place, the programme drafted by the group towards the end of 1884 contained the most important assertion – made independently of Plekhanov – that Russia had embarked after the emancipation of the serfs on the same path of economic competition which Western European countries had long since been following. 'Capitalism' had already been born in Russia and was growing. So, too, was a 'landless proletariat'.[55] The émigrés, for their part, contributed articles to the second number of *Rabochiy* and assured the Blagoyevtsy that their attitude to the group was 'most friendly' and that the group might count on them to be of use in whatever ways they could.[56]

The émigrés, however, lacking any other firm support in Russia in 1884–5, could not afford, for all their ideological purity, to be too discriminating in their choice of allies and it would be wrong on the basis of their friendly response to the Blagoyevtsy to attribute to the St Petersburg group the sort of Marxist orthodoxy which the émigrés would have liked them to cultivate. It is all too easy, given the uncompromising commitment of Plekhanov and his associates to Marxism and the subsequent ascendancy of a Marxian form of Social Democracy in Russia, to overlook the fact that Marxism had to compete vigorously at this period not only with Populism but also with other Western European streams of socialism, notably with the socialism of Lassalle. Lassalle had, after all, become known to Populists no later than Marx. Indeed, the quixotic character of his political career was bound to fire the Populist imagination as Marx's erudite treatises could not. And the portrait of Lassalle, in the guise of Leo, in Spielhagen's novel, *In Rank and File*, known in Russia from the late 1860s, had seemed to Populists such as Vera Figner no less inspiring than the 'positive heroes' of their native literature.[57] It is significant, then, that Blagoyev, even when writing much later from a more orthodox Marxist viewpoint, admitted that Lassalle, as well as Marx, had engaged his attention in 1883 when, dissatisfied with Populist teachings, he was examining other streams of socialist thought, and that Lassallean socialism merged with Marxism in the group's draft programme.[58] Indeed, numerous propositions in the programme reflected the distinctive influence of Lassalle. Firstly, the state was viewed as the 'embodiment of a certain moral principle'. Secondly, socialism was considered attainable only by means of the intervention of the state in the economic life of the nation. The state would have to undertake the expropriation of the land and the means of production and would oversee the 'organisation of labour' on collectivist lines, replacing capitalism with 'associations of workers'. Thirdly, if the state power were really to serve the people as a whole rather than represent narrow sectional interests, then it was essential that it should be an 'expression of the people's will', and this objective could only be secured through the institution of universal suffrage. In accordance with all these beliefs, the ultimate demands set out in the draft programme of the Blagoyevtsy included, *inter alia*, the surrender of landed property to the state and of the factories to workers' associations and the transfer of state power to a representative assembly elected by direct and universal suffrage.[59]

This conception of the state and its role in the introduction of socialism were unmistakably Lassallean rather than Marxist, as was the expression of faith in a democratically elected body expressing the wishes of the majority – an institution in which Marx had no confidence. Even the nature of the capitalist growth that had been occurring in Russia seemed to the Blagoyevtsy to reinforce the arguments in favour of the adoption of a Lassallean strategy. Since Russia had embarked on a capitalist path at a much later date than the Western nations, the Blagoyevtsy argued, it was difficult for her to compete in established markets. As for the internal market, that was very limited since the majority of Russia's inhabitants were so poor. Furthermore, the class relationships were less clearly defined in

Russia than elsewhere; and the peasant population was scattered and difficult to organise. For all these reasons the 'process of the socialisation of labour', if left to develop naturally, would be much slower in Russia than the West, and state intervention was therefore all the more necessary if a new social order was to be created.[60] So pronounced are these Lassallean elements in the programme of the Blagoyevtsy and so important are they in the strategy the Blagoyevtsy recommend that it seems wrong to attribute to the Blagoyevtsy any very specific Marxist leanings. Indeed, their draft programme altogether lacks such fundamental Marxist concepts as class struggle and class consciousness, and, although the term 'proletariat' is used, we also find the expression 'workers' estate', which does not belong in the Marxist lexicon. The use of the phrase 'organisation of labour', finally, recalls Louis Blanc, whose advocacy of a peaceful democratic path to socialism the doctrines of Lassalle to some extent reflect.[61]

It is arguable that Lassallean socialism contained much that was congenial to revolutionaries active in an environment in which Narodnaya Volya was still revered. Lassalle's socialism, like Narodovolchestvo, postulated the necessity of political freedom if the struggle for socialism was to be successful; it envisaged the possibility of state intervention against the interests of the bourgeoisie; and it laid emphasis on the importance of an institution which would give democratic expression to the 'people's will' (the phrase *vyrazheniyem narodnoy voli* was indeed used in the draft programme of the Blagoyevtsy).[62] Nor were the Blagoyevtsy able to free themselves altogether from the attraction of Narodovolchestvo, which remained so strong in the St Petersburg environment from which they sprang (although, like the majority of Narodovoltsy themselves, they argued against the seizure of power by a minority or through a military conspiracy).[63] One of the first writings reproduced by the group on the hectograph they set up was a biography of Perovskaya.[64] More importantly, the Blagoyevtsy were unable to dissociate themselves altogether from terrorism, and their differences with the Narodovoltsy on this subject concerned emphases rather than fundamental principles. They did not consider political terrorism – supposedly a means of wringing concessions from the government – to be productive in the present conditions, that is to say in the absence of a strong workers' organisation capable of backing up the terrorists. However, they did envisage circumstances in which terrorism might still be appropriate: firstly, if the people themselves suggested victims from the authorities; secondly, if the party itself could find suitable targets whose assassination would not excite public antipathy towards the revolutionaries; and, thirdly, if it were used as a means of self-defence against spies.[65]

This approval of terrorism, provided that it was linked in some way to the activity which the Blagoyevtsy considered of paramount importance – propaganda among the urban workers – gave the draft programme of the group at least a superficial similarity to that of the 'young' Narodovoltsy with whom the Blagoyevtsy had connections and towards whom they adopted a most conciliatory attitude. Talks between the two groups revealed that in their views on 'activity among the workers' there was 'absolutely no difference' and it was agreed to pool 'resources' for this activity (though no formal union of the two groups was ever achieved).[66] That was not to say that the Blagoyevtsy were at pains to distance themselves even from the 'old' Narodovoltsy. On the contrary, they wrote to the party's émigré leaders on the editorial board of *Vestnik 'Narodnoy voli'* expressing the hope that they might be able to reach an agreement with them, too, and that it might be possible for the two groups to render each other useful services.[67] In making these overtures, however, the Blagoyevtsy evidently underestimated the extent to which their affinities with Narodovoltsy, both 'old' and 'young', as well as the Lassallean complexion of their socialism, served to set them apart from the émigré Social Democrats. The latter, for their part, could not approve the first draft of the programme of the Blagoyevtsy and must have been irritated by the request from St Petersburg for copies of *Vestnik 'Narodnoy voli'* as well as other literature.[68]

Nor was the thinking of the Blagoyevtsy free of classical Populist assumptions, which tended to tinge Social Democratic ideas as they first percolated into Russia. For example, the Blagoyevtsy continued to regard the peasantry as a revolutionary force of no less importance than the proletariat. Both in the draft programme and in the first number of *Rabochiy* attention was drawn to the fact that the Russian popular masses were made up of both peasants and industrial workers (and in both instances the two categories were mentioned in that order, the peasantry having precedence). It was stressed that the urban workers should be 'at one with the peasants' and a 'union' of the two was envisaged which would constitute an 'invincible force'.[69] Moreover, the Blagoyevtsy tended, in the early stages of the group's existence at any rate, to take the traditional Populist view of the working class as a bridge-head among the peasantry, the 'best conductor of revolutionary ideas and political development' to the countryside.[70] Social Democracy commended itself to them as a new approach to the masses.

Finally, as Blagoyev himself admitted, the group's thinking was also coloured to some extent by the influence of Lavrov.[71] The leading article of the first number of *Rabochiy*, for instance, described the purpose of the paper as the dissemination of the most necessary knowledge among the working people, who needed such knowledge if they were to look into the causes of their poverty and seek means of improving their lot.[72] A similar theme underlay the leading article of the second number of the paper, entitled 'Knowledge and Critical Thought'.[73] And it is perhaps worth noting in this connection that even in the middle of 1885 Blagoyev, by this time back in Bulgaria and editing another socialist paper in Sofia, was still tending to equate the march of civilisation with the dissemination of knowledge and to uphold Buckle's thesis that ignorance brought on a people more ills than did the ills themselves.[74]

The eclecticism of the socialism of the Blagoyevtsy was reflected too in the programme of reading which they used as a basis for their propaganda among the St Petersburg workers. The works of fiction with which the propagandist was advised to begin were mainly stories by writers such as Grigorovich, Levitov, Naumov, Reshetnikov and Zasodimsky (Nekrasov's poetry was recommended, too), who had been favoured by the Populist predecessors of the Blagoyevtsy and dealt in the main with life in the countryside rather than with the condition of the workers in the towns. Bervi-Flerovsky headed the list of writers whose work might be used when the propagandist came to deal with the 'workers' question'. Shchapov, Mordovtsev and Maksimov were recommended in connection with study of Russian history. Works by Chernyshevsky, Mikhaylovsky and Lavrov appeared under several headings, and in general it was clear from the list that, even if the Blagoyevtsy were beginning to abandon Populism, nevertheless they still intended the workers to have a thorough grasp of all the basic Populist assumptions. It is true that *The Communist Manifesto* and Plekhanov's polemics with the Populists were also to be studied, that works by Marx were to play a most important part in the instruction of the workers in political economy and that detailed reference was to be made to the first volume of *Capital*. But there were at least as many references in the reading list to Lassalle as to Marx, and yet other non-Marxist European socialists were included, notably Louis Blanc, whose *Organisation of Labour* evidently remained popular.[75]

The Blagoyevtsy, then, hardly merited the appellation 'Party of Russian Social Democrats' which they gave their group, for they remained the victims of the theoretical confusion characteristic in their period. Nor did the group really constitute a party. It is worth noting that their draft programme concentrated on theoretical issues and practical demands but paid no attention to the organisational matters with which a party would have to preoccupy itself. And the paper *Rabochiy* was too indeterminate in character to be the political organ of a distinctive political grouping. Nevertheless, the group undoubtedly did represent a significant new departure in the movement inside Russia, for in effect it helped to change the direction of the movement, concentrating attention on the urban workers to the virtual exclusion of other groups and envisaging a long 'preparatory period' of activity among them.[76]

THE 'MOROZOV STRIKE' OF 1885

While the Blagoyevtsy were conducting their propaganda in workers' circles in St Petersburg there took place quite independently of the intelligentsia a portentous event which served to underline the significance of this movement towards Social Democracy. Early in 1885, in Nikolskoye, a village of the industrial heartland of the country in the province of Vladimir, a serious strike broke out in a cotton-mill owned by Savva Morozov and Company.[77]

The picture of life in the cotton-mill which emerged as a result of the strike gave the public a good insight into the conditions in which the growing Russian proletariat dwelt and worked. The workers were accommodated in barracks. Most would live in a dormitory, although a man with a family might have a small room. Many workers slept on clothing laid out on the bare floor-boards. The working day would last for a minimum of fourteen hours and passed in an unventilated atmosphere. A worker's vision might deteriorate in the poor light and the continuous din of machinery might impair his hearing. It was not improbable that he would suffer some injury, perhaps crippling, from the unguarded machinery which it required considerable expertise to operate properly. In the event of his disablement he or his next of kin might, depending on the disposition of the factory management, receive some compensation, like the boy Fillip Nikitin, who in 1871 had received the sum of five roubles and twenty-six kopecks (little more than an average weekly wage for the period) when he had lost a foot in a machine, or the woman who received a similar sum after her husband had fallen into a vat of boiling liquid. Wages would not be paid with any regularity, with the result that there were always plentiful customers for the factory shop, where provisions were sold on credit at exorbitant prices. A worker might in any case be deprived of part or even all of his earnings by the factory management, which retained the right to impose fines on him for the most trivial misdemeanours.[78] T. S. Morozov, son of the company's founder and managing director of the Nikolskoye mill, managed to conceal the more unattractive aspects of this régime from the inspectors who occasionally called. But the factory inspectorate was in any case in its infancy in Russia in the 1880s and the authorities were generally speaking uninterested in the welfare of the workers, provided that social stability was not threatened by eruptions of the sort which now occurred at Nikolskoye, prompting the provincial governor immediately to request the assistance of troops.[79]

Strikes and disorders had occurred at Nikolskoye with some regularity for more than twenty years, but the seriousness of that which broke out in 1885 was due in particular to the presence in the factory of experienced agitators. The leading role in the preparation of the strike was played by Moiseyenko, a worker who had participated in the demonstration in Kazan Square in 1876 and in the activities of the North–Russian Workers' Union. Since his return from political exile in Siberia in 1883 Moiseyenko had worked at Nikolskoye, where he was helped by another former member of the Union, V. I. Ivanov, and another young employee, Volkov. Their opportunity to bring the workers out on strike presented itself when the factory management refused to grant the traditional Christmas holiday on 7 January. Although the management had been forewarned of the workers' plans, the agitators succeeded in leading out the workers on the morning of that day and in presenting demands, formulated in advance. The demands included the return of wages taken back in fines since the previous Easter and undertakings from the management to the effect that fines should not in future constitute more than 5 % of a worker's wages and that not more than one rouble should be subtracted for one day's absence. In the main, the strikers were well organised and disciplined, owing largely to the restraint of their leaders. But, determined as they were, they could hardly resist the armed force of the three battalions of soldiers and 600 Cossacks which was called in to suppress the disturbance. Arrests were made and the workers, lacking the funds to finance a long strike, drifted back to work. Moiseyenko was arrested on 18 January and the strike petered out. By 20 January Count Tolstoy could report to Alexander that order was quite restored.[80] About six hundred workers were exiled from the region and thirty-three committed for trial. When their case finally came up in May 1886, however, a graphic picture of conditions in the Morozov factory was painted not only by the workers themselves but also by the factory manager who, having been sacked by Morozov after twenty years' faithful service, was not of a mind to assist the prosecution. The jurors dismissed the 101 charges which had been brought against the workers. (All the same, Moiseyenko and Volkov were taken back into custody and sent into exile, where Volkov died in 1887.)

Conservative circles were understandably enraged by the acquittal of the workers. 'Yesterday in ancient Vladimir, "city in the keeping of God",' wrote Katkov in his *Moskovkiye vedomosti* (*Moscow Gazette*) on the morrow of the jury's verdict, 'a 101-gun salute was fired in honour of the labour question which has reared its head in Rus.' The emergence of a labour movement was the inevitable accompaniment, Katkov regretfully supposed, of other Western innovations which augured only ill for Russia.[81] To socialists, on the other hand, the Morozov strike and the subsequent trial were naturally sources of encouragement rather than anger and despondency. Plekhanov, for example, optimistically declared that these events signalled the beginning of a new phase in the labour movement in Russia.[82] And in general the 'Morozov strike', as the outbreak of January 1886 came to be known, provided lessons of the utmost importance both to the workers themselves and to the revolutionary intelligentsia. Firstly, the official response to the strike made it abundantly clear that the tsarist government would unite with factory owners against the working class; it would send in troops when disturbances broke out in the factories of the new bourgeoisie just as it had when there had been disorders on the rural estates of the gentry. Secondly, the eventual failure of the strike pointed up the need for closer contact between intelligentsia and workers. Left to themselves, the workers were unable either to raise funds or as yet to produce the agitational literature which might help to sustain their morale. Thirdly, and most importantly, the strike forcibly underlined for the intelligentsia the revolutionary potential of the proletariat. Concentration of the workers in one locality and the rupture of their connections with the countryside made for the rapid growth of discontent among them. Their antagonism towards the capitalist tended also to be accentuated by the very nature of Russia's new industrial centres. Towns would spring up around a factory; there would be little in them that was not called into existence by the enterprises they accommodated. Moreover, the mobility of the proletarian work force helped both to confirm the impression that conditions were everywhere the same and to broadcast news of rebellion, thereby promoting a class consciousness as opposed to a mere sense of individual or local grievance. Finally, whereas no politically conscious individuals were to be found among the peasantry, men were emerging in the working class who were capable of formulating demands of a general political as well as of a local economic nature.

TOCHISSKY'S 'ASSOCIATION OF ST PETERSBURG ARTISANS'

The increasing interest of socialists in the working class was illustrated by the fact that in the autumn of 1885 another young organiser, Tochissky, began independently of, but just as single-mindedly as, the Blagoyevtsy to build a network of circles among the workers of St Petersburg. Designated in the first instance a 'society to help raise the material, intellectual and moral level of the working class in Russia', Tochissky's group subsequently adopted the less cumbersome name 'Association of St Petersburg Artisans', by which it has since been generally known.[83]

Tochissky was born in 1864, of a father of Polish origin and a French mother, in Yekaterinburg, one of the industrial cities of the Urals. In spite of his background – he was not himself of proletarian origin – he took work in factories in the region, where he was able to observe conditions for himself, and came into contact with an Englishman working there from whom he learnt something of the contemporary Western labour movements.[84] At the end of 1884 he arrived in St Petersburg and entered an industrial school in order to learn the metal worker's trade. Already he had both the ascetic bearing and the desire to 'simplify oneself' and to cultivate contact with the common people which had characterised the generation inspired by Lavrov a decade before. 'He lived extremely poorly,' recalled a close associate, 'nourishing himself with tea and bread and dining on almost nothing. He refused to take any money from his father . . . He dressed like a real worker, in a dirty blue smock, wretched leather trousers and ragged footwear on bare feet.'[85]

The year after his arrival in St Petersburg Tochissky began to build his 'Society', which was eventually to include three brothers by the name of Breytfus (the sons of a Russified German), Lazarev, Shalayevsky, and several women students (Arkadakskaya, Danilova, Lazarev's sister and Tochissky's own sister). Alongside this group of *intelligénty*, however, there also existed a workers' organisation which was deliberately kept quite distinct from the circle of *intelligénty*, and which led a very independent existence. This workers' organisation included leaders such as Buyanov, Klimanov, V. A. Shelgunov, Timofeyev and Vasilyev, most of whom were for some time to come to play a prominent role in the labour movement which was already beginning to acquire a momentum of its own in the St Petersburg factories. It appears to have embraced workers' circles, or at least had connections in a considerable number of enterprises, notably the Baird plant, the Stritter works, the artillery arsenal, the Vargunin paper-mill, the Aleksandrov plant, the Baltic plant, the Putilov metal works and the New Admiralty shipyard. Propagandists from the circle of *intelligénty* had limited access to these workers' circles and were evidently considered rather privileged to be introduced to them. The only significant activity undertaken by Tochissky's Association apart from propaganda among the workers was the accumulation of a large library, which eventually contained some 700 volumes and which was designed to support the propagandistic effort. The Association had no programme, only a code of rules, written by Tochissky himself, which has not survived. An attempt was made in 1887 to set up a press but in that year Tochissky was arrested and the Association was broken up by the police in 1888.

The fact that a sharp distinction was drawn between the two branches of the Association – the circle of *intelligénty* on the one hand and the workers' organisation on the other – and that only limited contact between them was permitted does not in this case serve to support Richard Pipes' contention that the leaders of a proletarian élite in St Petersburg were beginning in the mid 1880s to show a certain coolness, even hostility, towards the less mature student propagandists who visited their circles.[86] Rather, it reflects the importance attached by the Association – and by Tochissky in particular – to the workers' organisation. In the first place, such separation was prudent in the interests of conspiracy. It reduced the danger of the destruction of workers' circles by the police. All too frequently the surveillance of revolutionaries from the intelligentsia resulted in the arrest of all who were associated with them. In this instance, however, the police gathered no substantial information on the workers. The conspiratorial nicknames of some ('Klim', 'Semyonych' and 'Fimka', for example) were mentioned in testimonies during the investigation, but the police failed to establish the identity of the workers concerned and managed to arrest only one of their number, Vasilyev, even though they quickly broke up the Association's circle of *intelligénty* once they had detected its existence in 1888. In the second place, the separation of the two branches of the Association had a strategical significance which becomes clear in the light of Tochissky's views on the relationship between the intelligentsia and the masses in the revolutionary movement, for Tochissky seems to have viewed the intelligentsia as a potentially corruptible force which might align itself with the bourgeoisie and which would only be a temporary ally of the workers in their journey towards the revolutionary goal. No doubt this attitude towards the intelligentsia was partly the product of Tochissky's own fondness for life among the masses and of his distaste, given the prevailing conditions at any rate, for the sort of cultural pursuits in which members of the intelligentsia were inclined to indulge. (He harangued A. Breytfus, who was a student at the conservatoire, when the two became acquainted, on the criminality of an interest in a musical vocation while music served only as a distraction for the affluent minority, and he put a stop to the 'slovenly habits' of the women in the Association who were fond of visiting the theatre.) More importantly, Tochissky did not consider the intelligentsia capable of remaining faithful to the interests of another class. He is said to have been in the habit of illustrating his point by quoting Christ's words, 'before the cock crow twice, thou shalt deny me thrice', as the workers might put it to the intelligentsia. Consequently Tochissky looked on the intelligentsia only as a 'coincidental guest at the revolution' and expected it to part company with the working class once the government granted the first constitution. For the time being, admittedly, the intelligentsia was necessary to the working class, since the latter was still at too low a level of development to proceed on its own. The workers needed knowledge, for they were not yet fully aware of their own interests. Moreover, it was easier for the intelligentsia to procure funds for the workers' organisation, since the clerical work they could undertake was better paid than manual labour. But even in the present the rules of the Association assigned to the intelligentsia comparatively menial tasks, such as securing funds and obtaining literature, while entrusting the workers themselves with basic organisational tasks. By the beginning of 1888 Tochissky seems even to have been planning to exclude the *intelligénty* from full membership of the Association and to transfer all the Association's funds to the workers.[87]

Tochissky's demeaning view of the intelligentsia may well have represented a reaction against the exalted role assigned to revolutionary heroes by the Narodovoltsy. Certainly Tochissky was most unusual in his time – and differed in this respect from the Blagoyevtsy – in his extreme aversion to Narodnaya Volya and in particular to the terrorism with which that party was associated. While most contemporary socialists, including A. Breytfus at the time of his first acquaintance with Tochissky in 1885, considered Narodovolchestvo the 'height of heroism', Tochissky was dismissing the terrorists as *poseurs* seeking glory for themselves and was arguing that their actions would in the final analysis merely help the growing bourgeoisie to win power for itself. The masses were as yet too backward to take advantage of any weakness on the part of the authorities which terrorism might bring about.[88] Danilova, too, stated in her testimonies that she considered attempts to assassinate the Tsar positively 'harmful' since they not only failed to affect the 'existing relations between capital and labour' but also tended to retard the 'development of the people' by precipitating increased repression.[89]

The Association rejected important aspects of Populism in general as well as the main tactic of Narodovolchestvo in particular, for not only did the members of the Association in practice concentrate their attention entirely on propaganda among the urban workers, but they also justified this emphasis theoretically by regarding the proletariat as 'the only revolutionary class'. The peasant masses were not considered capable of acting as the 'vanguard of revolution'. And if we are to believe the memoirs of A. Breytfus – who may, of course, be retrospectively endowing Tochissky's views with a Marxian tinge which they did not in fact have at the time of the existence of his Association – Tochissky already saw the peasant masses as a divided force, not one united by common interests.[90] There is not much evidence, though, to support the view of the early Soviet historian, Sergiyevsky, that the Association was 'one of the earliest Marxist organisations' in Russia.[91] It is possible, admittedly, that familiarity with Plekhanov's work *Our Differences* led Tochissky in the direction of Marxism, as some contend,[92] but material on the Association is too sparse for one to be able to argue this with any confidence. The programme of the 'Emancipation of Labour' group was not in the Association's library and appears not to have been discussed (though a copy of that of the German Social Democrats was obtained and debated in detail).[93] Neither the émigré Social Democrats nor the Blagoyevtsy had any contact with the Association; indeed, they were not even aware of its existence.[94] As for possible non-Marxist socialist influences on the Association, we are told by Tochissky's sister that he was familiar with Lassalle, even in his days in Yekaterinburg, but there is no other evidence to suggest that he was an advocate of Lassalle's schemes for the creation of workers' associations and the introduction of socialism through the agency of the existing state.[95] Quite probably Tochissky was guided most of all by the example of British trade-unionism, the tactics and achievements of which he had in his youth heard described by his English acquaintance in the Urals.[96] Whatever political forms of struggle he might have envisaged for the labour movement in the long term, the objective of the Association in the shorter term was the organisation of the workers for struggle in pursuit of their economic interests.[97] To this end one of the clauses in the rules of the Association proposed the establishment of a fund, accruing from the payment of membership dues, out of which workers would be able to take interest-free loans. (In fact, the Association had so few members that the coffers were nearly always empty.) Lazarev and Danilova both spoke in their testimonies of the need to unite the workers in unions, and Danilova mentioned the example of the unions in England and America.[98]

In the final analysis, however, it hardly mattered if the political complexion of the Association was unclear, because like many other groups of the period its approach was so gradualist as to make ultimate objectives seem rather irrelevant to immediate activity. Tochissky believed, in common with most members of other groups to lean at this period towards Social Democracy, that the workers should be very thoroughly prepared before being allowed to embark on any ambitious or overt revolutionary venture. Consequently the work of his group, as its original title suggested, was at least in the first instance of a largely pedagogical nature. Its library consisted in the main of legally permitted publications and even included some newspapers of a conservative complexion – which were used 'for information' – as well as purely educative items such as textbooks of French, German, English and classical languages. A little illegal literature was stocked – separately from the main collection – but some members of the Association opposed its use on the grounds that it served to excite the workers without furnishing any useful information. Tochissky was even reluctant to recruit workers already influenced by other organisations for he feared they might have been spoiled by revolutionary 'adventurism'.[99] It is not surprising, in view of the apolitical and gradualist nature of the Association's activity, present and proposed, that its members seemed almost as innocuous to the authorities as Bekaryukov's group in Kharkov and that they accordingly received rather light sentences.

FEDOSEYEV'S ACTIVITY IN KAZAN IN 1888–9

Conditions in St Petersburg, where there was a substantial and growing proletariat and where the writings of foreign socialist thinkers were relatively easy to acquire, were much more favourable than they were elsewhere for the development of Social Democracy. Nevertheless, there were individuals even in the provinces who also began towards the end of the 1880s to search for alternatives to the increasingly discredited Populism. Foremost among these was Fedoseyev, who in 1888, while only seventeen years of age, gained considerable influence in student circles in Kazan.[100]

The thinker chiefly responsible for Fedoseyev's conversion to Marxism was probably not Plekhanov but P. N. Skvortsov, who arrived in Kazan towards the end of the decade after a period of exile in Tver. Skvortsov himself seems to have come to Marxism under the influence of the scholarly writings of Ziber rather than the more overtly revolutionary tracts of Plekhanov, whom Skvortsov considered a more recent convert to Marxism than himself and with whom he did not agree on all questions. On his arrival in Kazan Skvortsov obtained work as a statistician, work which, though at first sight arid, was in fact assuming considerable importance for the revolutionary movement since the detailed statistical knowledge sought by the *zemstva* on the economic structure of the countryside was to be crucial to the argument about the economic, and hence the social and political, destiny of Russia as a whole. (Both local economic statistics themselves and the meticulous methodology required to compile them were shortly to be used by V. I. Ulyanov, who during his confinement at Kokushkino very probably became acquainted for the first time with the weighty surveys based on statistical research in the local press.) Skvortsov's own researches were published in the legal press, both in the journal *Yuridicheskiy vestnik* (*The Legal Herald*) and in the regional paper *Volzhskiy vestnik* (*The Volga Herald*). Deploying a wealth of statistical material relating to numerous provinces, Skvortsov examined such questions as the size of the peasant's plot and family and the exploitation of wage labour on the land, with the object of showing that the peasantry was being divided into rich and poor. It was no longer possible to look on the peasant masses as 'something uniform', Skvortsov wrote in an article on the commune which appeared in *Volzhskiy vestnik* late in 1888. Owing to the 'economic differentiation' which had been taking place 'three strata of householders' could now be detected in the countryside: 'well-to-do peasants' or '*kulaks*', 'middle peasants', and 'poor-peasant-proletarians', whose ranks were being filled by the 'working class' of householders who did not have a house of their own. The interests of these groups were antagonistic. Nor did the existence of the commune impede the transformation of the peasant into a proletarian. Russian agriculture, then, was already subject to the laws of development studied by Marx, and Russia, in short, was becoming a capitalist country, a view no doubt reiterated in a critique which Skvortsov wrote of Vorontsov's work on the fate of capitalism in Russia and which he read to a gathering in Kazan early in 1889.[101]

The conclusions which Skvortsov drew from his researches, academic as they might at first sight seem, had the most fundamental practical implications and provided much ammunition for early provincial Marxists in their debates with the Populists. However, the influence of Skvortsov, an erudite and scholarly but not a particularly practical person, was bound to be primarily theoretical, and a skilled propagandist and capable organiser, such as Fedoseyev, was needed in order that some vitality and wider currency be given to the sort of conclusions Skvortsov was reaching. Born in 1871 in a gentry family in Vyatka province, Fedoseyev entered a *gimnaziya* in Kazan in 1880 and was still a pupil when his first contacts with revolutionary circles in the city were made. A self-education circle which he attended in the *gimnaziya* had a connection with Golubev, the former teacher of mathematics at the Troitsk *gimnaziya*, who was resident in Kazan from 1885 to 1887 and prominent in 'Populist' circles there for several years. It is also obvious from surviving letters of Fedoseyev's that he was acquainted with, and influenced by, Motovilov, the student of the Veterinary Institute who belonged to the conspirators' nucleus in Kazan and to the circle of L. Bogoraz which V. I. Ulyanov had entered in the autumn of 1887.[102] Neither of these mentors, however, was still in Kazan in 1888 when Fedoseyev, having by now been expelled from the *gimnaziya*, began in earnest to undertake his own organisational work among the ample ranks of discontented youth in the city. It is difficult to form a very clear picture of this organisational work since there is doubt as to the status of the group which the police succeeded finally in apprehending. It has been suggested, for example, that the circle which has become known to historians as 'Fedoseyev's circle' — consisting in the main of immature former pupils of the Troitsk *gimnaziya* who were arrested in the same police operation in which Fedoseyev himself was taken — played a relatively unimportant, peripheral role in the network as a whole.[103] Moreover, the police appear to have implicated in the case people who, although of revolutionary sympathies, had no direct involvement in Fedoseyev's group. There is even dispute as to the size of the network which Fedoseyev controlled, if indeed there was a network at all. One of those close to Fedoseyev, Grigoryev, states that the Marxist circles numbered 'not just one dozen' (*ne odnim desyatkom*), but his memoirs are vague and sparse and he is almost certainly exaggerating. On the other hand, another memoirist, Mitskevich, who heard of Fedoseyev in 1891 from another member of his group, Grigoryev's sister, refers to only one circle.[104] A third account — which is the most plausible, because it accords well with our knowledge of student circles in general in Kazan at this period and with what can be deduced about the complexion of Fedoseyev's work – speaks of the existence of a number of circles (though certainly not dozens) at two different levels.[105] In the lower circles Fedoseyev would appoint a leader, recommend a programme of reading and generally supervise studies; in the more advanced circles he would take charge of studies himself. In order to guide this activity Fedoseyev would compile programmes of reading and draft notes for propagandists, and to support the studies he assembled a sizeable library based on those remnants of a student's collection which had escaped detection by the police after the disorders of December 1887. By the summer of 1889 foreign works were being translated for use in the circles and Fedoseyev had succeeded in obtaining some print from local typographical workers in the hope of setting up a press. In July, however, he was caught by the police *in flagrante delicto* in a village outside Kazan where the print was stored, and the arrest of other members of his group followed shortly.

The task of ascertaining whether the circles of Fedoseyev's network were Marxist in character is no less difficult than the task of establishing the network's nature and size. The difficulty stems not merely from lack of sound evidence but also from two other factors which need to be borne in mind. Firstly, circles in Kazan continued to adhere to very strict rules of conspiracy. The secretive habits inculcated by Fokin, Bekaryukov and others ensured that members of one circle would very often not know the names of members of other circles which they did not frequent. Fedoseyev undoubtedly approved of strict secrecy in revolutionary work; he would allow only a very few trusted collaborators, for example, to use the volumes from the store of illegal literature which he was in charge of. Given these circumstances the reliability of statements by memoirists about the political affiliations of others could be very questionable; they might be guesses hazarded on the basis of hearsay rather than logical conclusions deduced from known fact. Secondly, and more importantly, the theoretical distinctions between factions were at this time so blurred – especially in Kazan – and knowledge of Marxism so sketchy that socialists, when they referred to one of their contemporaries as a 'Marxist', did not yet necessarily mean that he had the clear and sharply defined outlook which such professions of faith were subsequently to imply. We know, for example, that Berezin did not possess such an outlook, and yet one of the students of Fedoseyev's group told the police that Berezin had the reputation of being an 'ardent Marxist'.[106] The assertion of 'Marxist' convictions might indicate that a socialist admired Marx's *Capital*, or that he endorsed Plekhanov's view that Russia had now embarked on a capitalist path; or it might merely imply antipathy to Narodovolchestvo and a gradualist approach to revolutionary activity. It would be misleading, therefore, to search for evidence of the existence in Kazan at this time of a network of circles that were 'Marxist' in any very exact doctrinaire sense. Indeed, the difficulty of establishing the size of Fedoseyev's network may itself partly be the product of misconceptions as to what the term 'Marxist' actually meant.

Fedoseyev's own absorption of Marxist doctrines may have begun as early as 1887. Already he seems to have felt some dissatisfaction with prevailing Populist attitudes and Gorky claims that in the summer of that year Fedoseyev was vigorously defending Plekhanov's work, *Our Differences*, in which Populist theories were authoritatively challenged.[107] In his testimonies to the police, moreover, Fedoseyev declared that he rejected fundamental tenets of both Narodovolchestvo and what at this time was known as 'Populism', namely latter-day Chernoperedelchestvo.[108] More importantly, we know that in the summer of 1889 Fedoseyev's close collaborator, Sanin, was translating Kautsky's *Economic Teaching of Karl Marx*, an accessible introduction to Marx's economic doctrines which was doubtless for use in Fedoseyev's circles. Sanin asked Fedoseyev to send him further works for translation such as Marx's *Poverty of Philosophy* and his *Contribution to the Critique of Political Economy* and Engels' *Origin of the Family, Private Property and the State*.[109] It is reasonable to suppose, therefore, that Fedoseyev (and Sanin), by the time of their arrest in the summer of 1889, had embarked on a serious study of Marxism as a distinct stream of socialist thought and that they spread interest in that stream of thought in Kazan as they extended their influence over existing student circles (which may well have included some from the network established by Fokin and Bekaryukov). The translation of works from the German original and the plan to set up a press on which to print these translations perhaps reflected Fedoseyev's success as a propagandist and the favourable reception of the new doctrines. Even at the time of his arrest, however, Fedoseyev's Marxist views had not finally crystallised; he and his associates, he wrote shortly afterwards, were 'only just *beginning*' to clarify their views.[110]

V. I. ULYANOV AT KOKUSHKINO AND IN KAZAN, 1888–9

The subject of Fedoseyev's propagation of Marxist views in Kazan in 1888–9 has come to be linked in the history of the revolutionary movement at this period with the assimilation of those views by V. I. Ulyanov, who returned to the city in the autumn of 1888 after the period of exile that followed his participation in the demonstration of 4 December 1887. Before we examine Ulyanov's renewed participation in revolutionary circles in Kazan, however, it would be as well to attempt, in so far as the available material allows, to find out in what way he had occupied himself during his absence.

On his expulsion from the University Vladimir had settled with his mother, three sisters and one remaining brother on an estate which had formerly belonged to his maternal grandfather at Kokushkino, some fifteen miles from Kazan. Here, in his enforced seclusion, he engrossed himself in study. Never in his life, he said in 1904, had he read so much as he did during the nine months he spent at Kokushkino.[111] In one wing of the property was a cupboard full of books and journals which had belonged to Ulyanov's maternal uncle, a well-read man with an interest in the intellectual life of his time. From this source Ulyanov was able to familiarise himself with the social and political ideas debated in Russia over the previous twenty or thirty years. Most importantly, he was able to study the writings of Chernyshevsky.[112]

That Ulyanov read Chernyshevsky's works voraciously, both at this period in his life and subsequently, is not in dispute. We know from various sources that he held Chernyshevsky in an esteem which he reserved for very few people. Krupskaya, his life-long companion from 1894, for example, tells us that everything Vladimir Ilich said about Chernyshevsky 'breathes of a particular respect for his memory'.[113] And in a conversation of 1904, which one of the participants, Vorovsky, later attempted to record, Lenin is quoted as having said that Chernyshevsky had an overwhelming influence on him before his acquaintance with Marxism and that he had 'deeply ploughed him over'.[114] An album in which Lenin kept the photographs of a few writers and thinkers for whom he had a special regard included several pictures of Chernyshevsky.[115] And in 1888 he actually sent a letter to Chernyshevsky, who had then been allowed to leave Siberia and live in Astrakhan.[116] It is not so much that Lenin derived from Chernyshevsky any single important idea as that his horizons were immeasurably broadened by him. Chernyshevsky was after all a many-sided and seminal thinker in the Russian revolutionary tradition and furnished pabulum for writers exploring several different fields over the two or three decades following his brief publicistic career in the late 1850s and early 1860s. It was through Chernyshevsky that Lenin became acquainted with materialism, with the dialectic method, and with political economy as a discipline directed against the bourgeoisie rather than supporting or legitimising its enterprise. He was also affected by Chernyshevsky's attitudes, particularly his uncompromising hostility to liberalism. Most importantly, however, he was impressed by the revolutionary spirit of Chernyshevsky's thought, his 'revolutionary flair'.[117]

All these dimensions of Chernyshevsky's thought were doubtless accessible to the young V. I. Ulyanov in 1888 through the articles published in *Sovremennik* (*The Contemporary*). But more influential than any other work was Chernyshevsky's novel, *What is to be done?* It was in defending this novel against the criticism that it was banal that Lenin spoke, according to Vorovsky, of his great indebtedness to Chernyshevsky. After the execution of his brother, who had been captivated by Chernyshevsky, Lenin, too, had started to read the novel seriously, for he knew that it had been one of Aleksandr's favourite books. He spent not a few days but weeks reading it, he is reported to have said. Only then did he understand its depth. It was a novel which provided 'inspiration for a lifetime'. Hundreds of people had become revolutionaries under its influence.[118] And, although Ulyanov may have read it carefully in the summer of 1887, he is said to have read it four or five times more in the following year.[119] Nor, incidentally, was his interest in it exhausted even then. 'I was surprised to see how attentively he read that novel', recalled Krupskaya, who did not meet him until 1894, 'and how he took note of all the very fine nuances that are to be found in it.'[120]

What gave rise to this especial enthusiasm for Chernyshevsky's novel? Chernyshevsky gave fictional expression in the work to much that was fundamental to his publicism, for instance the ethical doctrine of rational egoism, the reverence for scientific method, and his hatred of the existing order, particularly its bourgeois manifestations; he also provided an optimistic depiction of a society based on co-operation. More important than any of these elements, however, was another that was lacking in Chernyshevsky's publicism, namely an inspiring portrait of the revolutionary whose appearance in Russian reality Chernyshevsky in 1863 already – rightly – considered imminent. Chernyshevsky's hero, Rakhmetov, represented the 'flower of the best people'; he and his ilk were the 'salt of the salt of the earth'. They were to the masses as was the theine in tea or the bouquet in a noble wine: from them the larger entity derived its strength and flavour. As a result of their efforts the life of all would blossom; without them it would decay. There were few of them, but they enabled all to breathe; without them people would suffocate.[121] It would not be quite correct to deduce, as Valentinov does, that Chernyshevsky is giving voice through his portrait of Rakhmetov to a crude Jacobinism which found its clearest expression in Zaichnevsky's proclamation 'Young Russia' and which Ulyanov himself derived from his reading of the novel.[122] The existence of a Jacobin strain in Chernyshevsky's thought as a whole is questionable and it is not obviously present in *What is to be done?* But it is reasonable to suppose that Chernyshevsky's portrait of a wilful individual who might be one of the moving forces of history served as a powerful spur to action for V. I. Ulyanov and accorded entirely with his own and other people's conception of his recently executed elder brother. *What is to be done?* yielded for him not a specific revolutionary strategy but the same meaning which Populists had been finding in it for more than fifteen years. It was a call for self-discipline, resolution, single-mindedness and self-sacrifice. Revitalised by this source of inspiration, as well as much more widely read in Russian socialist thought in general, Ulyanov resumed his contact with revolutionary circles in Kazan.

It was undoubtedly during the course of his second stay in Kazan, which lasted from October 1888 to May 1889, that Ulyanov for the first time read Marx's *magnum opus*, the first volume of *Capital*. His sister, Anna, tells us that during that winter he studied this work and began to describe its contents to her with all the enthusiasm of a new convert to the doctrines contained in it.[123] Valentinov, too, although he believes Anna's account is rhetorical and vacuous, dates Ulyanov's acquaintance with *Capital* to the beginning of 1889, claiming Lenin himself as the source of this information.[124] It is more problematical, though, whether Ulyanov immediately abandoned all other doctrines in favour of Marxism and whether he belonged to one of Fedoseyev's circles, which were supposedly designed to study the new stream of thought. Soviet biographers commonly assert that together with Fedoseyev, who held similar views to his own, V. I. Ulyanov represented a 'new generation of Russian Marxists' and that he 'joined one of the Marxist study circles' organised by Fedoseyev.[125] Only two pieces of evidence support these claims, however, and on examination they both prove brittle.

One such piece of evidence is Lenin's own description of his participation in revolutionary circles in Kazan in 1888–9 which he wrote in 1922 for a posthumous collection of articles on Fedoseyev (who had committed suicide in Siberian exile in 1898). 'I heard about Fedoseyev during my stay in Kazan, but I didn't meet him personally', wrote Lenin. 'In spring 1889 I went off to Samara province, where I heard at the end of the summer of 1889 about the arrest of Fedoseyev and other members of Kazan circles –

including, incidentally, the one in which I had taken part.'[126] Clearly Lenin gives the impression in this reminiscence that he took part in one of the circles organised by Fedoseyev. But he does not actually tell us that he did take part in such a circle, and his statement does not rule out the possibility that his own circle had no connection with Fedoseyev's. At any rate we may suggest that if indeed the circle in which V. I. Ulyanov took part did belong to Fedoseyev's network, then it could not have been among the more important ones in it, since in the whole period of Ulyanov's second stay in Kazan Fedoseyev, currently engaged in intensive dissemination of the new doctrine, evidently did not visit Ulyanov's circle as a propagandist. Nor, evidently, did Ulyanov show sufficient interest in Fedoseyev – whose Marxist leanings were widely known – to attempt to seek him out (although later, in 1893, when his own interest in Marxism had developed, Ulyanov did make a special journey to the city of Vladimir in order to try to meet Fedoseyev). It is even suggested by Trotsky that Ulyanov actually shrank from acquaintanceship with Fedoseyev, for the reason that he did not yet intend to break with the traditions of Narodnaya Volya and was reluctant to enter into controversy with an opponent known to be well versed in a current of thought that ran counter to those traditions.[127] We may add, finally, that Ulyanov's sister, Anna, tends to foster these doubts as to the existence of any connection between Vladimir's circle and Fedoseyev's. She also tells us that at the time of Fedoseyev's arrest some members of the circle to which her brother had belonged were arrested too and she mentions one of them, Chirikov,[128] a student at the University who had for some time moved in student circles and had acquired a certain celebrity with a facetious 'Ode to the Russian Tsar'. Chirikov was not at this time a Marxist, however; rather, he is described in one source as a 'Populist',[129] and he is nowhere mentioned in connection with Fedoseyev.

The second piece of evidence adduced in support of the view that Ulyanov was a 'Marxist' by the spring of 1889 is the supposed confirmation by Mandelshtam, a barrister who occasionally visited Kazan during this period to give lectures on Marx, that Ulyanov was in his audience. It is clear from his memoirs that Mandelshtam himself was not aware of Ulyanov's presence at the time. 'Only now have I learned', he said apologetically in 1928, 'that among my audience in my conspiratorial discussions in Kazan in the winter and spring of 1888–9 was Vladimir Ilich.'[130] All the same, it is quite possible that Ulyanov did attend Mandelshtam's talks, for his sister, Anna, tells us that when he began to visit circles more frequently at the beginning of 1889 he would mention the name of Chetvergova, who is named by Mandelshtam as the hostess of the gatherings he would address.[131] Chirikov, too, Mandelshtam recalls, was often present at these meetings. But it by no means follows from the fact that Mandelshtam gave lectures on Marx that all the members of his audience were convinced Marxists. Indeed, Mandelshtam himself tells us that, although there were circles of various complexions in Kazan at the time, including the 'Populist' circle of Berezin and the 'Marxist' circle of Fedoseyev, the one he personally frequented, Chetvergova's was closer in its sympathies to Narodnaya Volya. (One of its members, incidentally, was Kudryavtsev, the 'militarist'.) Even Mandelshtam himself can hardly have been a thoroughgoing Marxist, for he would argue about the need for terror with Chirikov (who as a 'Populist' would presumably have opposed the waging of violent political struggle).[132] As for Chetvergova herself, she was a Narodovolka (feminine of Narodovolets) and there is no evidence to suggest that Ulyanov argued with her. Indeed, he regarded her, writes Anna, 'with great sympathy'.[133] As late as 1900, when passing through Ufa on his return from Siberian exile, he paid her a visit; 'his voice and face,' Krupskaya recalled, 'seemed to become particularly gentle as he talked with her'.[134] In all probability, therefore, he looked on Chetvergova in 1888–9 not as an adversary but, to use Trotsky's words, 'as a green recruit looks at a scar-covered veteran'.[135]

What conclusions can we draw about Ulyanov's renewed involvement in student circles in Kazan in 1888–9? It is not disputed that Lenin came from a revolutionary background in which Narodovolchestvo was greatly respected and even that many of his early contacts in the revolutionary movement had deep sympathy for the terrorists of Narodnaya Volya. We cannot say for certain what his political views were during the period between his brother's execution in May 1887 and his departure from Kazan for Samara in the spring of 1889, for we have only scraps of circumstantial evidence. There is no concrete evidence available on which to base an argument to the effect that he had Jacobin sympathies during this period, though like everyone else in the revolutionary camp he would have been familiar with the essence of Jacobin theory. But nor is there any evidence to suggest that he took issue with people who remained loyal to the traditions of Narodnaya Volya. Indeed, we can say with confidence that he derived his initial inspiration as a revolutionary from the heroic political struggle of Narodnaya Volya, a struggle in which his own deeply respected brother had lost his life. He himself spoke in glowing terms of the example set by Narodnaya Volya when he came at the end of his own work, *What is to be done?*, to enumerate the stages through which Social Democracy had passed in Russia. Many of the young Russian Social Democrats who had led the movement to the workers in the mid 1890s, he wrote,

> began to think in a revolutionary way as Narodovoltsy. Almost all in their early youth enthusiastically worshipped the heroes of terrorism. Ridding oneself of the charismatic impression of this heroic tradition cost a struggle, it meant a break with people who wanted at all costs to remain faithful to Narodnaya Volya and whom the young Social Democrats greatly respected.[136]

Indeed, this passage had a special pertinence for Lenin himself, the brother of a terrorist and a leader of one of the early Social Democratic groups in St Petersburg; it was, as Krupskaya put it, a 'piece of the biography' of Lenin himself.[137] His sister, Anna, also tells us that Lenin 'always had a great respect for old Narodovoltsy' and that 'in no way did he renounce their "heritage"'.[138] This 'heritage' may have included a lingering sympathy for terrorism, which his close associate from his Samara days, Lalayants, says still persisted in 1893, causing some friction in their by now Marxist circle.[139] It was clearly reflected, too, in a fine knowledge of conspiratorial methods (though such knowledge, by the late 1880s, was not the exclusive property of Narodovoltsy). 'Of all our group,' Krupskaya wrote in her account of the activities of the Social Democrats in St Petersburg in 1894–5, 'Vladimir Ilich was the best equipped for conspiratorial work . . . one felt the benefit of his good apprenticeship in the ways of the Narodnaya Volya Party.'[140] But most important of all in the heritage of Narodnaya Volya was that same quality which Lenin found in Chernyshevsky's thought and in his novel, *What is to be done?*, in particular: revolutionary mettle, a wilful determination to fight to the end.

THE LABOUR MOVEMENT AND STUDENT CIRCLES IN
ST PETERSBURG IN THE LATE 1880s

Debates as to the respective merits of Populism and Social Democracy may have begun to take place in the provinces by the end of the 1880s, but it was natural that it should be in St Petersburg, the intellectual capital of Russia and her main industrial centre, that the adherents of the new stream of socialist thought emanating from Western Europe should make their strongest challenge. Here the growth of a Social Democratic movement was assisted by the emergence in the working class itself of leaders whose sympathetic attitude towards socialist teachings was only partly due to the efforts of groups, such as the Blagoyevtsy and Tochissky's Association, which had devoted their resources to propaganda in the factories. The more mature workers themselves undertook the task of acquiring suitable literature, combing the markets and secondhand bookshops for numbers of the old 'thick' journals in which the radical publicism of the previous three decades had first appeared. One worker, Timofeyev, who inherited the library built up by Tochissky's Association, is said to have amassed as many as a thousand volumes, from among which he would lend items not only to the converted but also to young workers who seemed likely to prove receptive to this propaganda. Under the direction of labour leaders such as Timofeyev, workers' circles proliferated more or less independently of the intelligentsia towards the end of the decade. Estimates of the number of such circles in existence vary, but it seems that at the very least there were by the beginning of 1889 ten circles, each with five to eight members, though in all probability the number was much higher. A revolutionary who returned to St Petersburg in 1890 after an absence of some years noticed the change that had taken place: whereas at the time when Blagoyev's group had been operating there had not been enough circles to occupy all the aspiring propagandists in the student body, now there were insufficient propagandists to serve all the workers' circles which needed them.[141] It is indicative of the increasing momentum of the workers' activity, moreover, that the labour leaders decided early in 1889 to set up a committee consisting of representatives of the various industrial regions in which circles had sprung up in order to co-ordinate their activity. The leaders of the existing circles met at the home of one of their number, Fomin, approved a set of rules and agreed the composition of this committee, designated the 'Central Workers' Circle', which would include Afanasyev, Bogdanov, Buyanov, Klimanov, Mefodiyev and Yevgrafov. All these workers would enjoy equal rights in the circle and would act in turn as host of their weekly meetings. One member of the intelligentsia (in the first instance, V. S. Golubev) would attend these meetings, but he would have no formal authority at them.[142]

For all their independence, however, the workers were by no means entirely out of touch with the intelligentsia, as the presence of a student representative on their central committee, albeit in a purely consultative capacity, clearly shows. In fact, connections between workers and intelligentsia had never been entirely broken off, and to a certain extent had continued independently of organisations such as the workers' group of Narodnaya Volya, the Blagoyev group and Tochissky's Association. Students had taught in workers' schools, of which a number existed in St Petersburg, providing workers with a grounding in reading, writing and other basic subjects and often introducing revolutionary propaganda into their lessons, or at least preparing the ground for such propaganda.[143] Other students, *odinochki* as they were known, had maintained contact with workers' circles on an individual basis, either because they disagreed with the programmes of existing groups or simply because they reasoned that it was easier to escape detection and to work effectively in isolation. And now, towards the end of the decade, a substantial portion of the student youth was again seized by the enthusiasm for communion with the masses that had infected the young generation of the early 1870s, though on this occasion it was the urban worker rather than the peasant on whom attention was to be concentrated. Once more the young took a stoical pleasure in rejecting the niceties of 'bourgeois' life and enthusiastically tried to live in the style of the common man. One memoirist relates how he went about in a *poddyovka*, rough boots and leather cap, trying to sleep on bare boards and eating only the most basic and essential food.[144] Others describe the elaborate though frequently unconvincing attempts made by students to disguise themselves as workers when they went to conduct propaganda in workers' circles: student uniform would be exchanged for high boots, a man's blouse, a threadbare coat and cap, and their faces would be smeared with soot.[145] At this time, too, another organisation developed among the students to renew and to direct serious activity in the masses. A number of Polish students – Rodzevich, Lelevel, Burachevsky, Tsivinsky and others – were among the first to attempt in 1888 to promote Social Democracy, about which they were comparatively well informed as a result of connections with Western European socialist circles. And in the course of the years 1889–92 some of these Poles joined numerous Russian students in the so-called 'Brusnev group', a loose collection of individuals adhering to no generally accepted programme but united by the common purpose of conducting propaganda among the proletarian masses.[146]

It has been argued by Richard Pipes that the aspirations of the St Petersburg workers, on the one hand, and the students who visited their circles as propagandists, on the other, were far from identical and that relations between the two groupings were less amicable than most memoirists and all Soviet students of the subject would have us suppose. The workers, Pipes contends, were interested primarily in the knowledge which the students could impart rather than in the political content of their propaganda; and while they 'eagerly learned sociology or biology from their contemporaries from the intelligentsia', they 'resented practical advice tendered them by bookish, naïve students'. This view is based to a large extent on evidence culled from the memoirs of one member of the workers' circles, V. A. Shelgunov, who recalled, in Pipes' words, 'how concerned the workers were that the "*intelligént* not insist too much on revolution, that is, that he communicate more knowledge and agitate less"'.[147] It should be said, however, that in the passage cited by Pipes Shelgunov is not speaking for the workers as a whole but describing his personal request for a propagandist who would help to prepare him to fulfil his ambition to qualify as a teacher.[148] From the memoirs of another worker who participated in circles in St Petersburg at this time, Norinsky, it is clear that it was not the students who took the initiative in introducing workers to literature of plainly revolutionary significance: Timofeyev gave Norinsky a copy of *The Religion of Capital* by Marx's son-in-law, Paul Lafargue, and would read to the workers a pamphlet by the Polish socialist, Diksztajn, *What does a man live on?*, which had been issued by the 'Emancipation of Labour' group in 1885.[149] We have, too, the report by the labour leader, Bogdanov, of the favourable impression made in a workers' circle by the propagandist, Pereverzin, a student at the Technological Institute; from the beginning Pereverzin won the confidence of the workers by his 'simplicity' and his ability to communicate with them at an appropriate level.[150]

In order to guide the studies of the workers' circles the students drew up a new reading programme. The propagandist would provide a very broad general education, touching upon physics, chemistry, botany, zoology, physiology, anatomy, hygiene, geology, cosmography, astronomy, and the various theories concerning the formation of the earth and the origin of the universe. He would discuss the history of man's culture, his food, occupations and customs, his society at various stages of evolution, the development of political power, religion, the family and private property. Political economy, the history of the various economic systems and the history of the workers' movement would be studied, too.[151] It is difficult to believe that the zealous students responsible for the compilation of this erudite and immensely detailed aid to propaganda can have seriously entertained the hope that the propagandist himself, let alone any of his pupils in the working class, might assimilate more than a fraction of this knowledge, even at a superficial level. The programme must surely reflect an element of wishful thinking on the part of the students as well as the influence on them of the tradition of *kruzhkovshchina*, or meticulous study in self-education circles, to which they themselves belonged. It also laid them open to the charge that their activity was in the last analysis pedagogical rather than revolutionary and seems at first sight to provide further support for Pipes' view that it was uncontentious information rather than revolutionary propaganda in which the workers themselves were interested. But in fact the programme did not reflect any concession on the part of the students to apoliticism in the masses. Rather, it was intended to prepare the ground for a Social Democratic movement, which required both a theoretical basis of supposedly scientific rigour and solidity and an abundant supply of knowledgeable and articulate propagandists in the working class itself. The socialist ideal, one of the propagandists told his workers' circle, would be attained as a result not of the efforts of revolutionary 'heroes' but of a movement of the entire, organised working class. And to be capable of organising the working class the socialist leader required knowledge, which he would gain through study according to a broad programme.[152]

Nor did the period of painstaking theoretical preparation last for long. Propaganda of a largely pedagogical nature soon began to give way to agitation, in which the workers, far from being reluctant participants, played a prominent role. When a strike broke out in the docks in 1890, for example, a worker from the central circle was sent to one of the workshops of the New Admiralty with funds which the workers had collected in order to help the strikers. The need was now felt for a paper which would provide news of the development of the movement in the various factories and regions and it seems that two numbers of such a paper were produced, though only in manuscript form. A deputation of workers delivered an address to the dying publicist, N. V. Shelgunov, who had consistently championed their cause; some took part in his funeral procession and contributed a wreath, and one of the speeches was made in their name. Shortly afterwards, in 1891, it was decided to mark 1 May with an appropriate gathering and seventy or eighty people, the vast majority of them workers, attended a meeting on the first Sunday of the month in a secluded spot by the Yekateringofka River. A further, larger, gathering of this type was arranged in May 1892 and in the same year the St Petersburg workers sent an open letter expressing solidarity with Polish workers who had launched a series of strikes.

Taken by themselves these incidents were more or less trivial. But they did help to increase the workers' consciousness of their potential strength and of their common interests. Moreover, seen in the broadest perspective, they mark the beginning of a new phase in the revolutionary movement in Russia. The age of *kruzhkovshchina*, when students and sometimes workers, too, had gathered secretively in small circles was coming to an end. So, too, was the age of Populism, when revolutionaries had concentrated their energies in the towns not because that was where they found a class capable of generating the revolution but primarily because they had been frustrated in the countryside. Relatively numerous members of the St Petersburg intelligentsia now began to ask themselves not whether Social Democracy could possibly have any application in Russian conditions, but by what method, 'legal', 'spontaneous', or 'economist' it was best to pursue its objectives. And in the provinces the exponents of Marxism (in the proper sense of the word, no longer in its sense of peaceful Populist or opponent of Narodnaya Volya) now began impatiently and petulantly to denounce the old beliefs and to challenge the Populists even in the most isolated towns, which only a few years before had been their strongholds.

CONCLUSION

There is no doubt but that after 1 March 1881 revolutionary Populism entered a decadent phase and that the Russian revolutionary movement as a whole, having suddenly flourished in the 1870s, went into a temporary decline. For one thing, terrorism abated, even though certain groups did continue to contemplate its application. Meanwhile, those groups which were in any case opposed to violence (albeit on tactical rather than moral grounds), realising that the advent of socialism was not so imminent as their predecessors had hoped, accepted that the patient and unheroic activity of many generations would be necessary before revolution would take place, and set themselves correspondingly limited objectives. Activity came to be hampered, moreover, by confusion and lack of purpose as the weakness of the major theoretical premises of Populism became increasingly apparent. After all, it seemed unlikely now that 'critically thinking' individuals could generate far-reaching social change by means of patient propaganda, inflammatory agitation or terrorism – political or economic – or indeed that they could obliterate distinctions between themselves and the peasantry, as Populists had once hoped. As for the peasants themselves, they, as revolutionaries had already begun to their chagrin to learn in the 1870s, were not exceptionally amenable to socialism or ready to carry out revolution from below, be it peaceful, as Lavrov had hoped, or violent, as Bakunin had imagined. It was also questionable whether the commune could any longer be plausibly presented as a possible foundation for socialism in Russia (indeed, certain Populist writers, such as Gleb

Uspensky, as well as the Marxist Plekhanov, pointed to the beginning of its disintegration under new economic pressures after the emancipation of the serfs), and whether Russia would be able to bypass the capitalist path of development on which she seemed to some by 1890 to be firmly embarked.

Yet another indication of the decadence of Populism in the 1880s, besides the abatement of terrorism and the increasing patience and theoretical confusion of its adherents, was the fact that certain revolutionary groups which did try to uphold established beliefs patently lost their *raison d'être*. The Narodovoltsy of the late 1880s, for example, while continuing to declare as their objective the overthrow of the autocrat and his government, failed to sustain the strong metropolitan base which the pursuit of this objective required, so that by 1890 their remaining cadres were operating in Vladimir and Kostroma, ancient towns of the 'golden ring' in which the Muscovite princes had built their fortifications against the marauding Tartars, and in Vologda, a religious and trading centre founded by monks in medieval times some 250 miles to the north of Moscow in the forest wilderness and still in the 1860s so remote that the tsarist authorities deemed it a suitable place of exile for opponents such as Pisarev and Lavrov. Similarly, the members of the 'printers' circle' in Kazan, while attempting to sustain the Populists' sense of responsibility for bringing about a rapid improvement in the life of the masses, at the same time acknowledged the correctness and relevance to Russia of aspects of Social Democratic doctrine and abandoned the press on which they had hoped to print their defence of the old beliefs. Thus by the end of the 1880s the tsarist authorities, whose own vigorous persecution of the revolutionary movement had helped to turn back the revolutionary tide and who were threatened in that decade by none of the major popular disturbances which revolutionaries had dreamed of inciting, enjoyed a greater sense of security than at any time for perhaps thirty years. It is quite understandable, therefore, that the revolutionary groups of the 1880s, when compared to those of the 1870s and 1890s, should appear to have had little impact on their society and to have had an air of ineffectualness that accounts in large measure for the relative obscurity in which they have subsequently been shrouded.

It would be far from the truth, however, to say that Populism in its decadent phase and the movement of the 1880s in general had no usefulness in the struggle against the tsarist régime or that the period had no significance in the broader history of the revolutionary movement. For one thing a number of lessons were learned or reinforced during the decade, as revolutionaries came to attach importance to tendencies that may have been already apparent in the 1870s but were not readily accepted by a majority of revolutionaries in that decade. By the end of the 1880s, for example, many acknowledged that their struggle required a 'political' aspect in Russia, where the expression of any independent thought inevitably entailed conflict with the government. Some Zemlevoltsy had already begun in the 1870s to recognise that the propagation of socialism was not merely, perhaps not primarily, an 'economic' or moral question, as Lavrov, Bakunin and the Chaykovtsy had supposed. But it was the party Narodnaya Volya which first gave the concept of 'political' struggle wide currency in Russia and their epigones of the 1880s who kept alive the concept. It is arguable that the Narodovoltsy helped by this means to introduce a greater pragmatism into revolutionary circles and also even prepared the ground to a certain extent for the later promotion of Marxism, in which the concept of political struggle, albeit in a different sense, played a central role.

A second and perhaps more important lesson that was properly absorbed during the 1880s concerned organisation. It became customary during this decade for groups of quite diverse complexions to attach far greater importance than had been usual in the early and mid 1870s to organisational tasks. It was no longer merely the Narodovoltsy who emphasised the need for centralised organisation of revolutionary forces, rigid discipline and strict observation of the rules of secrecy; rather, a majority of revolutionaries in the 1880s — 'militarists' such as Raspopin, 'conspirators' such as Fokin and Bekaryukov, and even peaceful advocates of propaganda among the urban workers such as Tochissky now regarded a sound and tightly knit organisation that could protect its members from the attentions of the police as a prerequisite for any other activity. Indeed, several groups were prepared to devote their main energies for the foreseeable future to painstaking organisation work.

A third and equally important factor of which revolutionaries became increasingly aware in the 1880s was the receptivity of the urban workers to socialist propaganda, a factor which naturally made expeditions to the industrial regions of the cities seem more useful than pilgrimages to the countryside. Admittedly, even the Chaykovtsy had stumbled across this fact at the beginning of the 1870s, and their experience was confirmed by the Zemlevoltsy and the Chernoperedeltsy. But again, it was the Narodovoltsy in provincial towns such as Kiev, Kharkov, Rostov and Yekaterinoslav, as well as in St Petersburg, who in the 1880s came in practice to give propaganda among the workers priority over all other forms of activity.

Very gradually there appeared too during this decade groups of individuals who understood that Populism did not adequately account for the experience of revolutionaries among the urban workers and who therefore began to lean in the direction of Social Democracy. (These groups and individuals naturally tended to be resident in St Petersburg, where the growth of industry and a proletariat could be observed at first hand, though even in provincial towns, urban islets in a rural ocean, some socialists, such as Fedoseyev in Kazan, began also to accept elements of Social Democratic doctrine and to become amenable to the ideas being patiently advanced by Plekhanov in Switzerland.)

There is, however, a further factor of which it is even more important to take account when assessing the role of the groups of the 1880s in the history of the Russian revolutionary movement, namely that these groups simply existed and functioned, thus keeping alive a revolutionary tradition that could be reinvigorated in the 1890s when conditions were again propitious. The undoubted relative lack of impact of these groups on the government and on such public opinion as existed in Russia at the time and the resignation of many individuals to more cautious and patient activity than their predecessors had tolerated make it all too easy to incline to the view of Arthur Mendel that 'radical socialism', faced as it was in the 1880s

> with the combined opposition of Tolstoyan pacifism, the beginnings of the art-for-art's-sake movement, small-deeds reformism, and the intensified police reaction and popular disillusion resulting from the assassination of 1881 . . . all but disappeared as a serious contender for the allegiance of the intelligentsia.[1]

But in reality support for the socialist ideal did not diminish (though the nature of that support changed and expectations became more modest), as the profusion of groups which we have surveyed amply demonstrates.

These groups maintained and even strengthened the movement in various ways. In the first place, they perpetuated and developed the practical skills that were necessary to revolutionaries if they were to operate effectively in the tsarist state: they composed material to assist propaganda among the masses, they established secure headquarters and clandestine printing presses, they mastered techniques for duplicating illegal literature and producing false documents and they devised means both of avoiding detection by the police and of communication with other groups. These skills were the stock-in-trade of the revolutionary of the 1890s, but he did not devise them himself; rather, he received them, adapted and improved over many years, from his predecessors. In the second place, the groups of the 1880s ensured that socialism retained a strong base in the nation's higher educational institutions. The frequent disorders in the major universities and institutes and the public demonstrations on important anniversaries and other occasions, in which students were always prominent, were one expression of this continuing radical commitment among the student youth, and an important expression at that, which helped periodically to recharge the political atmosphere. But behind these more visible manifestations of student discontent the earnest *kruzhki* of the universities in St Petersburg, Moscow, Kiev, Kharkov, Kazan and Odessa, the veterinary institutes of Kharkov and Kazan, the Agricultural College in Moscow, and the technical institutes in St Petersburg continued to prepare a politically conscious section of the population that not only grew in size but spread ever more widely as students were banished from these centres or graduated and took up employment, so that by the 1890s hardly a provincial town of any importance was without its revolutionary propagandists and sympathisers. And in the third place, and no less importantly, numerous groups of the 1880s – Narodovoltsy and 'conspirators' such as Bekaryukov, as well as the Blagoyevtsy, Tochissky's 'Association' and Fedoseyev's disciples in Kazan – through their work in circles in factories in all the major industrial centres, maintained a connection with the masses and thereby facilitated the building of a working-class movement when the pace of industrialisation quickened in the 1890s and when the growth of unrest among the urban workers made it more than ever desirable for the revolutionaries to cultivate them.

The Russian revolutionary groups of the 1890s, then, did not have to begin at the very beginning, although there was of course much painstaking work to be done. They had precedents to follow, foundations to build on and, perhaps most important of all, examples to emulate. This heritage they received from groups of various complexions which linked them to the revolutionaries of the 1870s in a continuous revolutionary tradition. In the absence of groups such as those we have examined, and in which many revolutionaries who remained active in the 1890s and beyond gained their earliest political experience, the great events of early Russian revolutionary history, the 'going to the people' and the 'heroic' feats of the Narodovoltsy, would have become but a distant memory. As it happened, though, these events remained a fresh source of inspiration and their exemplary potential was undiminished. Moreover, Populism in general and Narodovolchestvo in particular, despite their shortcomings, which became increasingly apparent in the 1880s, proved highly suitable vehicles for the transmission of the social ideal in a revolutionary dark age when it was important to preserve it for future generations. For Populism was, as Oliver Radkey has put it, 'less an ideology than a state of mind which brought men together in the absence of concrete formulas and held them together despite divergences over programme and tactics'.[2] Its capacity to inspire was therefore strong and durable, as we have seen, even for revolutionaries, such as the young Lenin, who were in due course to reject the major theoretical assumptions on which it rested.

If one loses sight of the continuity in Russian revolutionary history, of the fact that the groups of the 1880s kept a socialist tradition alive in a difficult period, then it becomes easy to exaggerate the distinction between the Populism which held sway in the revolutionary camp in the 1870s and the Social Democracy which came to exert such a strong influence there in the 1890s. It is a tendency that Venturi, in a recent survey of historical writings on Russian Populism, has detected in numerous works of Western as well as Soviet scholarship which, despite 'their considerable value . . . often risk perpetuating the deep division and separation established in Russia between the history of social democracy and the history of the previous revolutionary movement' and of 'severing the profound psychological and political unity between the various phases of the struggle against czarist absolutism'.[3] This division and separation, though, should not be overemphasised. As Robert Service has pointed out, there was 'no butcher's blow which severed the two traditions neatly and irreparably. Rather there was a messy, complex fracture.'[4] In practice the distinctions between Populism and Social Democracy were from the beginning very blurred, however much some thinkers, particularly Plekhanov, tried for polemical purposes to clarify them.

This blurring of divisions is particularly noticeable in the period with which the present study has been concerned. Indeed, to a certain extent even the drawing of the distinctions implicit in the classification of the groups of the 1880s under the various headings given to the chapters of this study involves an oversimplification, albeit a necessary one, a retrospective imposition on the movement of that decade of a greater order and clarity than it in fact possessed. Just as supporters of Narodnaya Volya and the opponents of violence within the Populist movement tended during the 1880s to co-operate so freely that it is often difficult to decide to which faction in the Populist camp a group should properly be assigned (as is especially the case with groups in Kharkov, Kiev and Kazan), so a number of groups or individuals who appear to belong to one or other of the Populist factions exhibit certain Social Democratic tendencies, whilst other groups which it is customary to describe as at least forerunners of Social Democracy retain a strong Populist colouring. Thus many groups of Narodovoltsy in practice concentrated in the 1880s on that form of activity, propaganda among the urban workers, to which Social Democrats were also to give the greatest emphasis; Aleksandr Ulyanov, while resolving to undertake another attempt at tsaricide, pondered the applicability of a Marxian analysis to Russian society; the Muscovite 'translators and publishers', while commending a 'militarist' conspiracy, propagated Marxist ideas among the student youth; and 'Populists' in Kazan, while tenaciously upholding the Populist view that the intelligentsia should work among the peasantry, appear to have sensed the grave weakness of Populism and the comparative strength of Marxian social analysis. Meanwhile the Blagoyevtsy, despite their decision, bold for its time, explicitly to align themselves with the Social Democratic stream of socialist thought, showed a predilection for terrorism of which Plekhanov could not approve and which gave them an affinity with Narodnaya Volya, with whose epigones they in any case collaborated and maintained close contact. Nor were the groups of the 1880s whom it is conventional to dissociate from the prevailing Populist tendencies nearly so clearly Marxian in complexion as it has been customary, in Soviet scholarship at any rate, to portray them. Blagoyev's group appears to have had at least as strong a Lassallean hue as a Marxian one. Tochissky's 'Association' was probably inspired more by the model of Owenism and British trade-unionism than by any stream within German Social Democracy. And while Fedoseyev himself may have adopted a more thoroughgoing Marxist position than most of his contemporaries, it is unlikely that the circles over which he extended his influence altogether freed themselves during his short propagandistic career in Kazan from the miscellaneous Populist influences prevalent in that city throughout the 1880s.

It is perhaps particularly useful to bear in mind the complexity of these relationships and the indistinctness of affiliations among the revolutionaries of the 1880s when we come to consider the earliest experience of the future Lenin in the movement. Far from being a clear-minded Marxist from the age of seventeen, young Vladimir Ulyanov did not stand out conspicuously against the confused revolutionary background at the very beginning of his career, nor did he move towards Marxism at the end of the 1880s in such a decisive fashion as is usually implied in Soviet biography. (When he did move towards Marxism, moreover, he was following a prevailing current in revolutionary circles, not directing it.) On the contrary, historical fact, as opposed to hagiographical legend, tells us that he was at first unobtrusive in a milieu in which Populist example remained powerful even while uncertainty began to be expressed about Populist doctrine. That is not to say that there is firm evidence of clear traces, in his early years in the revolutionary movement, of the 'Jacobin' sympathies often imputed to him, although V. G. Bogoraz, the elder brother of one of his earliest associates, certainly did express such sympathies in his pamphlet on the 'struggle of social forces in Russia'. But it is safe to surmise that the example of active struggle so pronounced in revolutionary Populism and in Narodovolchestvo in particular, and passed on by Aleksandr Ulyanov, combined with Vladimir's own temperament to lead him to interpret in a dynamic way the Marxism which was beginning to attract the Russian intelligentsia in the early 1890s and which many of his contemporaries tended to see as a deterministic doctrine rather than one giving free rein to the individual or the élite group in the historical process. For the impatient and forceful Lenin, Marxism held out little more hope than it had to his brother or other Narodovoltsy unless it could be adapted for use in a backward country where capitalism was only just beginning to develop. Unlike Plekhanov, Lenin found it impossible, in Haimson's words, to

> accept a view of the world that imposed such rigid restraints on the initiative of the revolutionist. Concerned as he was with the effectiveness and ultimate success of his revolutionary activity he too had to hold on to a belief in historical necessity, but this vision had to make infinitely more room for the role of the individual's will.[5]

Like the Narodovoltsy, Lenin therefore laid emphasis on 'subjective factors' such as initiative, intention and will and accepted to a greater extent than most fellow Marxists that it might be necessary to give history a push. To this dynamism we may add other factors prominent in Lenin's revolutionary biography and doubtless inculcated in him from his earliest years in revolutionary circles in Kazan in the late 1880s: his belief in the importance of strict rules of conspiracy and his adeptness at applying them, to which Krupskaya refers; and his insistence on sound and disciplined revolutionary organisation, for which he himself applauds Populist revolutionaries in *What is to be done?* One should, of course, also mention his awareness of the need to take account of the peasant masses and utilise them as a revolutionary force, an awareness that became clear in the early years of the twentieth century, when, despite competition between the Social Democrats and the Socialist Revolutionaries, Lenin showed a willingness to appropriate what was useful in the thought of these heirs to the earlier Populism.

Although the relationships among revolutionaries of nominally different factions and their political affiliations would appear, in the light of the evidence we have adduced, to be exceptionally complex in the 1880s, it is nevertheless reasonable to add, finally, that they still remained anything but straightforward when Social Democracy began to win numerous adherents and indeed to prevail over Populism inside Russia from the beginning of the 1890s. Groups of Narodovoltsy active in St Petersburg in the 1890s, for example, considered themselves followers of 'scientific socialism' and maintained close links with Marxist circles, and in the middle of the decade one such group published a series of leaflets that took on such a Marxist colouring that the last leaflet was distributed by Marxists but disavowed by other Narodovoltsy.[6] Again, Chernov, the leader of the Party of Socialist Revolutionaries, which was founded in 1901 and which followed earlier Populist groups in its insistence on the need for agrarian revolution and its enthusiasm for terrorism, 'drew heavily on Marxism and its revisionist offshoot' all the same, as the party's main historian has pointed out, while 'the reverse is also true', in that Russian Marxism, or rather its Bolshevik variant, 'betrays increasing evidence of the influence of the rival ideology' after the turn of the century.[7] Russian Social Democracy itself was hardly a clearly delineated stream of thought, but was riven from the beginning by its own factional controversies, some of which – for instance, the debates about whether revolutionaries should follow the 'spontaneous' example of the stirring factory workers, whether they should pursue mainly 'economic' as opposed to 'political' goals, and to what extent they should bring socialist consciousness to the masses from without – have a familiar ring to the student of the Populist movement. And, of course, the durability of Populism to a considerable extent determined the preoccupations of the early theoreticians of Social Democracy in Russia. A generation of intellectuals, as Haimson has observed, 'lay their imprint on their successors, if only by defining the intellectual grounds on which the succeeding generation may challenge them'.[8] Hence the great interest in the Social Democratic camp in the 1890s in that same question to which Plekhanov had addressed himself in the 1880s: was capitalism developing in Russia, or was it a stunted or coincidental growth? This was the central problem tackled by Struve in his *Critical Notes on the Question of the Economic Development of Russia* (1894) and by Lenin in his work *The Development of Capitalism in Russia* (1899), because the Populists had made its examination unavoidable.

Thus in 1890 the revolutionary movement in Russia, despite some superficial indications to the contrary, remained vigorous after almost a decade of retrenchment. True, the movement was now tending in a direction which the impetuous libertarian socialists of the early 1870s, with their immediate concern for the suffering peasantry, had not foreseen and was taking a course which they would not entirely have approved of. (Indeed, Mikhaylovsky and others of his generation could not look in a more or less disengaged way, as could the younger Social Democrats, at the plight of the peasantry during the famine of 1891–2.) An idealistic vision was giving way to sober pragmatism. The great ambitions generated by humanitarian impulses were being supplanted by prudent calculation as to what it was possible to achieve in given circumstances. The socialists of the late 1880s and early 1890s may consequently have been less attractive in some respects than their quixotic predecessors. But they were able to make sounder judgements about the relative revolutionary potential of various sections of the Russian population and were more deeply aware of the value of a secure organisational base and thorough theoretical preparation. They were therefore better equipped to seize the opportunities which Russia's new industrial age was about to offer them. And yet, for all the novelty of their approach, they remained the heirs to a now considerable revolutionary tradition, to which they owed much in terms of operational practice, contacts, inspiration, determination and confidence, a tradition which it had been the unglamorous but invaluable service of the revolutionary groups of the 1880s to preserve.

❀ KEY TO ABBREVIATIONS USED IN THE NOTES AND BIBLIOGRAPHY

AIU   *Aleksandr Il'ich Ul'yanov i delo 1 marta 1887g.*, compiled by A. I. Ul'yanova-Yelizarova, Moscow–Leningrad, 1927

GM   *Golos minuvshego*

GOT   *Gruppa 'Osvobozhdeniye truda'*, ed. L. G. Deych, 6 vols., Moscow–Leningrad, 1924–8

IRS   *Istoriko-revolyutsionnyy sbornik*, ed. V. I. Nevsky, 3 vols. Moscow–Leningrad, 1924–6

IS   *Izbrannyye sochineniya*

KA   *Krasnyy arkhiv*

KL   *Krasnaya letopis'*

KS   *Katorga i ssylka*

LN   *Literaturnoye nasledstvo*

LPNV   *Literatura partii Narodnoy voli*, Moscow, 1907

LR   *Letopis' revolyutsii*

MG   *Minuvshiye gody*

NV, I   *Narodovol'tsy posle 1-go marta 1881 goda*, ed. A. V. Dikovskaya-Yakimova, Moscow, 1928

NV, II   *Narodovol'tsy 80-kh i 90-kh godov*, ed. A. V. Dikovskaya-Yakimova, Moscow, 1929

NV, III   *Narodovol'tsy, sbornik III*, ed. A. V. Dikovskaya-Yakimova, Moscow, 1931

Obzor   *Obzor vazhneyshikh doznaniy, proizvodivshikhsya po delam o gosudarstvennykh prestupleniyakh v zhandarmskikh upravleniyakh imperii*

PR	*Proletarskaya revolyutsiya*
PSS	*Polnoye sobraniye sochineniy*
RN	*Revolyutsionnoye narodnichestvo 70-kh godov XIX veka*, ed. S. N. Valk *et al.*, 2 vols., Moscow–Leningrad, 1964–5
RZh	*Revolyutsionnaya zhurnalistika semidesyatykh godov*, ed. B. Bazilevsky, Paris, 1905
SEER	*The Slavonic and East European Review*
Soch.	*Sochineniya*
SR	*The Slavic Review* (formerly *The American Slavonic and East European Review*)
SS	*Sobraniye sochineniy*

Note: For the sake of consistency, titles of works published in Russian before the orthographic reform of 1917–18 have been treated as if they had appeared in their modernised form.

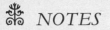 *NOTES*

PREFACE

1 See the bibliography for details of all works to which reference is made in the preface.

I RUSSIAN REVOLUTIONARY POPULISM BEFORE I MARCH 1881

1 The precise content of 'Populism' (*narodnichestvo*) has been the subject of much debate. Marxist historians, with their interest in the economic realities which they believe lie at the core of any social or political doctrine, see as central to Populism the view that Russia could follow a distinctive path of economic development and build an agrarian socialism based on the existing peasant commune. Thus Walicki, following Lenin, defines Populism as an 'ideological reaction to the development of capitalism' in Russia and 'to the capitalist economy and socialist thought of the West'. This ideology, he contends, expressed the 'class standpoint of small producers (mainly peasants)' who were 'willing to get rid of the remnants of serfdom' but who were at the same time 'endangered by the development of capitalism' (Andrzej Walicki, *The Controversy over Capitalism: Studies in the Social Philosophy of the Russian Populists* (Oxford, 1969), pp. 1–28, esp. 26, 12); see also B. Koz'min, '"Narodniki" i "narodnichestvo"', *Voprosy literatury*, 9 (1957), pp. 116–35. Some non-Marxist historians, on the other hand, see a quasi-religious preoccupation with moral issues as more fundamental to Populism than any economic doctrine or 'class standpoint' (see, for example, James P. Scanlan, 'Peter Lavrov: an intellectual biography' in his English edition of Lavrov's *Historical Letters* (Berkeley and Los Angeles, 1967), pp. 40–1). Use of the term 'Populism' is further complicated by its ambiguity. It perhaps most commonly denotes a particular set of views on certain economic and sociological questions, but is also often used loosely to define the outlook of almost all revolutionaries or revolutionary groups active in Russia between the period of reforms, the early 1860s, and the early 1890s when a Social Democratic movement began properly to develop there. The point has also been made

173

that the name 'Populist' (*narodnik*) was not adopted by the revolutionaries of the early 1870s, whom it is now common to describe as 'Populists', and that when it was given currency it tended to be used in rather narrow meanings to refer to particular factions within the broad socialist movement (see Richard Pipes, 'Narodnichestvo: a semantic enquiry', *SR*, 23: 3 (1964), pp. 441–58). The fact that the use of the term 'Populism' is fraught with such difficulties is perhaps reflected in the modification of the title of the monumental work by the Italian historian, Franco Venturi, when it appeared in English translation (*Il Populismo russo* (Turin, 1952), translated as *The Roots of Revolution: A History of the Populist and Socialist Movements in Nineteenth-Century Russia* (London, 1960)).

In the present study the term 'Populism' is used in two senses, one broad and one narrow. Firstly, it refers to something larger than a set of economic and sociological views, namely to a general outlook of which these views were an integral part and which it is the purpose of the first section of Chapter 1 to describe. Secondly, in accordance with Russian usage of the 1880s, it refers to the thought of those socialists who in that decade saw themselves as opponents of Narodnaya Volya and supporters of the position adopted in 1879–80 by Chornyy Peredel. The term 'Populist' has two corresponding meanings. Where the terms are used in any other sense, then their particular meaning in the context is explained.

2 See Baron A. von Haxthausen, *The Russian Empire: Its People, Institutions, and Resources* (2 vols., London, 1856), I, pp. 123–35.

3 See Bakunin's speech of November 1847 at a Parisian banquet on the anniversary of the Polish uprising of 1830 in his *IS* (5 vols., Petersburg–Moscow, 1919–21), III, pp. 43–5; his 'Vozzvaniye k slavyanam', *ibid.*, pp. 57–9; and his article 'Russkiye dela' (originally published in German) in *Sobraniye sochineniy i pisem 1828–1876* (4 vols., Moscow, 1934–5), III, esp. pp. 405–9.

4 See A. I. Gertsen [Herzen], 'La Russie', *SS* (30 vols., Moscow, 1954–65), VI, pp. 150–86, esp. 162–4; 'Du développement des idées révolutionnaires en Russie', *ibid.*, VII, pp. 9–132, esp. 25, 125; 'Le peuple russe et le socialisme', *ibid.*, pp. 271–306, esp. 288, 291; and 'La Russie et le vieux monde', *ibid.*, XII, pp. 134–66, esp. 144, 152.

5 See, for example, N. G. Chernyshevsky's review of Haxthausen's book in his *PSS* (15 vols., Moscow, 1939–50), IV, pp. 303–48, esp. 316–17, 328, 334, 340–1. See also his article on the Slavophiles and the commune (*ibid.*, pp. 737–61, esp. 744–6, 756, 760); 'Kritika filosofskikh predubezhdeniy protiv obshchinnogo zemlevladeniya', *ibid.*, V, pp. 357–92, esp. 362–3; 'Ekonomicheskaya deyatel'nost' i zakon-odatel'stvo', *ibid.*, pp. 576–626, esp. 615ff; and 'Suyeveriye i pravila logiki', *ibid.*, pp. 686–710.

6 See, for example, N. A. Dobrolyubov, 'O stepeni uchastiya narodnosti v razvitii russkoy literatury', *SS* (9 vols., Moscow–Leningrad, 1961–3), II, pp. 218–72; 'Narodnoye delo', *ibid.*, V, pp. 246–85, esp. 284–5; 'Cherty dlya kharakteristiki russkogo prostonarod'ya', *ibid.*, VI, pp. 221–88, esp. 224ff, 240ff, 266ff. The article 'Cherty dlya kharakteristiki' was written *à propos* of the stories of Marko-Vovchok. See also 'Povesti i rasskazy S. T. Slavutinskogo', *SS*, VI, pp. 49–64, esp. 52ff, and the letter in IX, p. 402.

7 On the popularity of the work of the little-known economist and publicist Bervi, see, for example, O. V. Aptekman, *Obshchestvo 'Zemlya i Volya' 70-kh godov* (Petrograd, 1924), pp. 72–5; M. F. Frolenko, 'Dvizheniye 70-kh godov', *SS* (2 vols., Moscow, 1932), I, p. 172; and N. A. Charushin, *O dalyokom proshlom* (Moscow, 1973), p. 64.

8 N. Flerovsky [V. V. Bervi], *Polozheniye rabochego klassa v Rossii* (St Petersburg, 1869), pp. 191–2, 204–5, 80ff; N. K. Mikhaylovsky, *Soch.* (6 vols., St Petersburg, 1896–7), I, col. 807.

9 See, for example, S. V. Maksimov, *Lesnaya Glush'. Kartiny narodnogo byta iz vospominaniy i putevykh zametok* (2 vols., St Petersburg, 1871); D. L. Mordovtsev, *Gaydamachina* (1870); *idem, Politicheskiye dvizheniya Russkogo naroda* (1871); F. V. Livanov, *Raskol'niki i Ostrozhniki; ocherki i rasskazy* (4 vols., St Petersburg, 1868–73); and V. V. Andreyev, *Raskol i yego znacheniye v narodnoy Russkoy istorii* (St Petersburg, 1870). A. P. Shchapov's pioneering work on the schism, a dissertation written at Kazan' University, had been published in 1859 under the title *Russkiy Raskol Staroobryadstva . . . .*

10 On the influence of Nekrasov on revolutionaries of the 1870s and 1880s see, for example, Charushin, *op. cit.*, p. 43; Vera Figner, *Zapechatlyonnyy trud* (2 vols., Moscow, 1964), I pp. 91–2; P. Kropotkin, *Memoirs of a Revolutionist* (2 vols., London, 1899), I, p. 111; N. A. Morozov, *Povesti moyey zhizni* (2 vols., Moscow, 1961), I, pp. 352–3; G. V. Plekhanov, 'N. A. Nekrasov', *Soch.* (24 vols., Moscow–Leningrad, 1923–7), X, pp. 377–95, esp. 379, 386ff.

11 N. I. Ziber, *Teoriya tsennosti i kapitala D. Rikardo v svyazi s pozdneyshimi dopolneniyami i raz'yasneniyami* (Kiev, 1871). There is a Soviet edition of Ziber's works, *Izbrannyye ekonomicheskiye proizvedeniya* (2 vols., Moscow, 1959). On Ziber, see A. L. Reuel', *Russkaya ekonomicheskaya mysl' 60–70-kh godov XIX veka i marksizm* (Moscow, 1956), pp. 287–341. For Mikhaylovsky's discussion of Ziber's dissertation, see his *Soch.*, I, col. 814.

12 G. Z. Yeliseyev, 'Plutokratiya i yeyo osnovy', in *Narodnicheskaya ekonomicheskaya literatura*, ed. N. K. Karataycv (Moscow, 1958), p. 125.

13 Mikhaylovsky, 'Chto takoye progress?', *Soch.*, I, cols. 1–150, esp. 56, 132ff, 141, 148.

14 On the impact of the *Historical Letters* on revolutionaries of the time, see, for example, Charushin, *op. cit.*, p. 53; Aptekman, *op. cit.*, pp. 74–5; Frolenko, 'Dvizheniye 70-kh godov', p. 172; Vl. Debagoriy-Mokriyevich, *Vospominaniya* (Paris, 1894), p. 14.

15 P. L. Mirtov [Lavrov], *Istoricheskiye pis'ma* (St Petersburg, 1870), pp. 50–64. This text is reproduced in a so-called 'second' edition printed in St Petersburg in 1905 under the pseudonym S. S. Arnol'di. The actual second edition (the so-called 'second edition, supplemented and corrected' and sometimes known also as the 'Paris edition') was published in Geneva in 1891. It is this actual second edition that is reprinted in P. L. Lavrov, *IS* (4 vols. published, Moscow, 1934–), I, pp. 163–394, and in *idem, Filosofiya i sotsiologiya: Izbrannyye proizvedeniya* (2 vols., Moscow, 1965), II, pp. 19–295; but since it contains much material added by Lavrov in 1872, 1881 and 1891 and unknown to the revolutionaries examined in this study it cannot be used here.

16 The most influential ethic in the radical camp in the 1860s was the 'rational egoism' expounded by Chernyshevsky in works such as 'The anthropological principle in philosophy' ('Antropologicheskiy printsip v filosofii', *PSS*, VII, pp. 222–95). Chernyshevsky contended that all one's actions are governed by self-interest and that people should cultivate (or be taught) the ability to derive their selfish pleasure from acts of general utility. As has often been noted, though, it is tempting to interpret Chernyshevsky's own dedication of his life to a social and political cause (and the tendency of his own fictional characters and the characters of much other fiction of the period to do the same) as an expression of the altruistic impulses whose existence Chernyshevsky was questioning.

17 The demand for the translation of ideals into action found expression in Turgenev's essay on 'Hamlet and Don Quixote' (delivered as a lecture in 1860) and in a series of

three public lectures on the 'contemporary significance of philosophy' which Lavrov delivered in St Petersburg in 1860, at the very period when interest in the 'positive hero' was developing in literary circles. Lavrov emphasised the importance of a capacity for 'critical thought' (*kritika*) and of the 'firmness of character' (*reshimost' kharaktera*) without which any ideal that might give shape and purpose to one's life would remain sterile (see Lavrov's 'Tri besedy o sovremennom znachenii filosofii' in his *Filosofiya i sotsiologiya*, I, pp. 513–73, esp. 551ff).

18 Lavrov, 'Diagnoz i retsepty obshchestvennykh medikov', *IS*, IV, p. 166; 'Komu prinadlezhit budushcheye?' *ibid.*, III, p. 126; 'Poteryannyye sily revolyutsii', *ibid.*, p. 158. See also *Russkoy sotsial'no-revolyutsionnoy molodyozhi* (hereafter *Russkoy molodyozhi*), *ibid.*, p. 349.

19 *Idem*, 'Komu prinadlezhit budushcheye?', p. 126.

20 *Idem*, *Narodniki-propagandisty 1873–78 godov* (St Petersburg, 1907), pp. 93–6.

21 See, for example, 'Poteryannyye sily revolyutsii', pp. 158–60; and 'Znaniye i revolyutsiya', *IS*, II, pp. 68–9.

22 See the programme for *Vperyod!* in *'Vperyod!', 1873–1877*, ed. Boris Sapir (2 vols., Dordrecht, 1970), II, p. 162 (Lavrov's italics).

23 *Ibid.*, pp. 162–3; *idem*, *Russkoy molodyozhi*, pp. 342, 350–1; 'Znaniye i revolyutsiya', p. 68.

24 *Idem*, *Gosudarstvennyy element v budushchem obshchestve*, *IS*, IV, e.g. pp. 390–2.

25 *Idem*, 'Parizhskaya kommuna 1871 goda', *IS*, IV, pp. 24–5.

26 *Idem*, 'Uchonyye fantazii liberal'nykh optimistov', *IS*, IV, p. 175; 'Poteryannyye sily revolyutsii', pp. 157, 161; 'Otvet russkomu konstitutsionalistu', *IS*, IV, p. 170; *'Vperyod!', 1873–1877*, II, p. 161.

27 *Idem*, 'Sotsial'no-revolyutsionnaya i burzhuaznaya nravstvennost'', *IS*, IV, p. 64.

28 *Ibid.*, pp. 69–70; *idem*, *Russkoy molodyozhi*, p. 364; 'Znaniye i revolyutsiya', p. 75.

29 *Idem*, *'Vperyod!', 1873–1877*, II, pp. 155–6; *Russkoy molodyozhi*, p. 361.

30 *Idem*, 'Znaniye i revolyutsiya', pp. 69, 74–7, 79, 81; see also p. 120.

31 Evgeny Lampert, *Studies in Rebellion* (London, 1957), p. 133.

32 Bakunin, *Parizhskaya kommuna i ponyatiye o gosudarstvennosti*, *IS*, IV, p. 258.

33 *Idem*, *Gosudarstvennost' i anarkhiya*, in *Archives Bakounine*, ed. Arthur Lehning (7 vols. published, Leiden, 1961–), III, p. 114.

34 *Idem*, *Parizhskaya kommuna i ponyatiye o gosudarstvennosti*, p. 257. It should be noted, however, that Bakunin did not consistently subscribe to the view that the masses should be sole masters of their own destiny. During the period of his association with Nechayev in the late 1860s he had envisaged the formation of a 'secret organisation, inspired by one thought, one objective', operating everywhere according to a preconceived plan and lending order to the anarchy which would follow a popular uprising. Bakunin sought to reconcile this plan for 'collective dictatorship' with the axiom that the people themselves must carry out the revolution by attributing great dedication and the highest integrity to the members of the secret organisation and also by conceding to them no 'officially recognised power' (see Michael Confino, 'Bakunin et Nečaev', *Cahiers du monde russe et soviétique*, 7: 4 (1966), p. 660). It was the views propagated in *Gosudarstvennost' i anarkhiya*, though, which were known to the Russian revolutionaries of the 1870s and espoused by them (see also note 36 below).

35 See his pamphlet of 1862, *Narodnoye delo: Romanov, Pugachov ili Pestel'*, *IS*, III, pp. 75–91, esp. 82ff.

36 See, for example, *Protsess 193-kh* (Moscow, 1906), pp. 24, 29, 31, 65–70.

37 See Bakunin, 'Pribavleniye A' to *Gosudarstvennost' i anarkhiya*, pp. 164–79, esp. 168, 166, 170, 175.

38 *Ibid.*, pp. 168, 174, 177; Lampert, *op. cit.*, p. 148.

39 On the unpopularity of Tkachov's views among revolutionaries of the 1870s, see, for example, *Obshchina*, 8–9 (Geneva, 1878), p. 1; Morozov, *op. cit.*, II, p. 396; Figner, *op. cit.*, I, p. 129; [Ya. V. Stefanovich], 'Russkaya revolyutsionnaya emigratsiya', *GOT*, III, p. 284; L. G. Deych, *Russkaya revolyutsionnaya emigratsiya 70-kh godov* (St Petersburg, 1920), pp. 83–4; [P. B. Aksel'rod], *Perezhitoye i peredumannoye* (Berlin, 1923), p. 163. Even Tkachov himself admitted that the circulation of his journal, *Nabat*, in Russia was small (see 'Materialy dlya biografii P. N. Tkachova', *Byloye*, 8: 20 (1907), p. 165.

40 See, for example, Tkachov, 'Retsenziya na knigi Yu. Zhukovskogo', *IS* (5 vols. published, Moscow, 1932–), I, pp. 69–70; 'Podrastayushchiye sily', *ibid.*, p. 276; 'Rol' mysli v istorii', *ibid.*, III, pp. 214–15.

41 *Idem*, 'Retsenziya na sobraniye sochineniy Gerberta Spensera', *IS*, V, pp. 301–2; 'Nauka v poezii i poeziya v nauke', *IS*, II, pp. 93–4, 100–1; 'Rol' mysli v istorii', p. 215. See also 'Retsenziya na knigi Yu. Zhukovskogo', p. 69.

42 *Idem*, 'Retsenziya na knigu Teodora Grizingera', *IS*, I, pp. 260–1.

43 *Idem*, 'Otkrytoye pis'mo gospodinu Fridrikhu Engel'su', *IS*, III, pp. 90–2.

44 *Idem*, *Zadachi revolyutsionnoy propagandy v Rossii*, *IS*, III, pp. 69–70; 'Revolyutsionery-reaktsionery', *ibid.*, pp. 272–5.

45 *Idem*, 'Razbityye illyuzii', *IS*, I, pp. 350, 369.

46 *Idem*, 'Nashi illyuzii', *IS*, III, pp. 241–3 (Tkachov's italics).

47 *Idem*, 'Narod i revolyutsiya', *IS*, III, pp. 267–8.

48 *Idem*, *Zadachi revolyutsionnoy propagandy v Rossii*, pp. 55–6.

49 *Ibid.*, p. 71.

50 *Idem*, '"Nabat" (Programma zhurnala)', *IS*, III, pp. 223).

51 See, for example, *ibid.*, pp. 227ff; and *idem*, 'Organizatsiya sotsial'no-revolyutsionnoy partii', *IS*, III, pp. 285–94.

52 *Idem*, 'Zhertvy dezorganizatsii revolyutsionnykh sil', *IS*, III, pp. 382, 395–6.

53 One of Tkachov's early essays (which includes a review of Spielhagen's popular novel, *In Reih und Glied* (1868) – see below, Chapter 4, p. 134) is entitled 'Lyudi budushchego i geroi meshchanstva' ('People of the future and the heroes of the *meshchanstvo* [lower middle class]', *IS*, I, pp. 173–233). See also 'Novyy fazis revolyutsionnogo dvizheniya', *IS*, III, p. 429.

54 *Idem*, 'Retsenziya na knigi Yu. Zhukovskogo', pp. 71–2.

55 See N. V. Chaykovsky, 'Cherez pol stoletiya: Otkrytoye pis'mo k druz'yam', *Golos minuvshego na chuzhoy storone*, 3:16 (1926), p. 184; Charushin, *op. cit.*, pp. 100, 108–9; Debagoriy-Mokriyevich, *op. cit.*, pp. 13–14; Aptekman, *op. cit.*, p. 202; Frolenko, 'Dvizheniye 70-kh godov', p. 168; *RN*, I, p. 85; Kropotkin, *op. cit.*, II, pp. 107–8, 116–17. 'Chaykovtsy' is rather a misnomer for the members of this group, for Chaykovsky himself was not in the first instance the leading organiser (Natanson played that role), nor did he remain at the centre of the group throughout the period in which it was active.

56 Kropotkin, *op. cit.*, II, p. 107; Chaykovsky, *op. cit.*, p. 183 (Chaykovsky's italics).

57 See *RN*, I, pp. 80–4.

58 On the activity of the Chaykovtsy among the workers in St Petersburg, see especially Charushin, *op. cit.*, pp. 126ff, 141ff; Kropotkin, *op. cit.*, pp. 117–21; S. S. Sinegub, 'Vospominaniya Chaykovtsa', *Byloye*, 8 (1906), pp. 39–41; [I. Ye. Deniker], 'Vospominaniya I. Ye. Denikera', *KS*, 4: 11 (1924), pp. 29, 36; the testimony of Nizovkin (*RN*, I, pp. 245–51); and L. E. Shishko, *Obshchestvennoye dvizheniye v shestidesyatykh i pervoy polovine semidesyatykh godov* (Moscow, 1920), pp. 83–4. See also Sh. M. Levin, 'Kruzhok chaykovtsev i propaganda sredi peterburgskikh rabochikh v nachale 1870-kh g.g.', *KS*, 12: 61 (1929), pp. 7–27.

59 See *RN*, I, pp. 86ff. Although Kropotkin's document is not a formal programme it is generally accepted as a fair summary of the consensus of opinion among the Chaykovtsy.

60 Frolenko, 'Dvizheniye 70-kh godov', p. 178; *idem*, 'Khozhdeniye v narod 1874 goda', *SS*, I, p. 202; A. I. Ivanchin-Pisarev, *Khozhdeniye v narod* (Moscow–Leningrad, 1929), p. 12; N. K. Bukh, *Vospominaniya* (Moscow, 1928), p. 54.

61 Debagoriy-Mokriyevich, *op. cit.*, p. 63.

62 Frolenko, 'Khozhdeniye v narod 1874 goda', p. 197; S. M. Stepnyak [Kravchinsky], *Podpol'naya Rossiya*, in *Izbrannoye* (Moscow, 1972), p. 395.

63 *Protsess 193-kh*, p. 172.

64 Ivanchin-Pisarev, *op. cit.*, p. 19; *Obshchina*, 6–7 (1878), pp. 25–6; *RN*, I, p. 262.

65 *Obshchina*, 8–9 (1878), p. 9; Bukh, *op. cit.*, pp. 89–90.

66 See, for example, Debagoriy-Mokriyevich, *op. cit.*, pp. 72–4; *Obshchina*, 8–9 (1878), p. 9; Bukh, *op. cit.*, p. 89; Deniker, *op. cit.*, p. 26.

67 A. Lukashevich, 'V narod!', *Byloye*, 3: 15 (1907), pp. 28, 35.

68 *Obshchina*, 8–9 (1878), p. 12.

69 Lukashevich, *op. cit.*, p. 30; Ivanchin-Pisarev, *op. cit.*, pp. 21–2.

70 See *RN*, I, p. 266; and Lavrov, *Narodniki-propagandisty 1873–78 godov*, p. 204.

71 *RN*, I, pp. 277–8.

72 *Obshchina*, 6–7 (1878), p. 25; Debagoriy-Mokriyevich, *op. cit.*, p. 74.

73 See, for example, Bukh, *op. cit.*, p. 87; and *Protsess 193-kh*, p. 171.

74 On the 'Muscovites', see B. Bazilevsky [V. Ya. Yakovlev] (ed.), *Gosudarstvennyye prestupleniya v Rossii v XIX veke*, 3 vols. (II, Stuttgart, 1904), pp. 157–415; and I. S. Dzhabadari, 'Protsess 50-ti (Vserossiyskaya sotsial'no-revolyutsionnaya organizatsiya 1874–1877g.)', *Byloye*, 8: 20 (1907), pp. 1–26; 9: 21 (1907), pp. 169–92; 10: 22 (1907), pp. 168–97. See also Sh. M. Levin, 'Obshchestvennoye dvizheniye v Moskve v 1868–1882gg.', *Istoriya Moskvy*, IV (Moscow, 1954), pp. 355–61.

75 The fullest memoirist's account of Zemlya i Volya is Aptekman's (see especially pp. 177–377). For secondary accounts, see Venturi, *op. cit.*, pp. 558–632; and P. S. Tkachenko, *Revolyutsionnaya narodnicheskaya organizatsiya 'Zemlya i volya' 1876–1879 gg.* (Moscow, 1961).

76 See *RN*, II, p. 27. See also p. 30 and *RZh*, pp. 71–2.

77 *RZh*, p. 153; A. P. Pribylyova-Korba and V. N. Figner (eds.), *Narodovolets Aleksandr Dmitriyevich Mikhaylov* (Leningrad, 1925) (hereafter *Mikhaylov*), pp. 105–6.

78 *RZh*, pp. 150–1.

79 *Ibid.*, pp. 240ff; *RN*, II, p. 28.

80 Pribylyova-Korba and Figner, *Mikhaylov*, pp. 101–2; *RZh*, p. 235.

81 *RZh*, pp. 76–7, 236.

82 See, for example, Pribylyova-Korba and Figner, *Mikhaylov*, pp. 47, 112; Aptekman, *op. cit.*, pp. 323–4; Plekhanov, *Vospominaniya ob A. D. Mikhaylove*, in *Soch.*, I, pp. 157ff; and *idem*, *Russkiy rabochiy v revolyutsionnom dvizhenii* (hereafter *Russkiy rabochiy*), in *Soch.*, III, p. 187. For a secondary account of this new 'going to the people', see V. N. Ginev, *Narodnicheskoye dvizheniye v srednem povolzh'ye* (Moscow–Leningrad, 1966), pp. 100–53.

83 On this episode, see Debagoriy-Mokriyevich, *op. cit.*, pp. 135ff; L. G. Deych, *Za polveka* (2 vols., Berlin, 1923), II, pp. 9ff; and Aptekman, *op. cit.*, pp. 277–82. The documents which Stefanovich composed are published in *Byloye*, 12 (1906), pp. 257–61.

84 Pribylyova-Korba and Figner, *Mikhaylov*, pp. 44 6, 96.

85 *RN*, II, pp. 34–42.

86 *RZh*, pp. 194ff.

87 *Ibid.*, p. 196; see also Aptekman, *op. cit.*, p. 315.

88 On the labour movement in St Petersburg and the 'North-Russian Workers' Union', see especially *RZh*, pp. 19–23, 140, 173–8, 206–15; Plekhanov, *Russkiy rabochiy*, pp. 159–86; *Rabocheye dvizheniye v Rossii v XIX veke*, ed. A. M. Pankratova (4 vols., Moscow, 1951–63), II, Part 2, esp. pp. 237–78; and E. A. Korol'chuk, *Severnyy soyuz russkikh rabochikh i revolyutsionnoye rabocheye dvizheniye 70-kh godov XIX v. v Peterburge* (Leningrad, 1946).

89 *RZh*, p. 258.

90 Aptekman, *op. cit.*, pp. 308ff; Plekhanov, *Russkiy rabochiy*, p. 164; *RZh*, p. 132.

91 On the Kazan' Square demonstration, see Plekhanov, *Russkiy rabochiy*, pp. 149–55; and the articles in *PR*, 4: 27 (1924), pp. 254–8, and *KS*, 7–8: 28–9 (1926), pp. 7–29.

92 See Bazilevsky (ed.), *Gosudarstvennyye prestupleniya v Rossii v XIX veke*, III (Paris, 1905); and *Protsess 193-kh*. The speeches of some of the defendants are printed in *RN*, I, pp. 352–67, 371–92. See also Dzhabadari, *Byloye*, 10: 22 (1907), pp. 192ff.

93 *RN*, II, pp. 30, 33.

94 See, for example, *RN*, II, p. 43; and *RZh*, pp. 29, 35, 46.

95 *RN*, II, p. 49.

96 *Ibid.*, p. 51.

97 S. M. Kravchinsky, *Smert' za smert'* (St Petersburg, 1878), esp. pp. 8ff.

98 *RZh*, p. 74.

99 *Ibid.*, pp. 104–5, 164, 228; see also *RN*, II, pp. 77–8. The pamphlet is entitled *Zazhivo pogrebyonnyye*.

100 *RZh*, pp. 237–41.

101 *Ibid.*, pp. 282–4.

102 *RZh*, pp. 293–4.

103 Pribylyova-Korba and Figner, *Mikhaylov*, pp. 127–8.

104 See Morozov, *op. cit.*, II, pp. 411–12.

105 On the final stages of the history of Zemlya i Volya, see especially Frolenko, 'Lipetskiy i voronezhskiy s'yezdy', *SS*, II, pp. 9–38; *idem*, 'Vozniknoveniye "Narodnoy voli"', *ibid.*, pp. 39–51; Morozov, *op. cit.*, II, pp. 407–32; Aptekman, *op. cit.*, pp. 365–77; and Figner, *op. cit.*, I, pp. 181–93.

106 See Plekhanov's leading article in *Chornyy peredel*, 2, pp. 1–4 (reprinted in *Soch.*, I, pp. 122–31; see especially p. 127).

107   See *S. V. Perovskaya* (London, 1882), pp. 21, 18–19.

108   *Obzor*, III (1882), p. 2.

109   *LPNV* pp. 148–9.

110   *Chornyy peredel*, 1 (London, 1880), p. 12.

111   See Plekhanov, *Soch.*, I, pp. 135–6.

112   *Dela i dni*, 2 (1921), p. 86.

113   Ye. Koval'skaya, *Yuzhno-russkiy rabochiy soyuz* (Moscow, 1926), pp. 13ff.

114   The main studies of Narodnaya Volya have been made by Venturi, *op. cit.*, pp. 633–720; S. S. Volk, *Narodnaya Volya, 1879–1882* (Moscow–Leningrad, 1966); M. G. Sedov, *Geroicheskiy period revolyutsionnogo narodnichestva* (Moscow, 1966); V. A. Tvardovskaya, *Sotsialisticheskaya mysl' Rossii na rubezhe 1870–1880 gg.* (Moscow, 1969). See also Tvardovskaya's 'Organizatsionnyye osnovy "Narodnoy voli"', *Istoricheskiye zapiski*, 67 (1960), pp. 103–44.

115   On the political crisis of the years 1879–81, see especially M. I. Kheyfets, *Vtoraya revolyutsionnaya situatsiya v Rossii: konets 70-kh – nachalo 80-kh godov XIX veka* (Moscow, 1963); and P. A. Zayonchkovsky, *Krizis samoderzhaviya na rubezhe 1870–1880-kh godov* (Moscow, 1964).

116   *RN*, II, pp. 221–2.

117   *LPNV*, p. 84.

118   *Ibid.*, pp. 45–8, 87–90.

119   *Ibid.*, p. 454.

120   *Ibid.*, p. 487.

121   *Ibid.*, p. 84; see also p. 434.

122   *Ibid.*, p. 42.

123   *Ibid.*, p. 4.

124   *Ibid.*, p. 7.

125   *Ibid.*, pp. 434–5.

126   *Ibid.*, p. 435 (italics in original). See also *RN*, II, pp. 200–9, 380–1 n. 115; and Volk, *op. cit.*, p. 253, where the authenticity of the rules is accepted.

127   On the organisation in the armed forces, see especially M. Yu. Ashenbrenner, *Voyennaya organizatsiya Narodnoy Voli i drugiye vospominaniya* (Moscow, 1924), pp. 169–70, 185–90; Figner, *op. cit.*, I, pp. 231–44, 293–7; and the testimonies of Zavalishin in *KS*, 5: 18 (1925), pp. 223, 227. Police findings are summarised in *Obzor*, VI and VII (1883). See also L. T. Senchakova, *Revolyutsionnoye dvizheniye v russkoy armii i flote v kontse XIX – nachale XX v.* (Moscow, 1972), pp. 35–57.

128   *LPNV*, pp. 5–6. Tikhomirov seems to be paraphrasing Hamlet:

> the dread of something after death –
> The undiscover'd country, from whose bourn
> No traveller returns – puzzles the will,
> And makes us rather bear those ills we have
> Than fly to others that we know not of.   (III, i, 78–82)

129   *Ibid.*, p. 84.

130   *Ibid.*, pp. 6–7, 10ff. See also Figner, *op. cit.*, I, p. 312.

131   *LPNV*, pp. 6, 7, 84.

132   *Ibid.*, p. 7.

133 *Ibid.*, p. 28.

134 *Ibid.*, pp. 40, 43–4.

135 Tkachov, 'Chto zhe teper' delat'?', *IS*, III, pp. 441–7. See also 'Materialy dlya biografii P. N. Tkachova', *Byloye*, 8: 20 (1907), p. 165.

136 [Morozov], *Terroristicheskaya bor'ba* (London, 1880); V. Tarnovsky [G. G. Romanenko], *Terrorizm i rutina* (London, 1880).

137 Figner, *op. cit.*, I, p. 312.

138 See S. N. Valk, 'G. G. Romanenko (Iz istorii "Narodnoy Voli")', *KS*, 11: 48 (1928), pp. 40–1.

139 See *KS*, 5: 18 (1925), p. 219; and *LPNV*, p. 170.

140 See, for example, Pribylyova Korba, *'Narodnaya Volya'. Vospominaniya o 1870–1880 kh g.g.* (Moscow, 1926) (hereafter *'Narodnaya Volya'*), pp. 48–9; Bukh, 'Pervaya tipografiya "Narodnoy Voli"', *KS*, 8–9: 57–8 (1929), p. 66; Aptekman, *op. cit.*, p. 323; and Figner, *op. cit.*, I, p. 201.

141 [Oshanina], 'K istorii partii Narodnoy voli', *Byloye*, 6: 18 (1907), p. 6.

142 *LPNV*, pp. 153, 3, 48n, 83–4, 454, 42, 52.

143 *Ibid.*, pp. 43, 61, 94–5, 4, 85, 437; Sedov, *op. cit.*, pp. 246–7.

144 *LPNV*, pp. 8, 6, 147.

145 Pribylyova-Korba, *'Narodnaya Volya'*, p. 49.

146 See L. G. Deych, 'Aaron Zundelevich', *GOT*, II, pp. 192ff; and M. R. Popov, *Zapiski zemlevol'tsa* (Moscow, 1933), p. 221.

147 See *LPNV*, pp. 146, 8, 6, 81; and Figner, *op. cit.*, I, p. 203.

148 F. M. Dostoyevsky, *Brat'ya Karamazovy*, Book I, Chapter 5.

2 NARODNAYA VOLYA AFTER 1 MARCH 1881

1 *Pis'ma K. P. Pobedonostseva k Aleksandru III* (2 vols., Moscow, 1925–6), I, pp. 318–19.

2 *LPNV*, p. 453.

3 N. R[usanov], 'Sobytiye 1-ogo marta i Nikolay Vasil'yevich Shelgunov', *Byloye*, 3 (1906), p. 44.

4 See *LPNV*, p. 487.

5 *Ibid.*, pp. 451–4.

6 On these proposals, see Michael T. Florinsky, *Russia: A History and an Interpretation* (2 vols., New York, 1953), II, p. 1083; H. Seton-Watson, *The Decline of Imperial Russia, 1855–1914* (London, 1952), p. 72; *idem, The Russian Empire, 1801–1917* (Oxford, 1967), p. 429; Kheyfets, *op. cit.*, pp. 166–91; and Zayonchkovsky, *op. cit.*, pp. 283–95. It is generally agreed that the proposals, if implemented, would not have resulted in any great diminution of autocratic power, for the commissions were intended to have only a consultative function, not a legislative one.

7 Florinsky, *op. cit.*, II, p. 1087.

8 *Ibid.*, p. 1089. The main work of Pobedonostsev in English is Robert F. Byrnes' *Pobedonostsev, His Life and Thought* (Bloomington, 1968).

9 Florinsky, *op. cit.*, II, pp. 1090–1.

10 *LPNV*, p. 209.

11 *Ibid.*, p. 200.

12 See *NV*, I, pp. 165–7.

13 *LPNV*, pp. 220, 224.

14 On activity among the workers in Moscow and St Petersburg after 1 March 1881, see Pankratov, *Iz deyatel'nosti sredi rabochikh v 1880–1884 gg.* (Moscow, 1906) (hereafter *Iz deyatel'nosti*), p. 7; Volkov [I. I. Maynov], 'Narodovol'cheskaya propaganda sredi moskovskikh rabochikh v 1881 godu', *Byloye*, 2 (1906), pp. 177ff; [V. S. Lebedev], 'Programma vospominaniy chlena Isp. k-ta "Nar. Voli" V. S. Lebedeva', *NV*, I, p. 161; and *Obzor*, I (1881), p. 23.

15 A. I. Georgiyevsky, 'Kratkiy ocherk pravitel'stvennykh mer i prednachertaniy protiv studencheskikh besporyadkov' in *Materialy po universitetskomu voprosu*, 2 vols. (I, Stuttgart, 1902), pp. 23–4; L. A. Kuznetsov, 'Iz dalyokogo proshlogo', *NV*, I, pp. 26–7.

16 P. P. Viktorov, 'Pervoye otkrytoye revolyutsionno-marksistskoye vystupleniye v Rossii (1881 g.)', *PR*, 6–7: 18–19 (1923), pp. 36–8; Lebedev, *op. cit.*, p. 162.

17 Demidov San-Donato, *Yevreyskiy vopros v Rossii* (St Petersburg, 1883), pp. 74ff.

18 Harold Frederic, *The New Exodus: A Study of Israel in Russia* (London, 1892), p. 116.

19 See the secret despatches of Ignat'yev and consular agents of the Pan-Slavic societies, published as a pamphlet under the title *Russian Intrigues* (London, 1877).

20 Frederic, *op. cit.*, pp. 127–8; Louis Greenberg, *The Jews in Russia* (New Haven and London, 1965), II, p. 30.

21 Greenberg, *op. cit.*, p. 25.

22 Frederic, *op. cit.*, p. 126.

23 *LPNV*, p. 193.

24 *Ibid.*, pp. 196–7.

25 Printed in Valk, 'G. G. Romanenko', pp. 50–2.

26 *Ibid.*, p. 49.

27 *LPNV*, pp. 215ff. On Romanenko's authorship of contributions to the party's publications, see Dmitriy Kuz'min, *Narodovol'cheskaya zhurnalistika* (Moscow, 1930), pp. 63–4, 207.

28 L. G. Deych, 'O sblizhenii i razryve s narodovol'tsami. (K istorii vozniknoveniya gruppy "Osvobozhdeniye truda")', *PR*, 8: 20 (1923), p. 10.

29 Pribylyova-Korba, *'Narodnaya Volya'*, p. 196.

30 V. Ya. Bogucharsky [Yakovlev], *Iz istorii politicheskoy bor'by v 70-kh i 80-kh gg. XIX v.* (Moscow, 1912), p. 223.

31 See Leonard Schapiro, 'The role of the Jews in the Russian revolutionary movement', *SEER*, 40: 94 (1961), p. 154; and Abraham Ascher, 'Pavel Axel'rod: a conflict between Jewish loyalty and revolutionary dedication', *The Russian Review*, 24: 3 (1965), pp. 253ff.

32 See *Byloye*, 25 (1924), pp. 284ff.

33 See Volk, 'Pis'mo Ispolnitel'nogo Komiteta "Narodnoy voli" k zagranichnym tovarishcham', in *Issledovaniya po otechestvennomu istochnikovedeniyu* (Moscow–Leningrad, 1964), pp. 178–85.

34 The letter was published in *GOT*, III, pp. 143–51; see especially 144–5, 149–50.

35 Pribylyova-Korba, *'Narodnaya Volya'*, pp. 211–20; see also Figner, *op. cit.*, I, p. 261.

36 *LPNV*, pp. 244–7.

37 See, for example, Plekhanov's remarks, which are printed in *Literaturnoye naslediye G. V. Plekhanova* (8 vols., Moscow, 1934–40), I, p. 142.

38 [Oshanina], *op. cit.*, p. 6.

39 L. G. Deych, 'Ya. V. Stefanovich sredi narodovol'tsev', *GOT*, III, p. 109. See also *RN*, II, pp. 299, 385–6.

40 See V. N. Svetlova, 'Proval narodovol'cheskikh kruzhkov v Tiflise v 1882 g.', *NV*, I, pp. 29ff; and Ashenbrenner, *op. cit.*, pp. 89–90. See also the sources listed in note 127 to Chapter 1 above.

41 *LPNV*, p. 444.

42 *RN*, II, pp. 298, 301–2.

43 Quoted by John F. Baddeley, *Russia in the 'Eighties'* (London, 1921), p. 186.

44 Ashenbrenner, *op. cit.*, pp. 95ff.

45 Figner, *op. cit.*, I, p. 344.

46 *Obzor*, VII (1883), pp. 5–6.

47 I. I. Popov, 'Revolyutsionnyye organizatsii v Peterburge v 1882–1885 godakh' (hereafter 'Revolyutsionnyye organizatsii'), *NV*, I, pp. 51ff; V. A. Bodayev, 'N. M. Flyorov i "Podgotovitel'naya gruppa partii Narodnoy voli"', *NV*, II, pp. 16ff.

48 I. I. Popov, 'Revolyutsionnyye organizatsii', pp. 52ff; V. L. Burtsev, 'Iz moikh vospominaniy', *Svobodnaya Rossiya*, 1 (Geneva, 1889), p. 48; *LPNV*, p. 480.

49 *Obzor*, II (1881), p. 37.

50 *Ibid.*, III (1882), p. 48; *ibid.*, IX (1884), p. 9; Gr. Borzyakov, 'Revolyutsionnaya molodyozh' v Odesse v 1882–1884 gg.', *KS*, 8–9: 57–8 (1929), p. 151.

51 L. S. Zalkind, 'Vospominaniya narodovol'tsa', *KS*, 3: 24 (1926), p. 93.

52 Pankratov, *Iz deyatel'nosti*, pp. 20–1.

53 *Ibid.*, p. 19; Plekhanov, *Russkiy rabochiy*, pp. 190–2.

54 P. K. Peshekerov, 'Propaganda narodovol'tsev sredi rabochikh v Rostov-na-Donu v 1882–1884 g.g.', *NV*, I, pp. 116ff.

55 Some of the contributions to the journal are printed in *LN*, 2, 1932, pp. 79–93. Others are described by Valk in his article, 'Zhurnal rostovskikh rabochikh', *ibid.*, pp. 98, 100. See also Pankratov, *Iz deyatel'nosti*, p. 21; and Burtsev, *Za sto let* (London, 1897), p. 121. (Burtsev wrongly attributes the journal to a group in Yekaterinoslav.)

56 *Obzor*, I (1881), p. 29; *ibid.*, 'Vedomost'', pp. 11–12; M. M. Polyakov, 'Razgrom yekaterinoslavskoy narodovol'cheskoy gruppy v 1886 g.', *NV*, I, p. 145.

57 M. I. Drey, 'Zametka o rabochem dvizhenii v Odesse v 1880–1881 gg.', *KS*, 5: 12 (1924), p. 75. See also 'Iz pokazaniy N. I. Rysakova', *KA*, 6: 19 (1926), p. 180.

58 Peshekerov, *op. cit.*, pp. 124, 127. On Rudomyotov, see Peshekerov's article in *KS*, 11: 60 (1929), pp. 164–71.

59 [S. A. Ivanov], 'Iz narodovol'cheskikh vospominaniy S. A. Ivanova', *NV*, II, p. 34.

60 *Obzor*, VII (1883), p. 19; *ibid.*, X (1885), pp. 37–9; I. Genkin, 'Predatel' S. P. Degayev v Amerike', *KS*, 9: 106 (1933), pp. 132–5.

61 B. D. Orzhikh, 'V ryadakh "Narodnoy voli"', *NV*, III, p. 79.

62 M. V. Bramson, 'Otryvki iz vospominaniy (1883–1886 gg.)', *NV*, I, pp. 82–3; Yakubovich's testimonies, published in *KA*, 1: 38 (1930), pp. 71, 76–7; *LPNV*, pp. 478–9; and I. I. Popov, *Pyotr Filippovich Yakubovich* (Moscow, 1930), p. 11.

63 V. I. Sukhomlin, 'Iz epokhi upadka partii "Narodnaya volya"', *KS*, 6: 27 (1926), pp. 66ff; A. V. Gedeonovsky, 'Yaroslavskiy revolyutsionnyy kruzhok 1881–1886 gg.', *KS*, 3: 24 (1926), pp. 95–109; F. V. Smirnov, 'Otgoloski "Narodnoy voli" v Yaroslavle i Rybinske v 1882–1887 godakh', *NV*, III, pp. 237–8.

64 See V. Antonov, *Russkiy drug Marksa. German Aleksandrovich Lopatin* (Moscow, 1962), pp. 4ff.

65 M. R. Gots, 'Moskovskaya tsentral'naya gruppa partii "Narodnaya volya"', *NV*, I, p. 107; A. N. Bakh, *Zapiski narodovol'tsa* (Leningrad, 1931), p. 102; Orzhikh, *op. cit.*, p. 91.

66 *LPNV*, pp. 338-9.

67 *Obzor*, IX (1884), p. 20.

68 *Ibid.*, 'Prilozheniye III', pp. 97-100.

69 *KA*, 1: 38 (1930), p. 74.

70 *Ibid.*, p. 96.

71 See S. N. Valk, 'K istorii protsessa 21', *KA*, 5: 36 (1929), p. 124; *idem*, 'Rasporyaditel'naya komissiya i "Molodaya partiya Narodnoy voli" ', *KS*, 2: 75 (1931), p. 131.

72 *Idem*, 'Molodaya partiya Narodnoy voli', *Problemy marksizma*, 1: 3 (1930), p. 101; M. P. Shebalin, 'Peterburgskaya narodovol'cheskaya organizatsiya 1882-1883 gg.', *NV*, I, p. 47.

73 I. I. Popov, 'Revolyutsionnyye organizatsii', p. 69; *LPNV*, p. 338. See also *KA*, 5: 36 (1929), pp. 136-7; and Burtsev, 'Iz moikh vospominaniy', p. 49.

74 Burtsev, 'Iz moikh vospominaniy', p. 51.

75 Gots, *op. cit.*, p. 106.

76 See *KA*, 5: 36 (1929), p. 169 n. 25.

77 Gots, *op. cit.*, p. 107.

78 *KA*, 1: 38 (1930), p. 99.

79 I. I. Popov, 'F. V. Olesinov', *KS*, 5-6: 114-15 (1935), p. 228.

80 *LPNV*, p. 479.

81 Shebalin, *op. cit.*, p. 47.

82 See Orzhikh, *op. cit.*, pp. 75ff, 88-9.

83 *Ibid.*, p. 141.

84 *Ibid.*, p. 105.

85 *Ibid.*, pp. 120ff; A. N. Shekhter-Minor, 'Yuzhno-russkaya narodovol'cheskaya organizatsiya', *NV*, I, pp. 134-5.

86 [V. G. Bogoraz], *Bor'ba obshchestvennykh sil v Rossii* ([Novocherkassk], 1886), pp. 32ff, 5ff, 16ff, 37, 25.

87 *LPNV*, pp. 370, 367.

88 [L. Ya. Shternberg], 'Politicheskiy terror v Rossii 1884', reprinted in *Lavrov: Gody emigratsii: arkhivnyye materialy v dvukh tomakh*, ed. Boris Sapir (2 vols., Dordrecht, 1974), II, pp. 572-94, esp. 585, 582, 574-8 (Shternberg's italics). Compare *LPNV*, pp. 5-6, and see Chapter 1, note 128 above.

89 Bogoraz, *op. cit.*, pp. 72-4; *LPNV*, p. 371.

90 *Obzor*, XI (1886), pp. 28-9.

91 Orzhikh, *op. cit.*, pp. 97-101.

92 *LPNV*, p. 364.

93 Shternberg, *op. cit.*, pp. 578, 594.

94 Orzhikh, *op. cit.*, p. 134.

95 *LPNV*, pp. 371, 387-93.

96 Bogoraz, *op. cit.*, p. 2.

97 *Ibid.*, pp. 5, 56, 3, 85.

98 Shternberg, *op. cit.*, pp. 587, 579.

99 There is much material on this demonstration. See, for example, *Svobodnaya Rossiya*, 1 (1889), p. 59; I. D. Lukashevich, *I marta 1887 goda* (Petersburg, 1920), pp. 9–10; A. I. Ul'yanova-Yelizarova, 'Vospominaniya ob Aleksandre Il'iche Ul'yanove', *AIU*, pp. 101–3; S. A. Nikonov, 'Zhizn' studenchestva i revolyutsionnaya rabota kontsa vos'midesyatykh godov' (hereafter 'Zhizn' studenchestva'), *ibid.*, pp. 151–2; I. N. Chebotaryov, 'Vospominaniya ob Aleksandre Il'iche Ul'yanove i peterburgskom studenchestve 1883–1887 gg.', *ibid.*, pp. 246–7; Ye. I. Yakovenko, 'O vtorom 1-ye marta', *KS*, 32 (1927), p. 16; and M. A. Braginsky, 'Aleksandr Il'ich Ul'yanov', *ibid.*, pp. 50–1.

100 See I. D. Lukashevich, *op. cit.*, pp. 10–11; Chebotaryov, *op. cit.*, pp. 244–5; and Braginsky, *op. cit.*, pp. 45–6. See also B. S. Itenberg and A. Ya. Chernyak, *Zhizn' Aleksandra Ul'yanova* (Moscow, 1966), pp. 58–72.

101 Ul'yanova-Yelizarova, *op. cit.*, p. 99.

102 Braginsky, *op. cit.*, pp. 51–2.

103 Nikonov, *op. cit.*, p. 152.

104 *Svobodnaya Rossiya*, 1 (1889), p. 59.

105 I. D. Lukashevich, *op. cit.*, p. 27; Braginsky, *op. cit.*, p. 52.

106 O. M. Govorukhin, 'Vospominaniya ob A. I. Ul'yanove, P. Ya. Shevyryove, V. D. Generalove, i P. I. Andreyushkine', *AIU*, p. 228.

107 *Ibid.*, p. 235.

108 *Obzor*, XII (1887), p. 14.

109 See *AIU*, pp. 303–4.

110 *Ibid.*, p. 351.

111 I. D. Lukashevich, *op. cit.*, p. 5.

112 Ul'yanova-Yelizarova, *op. cit.*, p. 96; S. A. Nikonov, 'Iz vospominaniy ob A. I. Ul'yanove', *PR*, 2–3: 85–6 (1929), p. 176.

113 *AIU*, pp. 375ff.

114 Semyon Khlebnikov, 'Vospominaniya ob Aleksandre Il'iche Ul'yanove 1886–1887 g.', *AIU*, p. 265.

115 On Ginsburg's attempt to revive Narodnaya Volya, see P. L. Lavrov, 'Vospominaniya o Sof'ye Mikhaylovne Ginsburg', *GM*, 7–8 (1917), pp. 225–56; L. V. Freyfel'd, 'Iz zhizni narodovol'cheskikh organizatsiy kontsa 80-kh godov', *NV*, II, pp. 143ff; *idem*, 'Delo i protsess Sof'i Mikhaylovny Ginsburg i yeyo tovarishchey', *Narodnaya Volya pered tsarskim sudom* (2 vols., Moscow, 1931), II, pp. 109–20; M. I. Drey, 'K delu S. M. Ginsburg', *ibid.*, pp. 121–5; *Obzor*, XIV (1889), pp. 9ff; and *Sotsial Demokrat*, 4 (Geneva, 1892), pp. 46–63, in which the charges are reprinted.

116 Kacharovsky's programme is printed in *Obzor*, XV (1890), pp. 27–37. The journeyings and arrests are chronicled in *ibid.*, pp. 8–13, 37ff. See also Freyfel'd, 'Iz zhizni narodovol'cheskikh organizatsiy kontsa 80-kh godov', pp. 149–53; 'K istorii sabunayevskoy revolyutsionnoy organizatsii 1889–1890 godov', *NV*, III, pp. 250–5, 257–63; and N. Narbekov, 'N. I. Alyakritskiy', *KS*, 4: 77 (1931), p. 202.

3 'POPULISTS', 'MILITARISTS', 'CONSPIRATORS' AND OTHER GROUPS IN
THE 1880s

1 Quoted by R. V. Ivanov-Razumnik (*Istoriya russkoy obshchestvenny mysli*, 2nd edn (2 vols.,
St Petersburg, 1908), II, p. 317), whose chapter 'The age of social philistinism'
characterises the cultural atmosphere of the 1880s.

2 James H. Billington, *Mikhailovsky and Russian Populism* (Oxford, 1958), p. 147.

3 V. B[artenev], 'Vospominaniya peterburzhtsa o vtoroy polovine 80-kh godov', *MG*, 10
(1908), p. 169.

4 V. S. Golubev, 'Stranichka iz istorii rabochego dvizheniya', *Byloye*, 12 (1906), p. 105.

5 Ivanov-Ruzumnik, *op. cit.*, II, p. 334.

6 The quotations are from Act IV.

7 Tikhomirov's pamphlet was entitled *Pochemu ya perestal byt' revolyutsionerom*. On his
defection, see Kyril Tidmarsh, 'Lev Tikhomirov and a crisis in Russian radicalism', *The
Russian Review*, 20: 1 (1961), pp. 45-63; and Abbot Gleason, 'The emigration and
apostasy of Lev Tikhomirov', *SR*, 26: 3 (1967), pp. 414-29.

8 S. Mitskevich, *Na grani dvukh epokh: ot narodnichestva k marksizmu* (Moscow, 1937)
(hereafter *Na grani dvukh epokh*), p. 44.

9 L. N. Tolstoy, 'V chom moya vera?', *PSS* (90 vols., Moscow–Leningrad, 1928–58),
XXIII, pp. 304–465.

10 See Billington, *op. cit.*, p. 150; and N. V. Shelgunov, *Soch.*, 3rd edn (3 vols., St
Petersburg, [1905]), III, pp. 973–94.

11 P. A. Argunov, 'Moskovskiy kruzhok "Militaristov"', *NV*, I, p. 88. See Chapter 3,
pp. 83–5, on this group.

12 See Richard Wortman, *The Crisis of Russian Populism* (Cambridge, Mass., 1967),
pp. 42ff.

13 See Mikhaylovsky's letter to Professor Tsitovich in *Soch.*, IV, cols. 633–4.

14 For example, A. I. Vasil'chikov, *Zemlevladeniye i zemledeliye v Rossii i drugikh
Yevropeyskikh gosudarstvakh* (2 vols., St Petersburg, 1876); and A. S. Posnikov,
Obshchinnoye zemlevladeniye, 2nd edn (2 parts, Odessa, 1877–8).

15 See Billington, *op. cit.*, pp. 95–6; Aptekman, *op. cit.*, pp. 303ff.

16 Nikolay-on [N. F. Daniel'son], *Ocherki nashego poreformennogo obshchestvennogo khozyaystva*
(St Petersburg, 1893). The treatise 'Kapitalizatsiya zemlevladel'cheskikh dokhodov'
was republished as the first part of this book; see especially pp. 77–8.

17 V. V. [V. P. Vorontsov], *Sud'by kapitalizma v Rossii* (St Petersburg, 1892). Extracts are
reprinted in N. K. Karatayev (ed.), *Narodnicheskaya ekonomicheskaya literatura* (Moscow,
1958), see especially pp. 417–26, 463–4. On Daniel'son and Vorontsov, see also
Walicki, *The Controversy over Capitalism*, esp. pp. 109ff.

18 S. Yuzhakov, 'Formy zemlevladel'cheskogo proizvodstva v Rossii' in Karatayev, *op.
cit.*, see especially pp. 591–2, 603–4.

19 See P. Anatol'yev, 'K istorii zakrytiya zhurnala "Otechestvennyye zapiski"', *KS*, 8–9:
57–8 (1929), pp. 169–202.

20 Argunov, 'Moskovskiy kruzhok "Militaristov"', pp. 87ff.

21 *Ibid.* See also *idem*, 'Yeshcho ob "Obshchestve perevodchikov i izdateley"', *KS*, 9: 106
(1933), pp. 72–5; P. Anatol'yev, 'Obshchestvo perevodchikov i izdateley', *KS*, 3: 100
(1933), pp. 82–141; Yu. Z. Polevoy, *Zarozhdeniye marksizma v Rossii 1883–1894 gg.*

(Moscow, 1959), pp. 262ff; and S. V. Utechin, 'The "Preparatory Trend" in the Russian revolutionary movement in the 1880s', *St Antony's Papers*, 12 (1962), pp. 10–11.

22 *Perepiska K. Marksa i F. Engel'sa s russkimi politicheskimi deyatelyami*, 2nd edn (Moscow, 1951) (hereafter Marx and Engels, *Perepiska*), pp. 275–6. For Engels' reply, see pp. 276–7.

23 See the note 'Ot izdateley', printed in *IRS*, II, pp. 172–3 (also in *GOT*, II, pp. 88–90), and the letter 'Pis'mo k tovarishcham', *ibid.*, pp. 173–81 (also in *GOT*, II, pp. 90–102). This letter was subsequently a source of controversy between the historian Sergiyevsky, who considered it to have been written by a socialist living in Russia and close to the Muscovite revolutionary circles (*IRS*, II, p. 168) and Deych, who insisted that the letter had been written by Aksel'rod (see 'Vmesto bibliografii', *GOT*, III, p. 354). For the disputants this apparently trivial issue assumed great importance when they came to assess the extent to which Russian revolutionary groups, when they moved in the direction of Marxism and Social Democracy, were acting independently of the émigrés of the 'Emancipation of Labour' group. Deych, of course, was anxious to prove that the émigré group, to which he himself had belonged, *was* influential in this respect.

24 See, for example, his article 'Chastnovladel'cheskoye khozyaystvo v Rossii po zemskim statisticheskim dannym', *Yuridicheskiy vestnik*, 11–12: 26 (1887).

25 V. I. Lenin, 'Razvitiye kapitalizma v Rossii', in *PSS*, 5th edn (55 vols., Moscow, 1958–65), III, pp. 19, 214, 232, 263, 286.

26 See Anatol'yev, 'Obshchestvo perevodchikov i izdateley', p. 129.

27 Argunov, 'Moskovskiy kruzhok "Militaristov"', p. 91.

28 *Ibid.*, pp. 91–2.

29 See *Vestnik 'Narodnoy voli'*, 4 (1885), pp. 260–1; *GOT*, I, p. 194; and M. Mazowiecki, *Historya ruchu socyalistycznego w zaborze rosyjskim* (Cracow, 1903), p. 150n.

30 *Vestnik 'Narodnoy voli'*, 4 (1885), pp. 260–1.

31 Figner, *op. cit.*, II, p. 169. See also M. V. Novorussky, *Zapiski shlissel'burzhtsa 1887–1905* (Petersburg, 1920), p. 190; and Feliks Kon, *Istoriya revolyutsionnogo dvizheniya v Rossii* (Khar'kov, 1929), p. 146. There is further material on Yanovich in the obituary to him in *Przedświt*, 4 (Lipiec, 1902), and in the article 'K istorii otnosheniy partii "Narodnoy Voli" i partii "Proletariat"', *Byloye*, 7 (1906), pp. 294–7. There is also a biography of Yanovich in Lithuanian (V. Merkys, *Liudvikas Janavicius* (Vilnius, 1964)).

32 Argunov, 'Moskovskiy kruzhok "Militaristov"', p. 90; *idem*, 'Yeshcho ob "Obshchestve perevodchikov i izdateley"', pp. 78–9; Burtsev, 'Iz moikh vospominaniy', p. 48n.; I. I. Popov, 'Revolyutsionnyye organizatsii', pp. 49–50.

33 On the circles in the armed forces and the 'militarist' element in them, see *Obzor*, XI (1886), pp. 53ff; XII (1887), pp. 52ff; XIV (1889), p. 17; Bartenev, *MG*, 11 (1908), pp. 186–7; M. A. Braginsky, 'Iz vospominaniy o voyenno-revolyutsionnoy organizatsii (1884–1886gg.)', *NV*, II, pp. 116ff; and Senchakova, *op. cit.*, pp. 62–3.

34 Nikonov, 'Zhizn' studenchestva', pp. 146–7; Smirnov, *op. cit.*, p. 245.

35 *Svobodnaya Rossiya*, I, 1889, p. 59; Smirnov, *op. cit.*, pp. 244–5.

36 Nikonov, 'Zhizn' studenchestva', p. 143; I. D. Lukashevich, *op. cit.*, pp. 5ff; L. I. Anan'ina, 'Pervoye marta 1887 goda', *NV*, I, p. 152; Yakovenko, 'O vtorom 1-marta', pp. 14ff.

37 Nikonov, 'Zhizn' studenchestva', pp. 136ff; Chebotaryov, *op. cit.*, pp. 242ff; T.

Garnak, '1 marta 1887 goda – vtoroye 1 marta', *AIU*, pp. 269–70.

38 Bartenev, *MG*, 10 (1908), p. 170.

39 See P. K[udelli], 'Iz perepiski gruppy "Osvobozhdeniye truda"', *KL*, 2: 11 (1924), p. 194.

40 See S. Mazurenko, 'Ot "Chornogo peredela" do kommunisticheskoy partii', *Puti revolyutsii*, 2–3: 5–6 (Kazan', 1926), p. 26.

41 Alekseyev [Yu. A. Bunin], 'Neskol'ko slov o proshlom russkogo sotsializma i o zadachakh intelligentsii', *IRS*, III, pp. 187–202.

42 *Obzor*, VIII (1884), pp. 27–8; *ibid.*, I (1881), 'Vedomost'', pp. 48–51.

43 The proclamations, 'Lyude dobri!' and 'Russkomu narodu', are reprinted in *KS*, 1: 74 (1931), pp. 50–2.

44 Aleksey Makarevsky, 'Revolyutsionnyy Khar'kov v 1882–1885 gg.', *LR*, 5 (1923), p. 67.

45 *Obzor*, IX (1884), p. 10.

46 Mazurenko, *op. cit.*, pp. 5ff; Lidiya Loyko [Kvashnina], *Ot 'Zemli i voli' k VKP(B)* (Moscow–Leningrad, 1929), pp. 61ff; *Obzor*, XI (1886), pp. 90–1; I. Veden'yev, 'V khar'kovskikh revolyutsionnykh kruzhkakh 1882–1889 gg.', *LR*, 5 (1923), pp. 99ff.

47 Mazurenko, *op. cit.*, pp. 15–16.

48 *Ibid.*, pp. 16–19; *Obzor*, XI (1886), p. 89; Loyko, *op. cit.*, pp. 62–3. The proclamations are reprinted in *KS*, 1: 74 (1931), pp. 53–8.

49 Mitskevich, 'Kazantsy v Nizhnem', *Puti revolyutsii*, 2 (1922), p. 11.

50 M. Ye. Berezin *et al.*, 'Vospominaniya iz zhizni narodnicheskikh kruzhkov v Kazani (1875–1892 gg.)', *KS*, 10: 71 (1930), p. 112.

51 *Ibid.*, pp. 112–13.

52 *Ibid.*, p. 116; Figner, *op. cit.*, I, p. 290.

53 N. I. Tezyakov, 'Iz perezhitogo – Studencheskiye gody', *Kazanskiy meditsinskiy zhurnal*, 5–6 (Kazan', 1930), p. 500.

54 Figner, *op. cit.*, I, p. 290; *Obzor*, VIII (1884), pp. 76–8.

55 Bakh, *op. cit.*, pp. 73ff.

56 *Obzor*, X (1885), pp. 47–51.

57 Bakh, *op. cit.*, p. 71.

58 *Obzor*, X (1885), p. 47.

59 Berezin, *op. cit.*, pp. 115ff; Loyko, *op. cit.*, pp. 35–6, 57–60; *Obzor*, VII (1883), 'Vedomost'', pp. 7–8. The leaflet is reprinted in *KS*, 1: 74 (1931), pp. 52–3.

60 Berezin, *op. cit.*, pp. 121ff; Loyko, *op. cit.*, p. 58; Vladimir Zolotnitsky, 'Materialy k biografii Maksima Gor'kogo (A. M. Peshkova)', *Prozhektor*, 5: 75 (1926), p. 14; I. N. Moshinsky [Yu. Konarsky], *Na putyakh k 1-mu s'yezdu RS-DRP* (Moscow, 1928) (hereafter *Na putyakh*), p. 23. Quotations are from Zolotnitsky and Moshinsky (who cites Fokin) respectively. On the 'Chelyabinsk index', see N. V. Zdobnov, *Istoriya russkoy bibliografii do nachala XX veka*, 2nd edn (Moscow, 1951), pp. 423ff. On the circle in the Troitsk *gimnaziya*, see Yu. Podbel'sky, 'Papiy Podbel'skiy', *KS*, 3: 52 (1929), pp. 42–5; Ivan Sazhayev, 'P. P. Podbel'skiy v yego gimnazicheskiye gody', *KS*, 8–9: 57–8 (1929), pp. 267–72.

61 Berezin, *op. cit.*, pp. 121–2.

62 See Zolotnitsky, *op. cit.*, p. 14.

63 Moshinsky, *op. cit.*, p. 14.

64 Quoted by Zolotnitsky, *op. cit.*, p. 14.

65 N. Ya. Bykhovsky, 'Bulochnik Aleksey Maksimovich Peshkov i kazanskaya revolyutsionnaya molodyozh' kontsa 80-kh gg.', *Byloye*, 4: 32 (1925), pp. 209, 220.

66 Berezin, *op. cit.*, p. 122; Vl. Vilensky-Sibiryakov *et al.* (eds.), *Deyateli revolyutsionnogo dvizheniya v Rossii* (5 vols., Moscow, 1927–34), V, vypusk I, pp. 218–19.

67 Bykhovsky, *op. cit.*, pp. 206–7; Mitskevich, 'Kazantsy v Nizhnem', p. 11.

68 See M. Gorky [A. M. Peshkov], *Moi universitety*, in *PSS* (25 vols., Moscow, 1968–76), XVI, pp. 29ff.

69 Bykhovsky, *op. cit.*, p. 207.

70 Count Witte, *The Memoirs of Count Witte*, tr. and ed. Abraham Yarmolinsky (London, 1921), p. 14.

71 A. I. Ivansky (ed.), *Molodoy Lenin: Povest' v dokumentakh i memuarakh* (Moscow, 1964), p. 337.

72 P. S. Tkachenko, *Moskovskoye studenchestvo v obshchestvenno-politicheskoy zhizni Rossii vtoroy poloviny XIX veka* (Moscow, 1958) (hereafter *Moskovskoye studenchestvo*), p. 167.

73 *The History of the Year. A Narrative of the Chief Events and Topics of Interest from October 1, 1882, to September 30, 1883* (London, 1883), p. 254.

74 See Georgiyevsky, *op. cit.*, pp. 42ff.

75 See G. Ye. Khait, 'V kazanskom kruzhke', *Novyy mir*, 4 (1958), pp. 189–90 (this article consists largely of valuable extracts from archive material); Ivansky, *op. cit.*, pp. 358–9, 361–3; *Obzor*, XII (1887), pp. 92–3, 69–70; Berezin, *op. cit.*, p. 123; R. Nafigov, 'A. I. Ul'yanov i yego yedinomyshlenniki v Kazani', *Kommunist Tatarii*, 4–5: 388–9 (Kazan', 1966), pp. 126ff; M. K. Korbut, *Kazanskiy gosudarstvennyy universitet* (2 vols., Kazan', 1929–30), II, p. 200.

76 On the demonstrations, see especially Georgiyevsky, *op. cit.*, pp. 44–9; Ivansky, *op. cit.*, pp. 369ff; Korbut, *op. cit.*, II, pp. 173–8; Tkachenko, *Moskovskoye studenchestvo*, pp. 163–73.

77 Reprinted in Ivansky, *op. cit.*, pp. 325–6.

78 *Ibid.*, p. 322.

79 *Ibid.*, p. 348; Nafigov, *Pervyy shag v revolyutsiyu* (Kazan', 1970) (hereafter, *Pervyy shag*), p. 81.

80 Ivansky, *op. cit.*, p. 371.

81 *Ibid.*, p. 362; Khait, *op. cit.*, pp. 190–1. Some of the archive material on the circle was first published in *KA*, 1: 62 (1934), pp. 65–6. See also Vilensky-Sibiryakov *et al.*, *op. cit.*, III, vypusk 2, p. 1517.

82 M. Ul'yanova, 'V gimnazii', *Vospominaniya rodnykh o Lenine* (Moscow, 1955), p. 85.

83 Nafigov, *Pervyy shag*, p. 86.

84 Polevoy, *op. cit.*, p. 362.

85 S. Shcheprov, *Vydayushchiysya revolyutsioner N. Ye Fedoseyev* (Moscow, 1958), p. 32.

86 *Vladimir Il'ich Lenin: A Biography* (Moscow, 1965), p. 10. See also B. Volin, *Lenin v Povolzh'ye*, 2nd edn (Moscow, 1956), p. 34; *Lenin* (a biography prepared by the Marx-Engels-Lenin Institute) (Moscow, 1943), p. 7; *Vladimir Il'ich Lenin: A Political Biography* (from the same source) (Moscow, 1944), p. 8.

87 M. Ul'yanova, *op. cit.*, p. 85.

88 Ul'yanova-Yelizarova, 'Vospominaniya ob Il'iche', *Vospominaniya rodnykh*, p. 14; *idem*, 'Vospominaniya ob Aleksandre Il'iche Ul'yanove', p. 95.

89 *Lenin*, p. 6; *Vladimir Il'ich Lenin*, p. 7; *Bol'shaya sovetskaya entsiklopediya*, 2nd edn, XLIV, pp. 214–15.

90 Ul'yanova-Yelizarova, 'Vospominaniya ob Aleksandre Il'iche Ul'yanove', pp. 96–7.

91 Leon Trotsky, *The Young Lenin*, tr. Max Eastman (Newton Abbot, 1972), pp. 107, 114. See also Neil Harding, *Lenin's Political Thought* (2 vols., London, 1977–81), I, p. 13.

92 I. Lalayants, 'O moikh vstrechakh s V. I. Leninym za vremya 1893–1900 gg.', *PR*, 1: 84 (1929), p. 49.

93 See Ivansky, *op. cit.*, p. 301.

94 Ul'yanova-Yelizarova, 'Vospominaniya ob Il'iche', p. 18.

95 See Korbut, *op. cit.*, II, p. 178.

96 V. Adoratsky, 'Za 18 let (Vstrechi s Vladimirom Il'ichom)', *PR*, 3: 26 (1924), p. 94.

97 Volin, *op. cit.*, p. 63.

98 See Nafigov, *Pervyy shag*, pp. 88–9.

99 Khait, *op. cit.*, pp. 190–1.

100 Pipes, 'The origins of Bolshevism; the intellectual evolution of young Lenin', in *Revolutionary Russia*, ed. Pipes (Cambridge, Mass., 1968), pp. 26, 28.

101 Rolf H. W. Theen, *Lenin: Genesis and Development of a Revolutionary* (London, 1974), pp. 49, 59.

102 Harding, 'Lenin's early writings – the problem of context', *Political Studies*, 23 (1975), p. 444.

103 *Leninskiy sbornik*, XX, ed. V. V. Adoratsky *et al.* (Moscow, 1932), p. 51.

104 Plekhanov, *Nashi raznoglasiya*, *Soch.*, II, pp. 153ff. On this work, see Chapter 4, pp. 127–30.

105 Berezin, *op. cit.*, pp. 127–30.

106 *IRS*, III, pp. 225–41 (italics in quotation in original).

107 *Ibid.*, pp. 219–25 (italics in quotation in original).

108 See *Obshchina*, 8–9 (1878), pp. 21–33.

109 Berezin, *op. cit.*, pp. 130–1; V. N. Golovkin, 'Iz vospominaniy narodnika', *NV*, III, pp. 228–9.

110 Berezin, *op. cit.*, pp. 131–3; Mitskevich, *Na grani dvukh epokh*, p. 61.

111 [M. D. Fokin, L. D. Sinitskiy, D. D. Bekaryukov], 'Istoricheskaya zapiska o taynom obshchestve "zagovorshchikov"', *KS*, 12: 49 (1928), pp. 49ff; Moshinsky, *Na putyakh*, pp. 10ff; *idem*, 'Devyanostyye gody v kiyevskom podpol'ye', *KS*, 5: 34 (1927), pp. 8–16; Vl. Sklyarevich, 'O kiyevskoy "gruppe zagovorshchikov" 1885–1892 gg.', *KS*, 5: 42 (1928), pp. 68–71; L. S. Fedorchenko, 'Pervyye shagi sotsial-demokratii v Kiyeve', *KS*, 6: 27 (1926), p. 23.

112 The police report is in *LR*, 3 (1923), pp. 194–6. See also V. Perazich, 'Yuvenaliy Mel'nikov i Khar'kovskiy rabochiy kruzhok' (hereafter 'Yuvenaliy Mel'nikov'), *LR*, 3 (1923), pp. 110ff; *idem*, *Yu. D. Mel'nikov* (Khar'kov, 1930), pp. 49–51; L. V. Freyfel'd, 'Zapozdalaya popravka', *KS*, 4: 113 (1934), p. 123; Veden'yev, *op. cit.*, pp. 106ff; and V. P. Denisenko, 'Khar'kovskaya gruppa partii "Narodnoy voli" (1885–1887 gg.)', *NV*, II, p. 131. A leaflet hectographed by Bekaryukov for distribution among railway workers is reprinted in *Ot gruppy Blagoyeva k 'Soyuzu bor'by' (1886–1894 gg.)*, ed. M.

Ol'minsky [M. S. Aleksandrov] (Rostov-on-Don, 1921) (hereafter *Ot gruppy Blagoyeva*), pp. 118–20.

113 Perazich, 'Yuvenaliy Mel'nikov', p. 108.

114 See V. I. Nevsky, 'Khar'kovskoye delo Yuvenaliya Mel'nikova i drugikh', *Ot gruppy Blagoyeva*, p. 105.

115 Denisenko, *op. cit.*, p. 131; Freyfel'd, 'Iz zhizni narodovol'cheskikh organizatsiy kontsa 80-kh godov', pp. 144–5.

116 See Bekaryukov's programme in *Ot gruppy Blagoyeva*, pp. 117–18.

117 Perazich, *Yu. D. Mel'nikov*, pp. 93ff (quotations from p. 97); *Obzor*, XV (1890), p. 61; Freyfel'd, 'Zapozdalaya popravka', p. 126. On the Rostov circle, see also the police report and testimony in *IRS*, II, pp. 215–22.

118 *Obzor*, IX (1884), 'Vedomost'', pp. 8–9.

119 See Perazich, *Yu. D. Mel'nikov*, p. 40; Samuel H. Baron, 'The first decade of Russian Marxism', *SR*, 14: 3 (1955), p. 321 and n. 25.

4 THE BEGINNINGS OF RUSSIAN SOCIAL DEMOCRACY

1 Marx and Engels, *Perepiska*, pp. 10–21.

2 *Ibid.*, p. 26.

3 P. N. Tkachov, 'Retsenziya na knigi Yu. Zhukovskogo', pp. 69–70.

4 There is a monograph on this subject by Koz'min, *Russkaya sektsiya pervogo internatsionala* (Moscow, 1957).

5 Marx and Engels, *Perepiska*, pp. 189–90.

6 Lavrov, 'Biografiya-ispoved'', *IS*, I, p. 95; 'Znaniye i revolyutsiya', p. 120.

7 Mikhaylovsky, 'Karl Marks pered sudom g. Yu. Zhukovskogo', *Soch.*, IV, cols. 165–206.

8 See Reuel', *op. cit.*, pp. 295ff.

9 Marx and Engels, *Perepiska*, pp. 251–2.

10 *Ibid.*, p. 246.

11 Marx and Engels, *The German Ideology*, in *Collected Works* (18 vols. published, London, 1975–), V, pp. 36, 53–4. Marx, *The Eighteenth Brumaire of Louis Bonaparte*, in *Collected Works*, XI, p. 103. See also 'From the Afterword to the Second German Edition of the First Volume of *Capital*' in Marx and Engels, *Selected Works* (2 vols., Moscow, 1962), I, p. 456.

12 Marx, *Capital* (3 vols., London, 1977), I, p. 715.

13 *The Communist Manifesto*, in Marx and Engels, *Collected Works*, VI, pp. 491–4.

14 *Ibid.*, p. 488.

15 Marx and Engels, *Perepiska*, pp. 195–207.

16 See, for example, Marx, *Letters to Dr Kugelmann* (London, 1934), p. 99; and Marx and Engels, *Perepiska*, p. 201.

17 This view is argued, for example, by Terrell Carver, *Engels* (New York, 1981), p. 50.

18 Marx and Engels, *Perepiska*, pp. 39, 48, 72, 90, 221; Marx, *Letters to Dr Kugelmann*, p. 112.

19 Marx and Engels, *Perepiska*, pp. 221–2.

20 Marx and Engels, *Selected Correspondence* (Moscow, 1953), p. 374.

21 See their review in *Collected Works*, X, p. 318.

22 Marx and Engels, *Perepiska*, p. 239.

23 Marx and Engels, *Correspondence, 1846–1895* (London, 1934), pp. 390–1.

24 Marx and Engels, *Selected Correspondence*, p. 405.

25 Marx and Engels, *Perepiska*, p. 253.

26 *Ibid.*, p. 260.

27 *Ibid.*, p. 301. See also the draft of this letter cited by David McClellan, *The Thought of Karl Marx: An Introduction* (London, 1971), p. 101.

28 Marx and Engels, *Selected Works*, I, pp. 23–4.

29 *Literaturnoye naslediye G. V. Plekhanova*, VIII, pp. 210–11.

30 *Dela i dni*, 2 (1921), pp. 90–1.

31 See Plekhanov, *Soch.*, I, pp. 135–6. See also *IRS*, II, p. 67.

32 On the relations of Plekhanov's group with the Narodovoltsy and on the emergence of the 'Emancipation of Labour' group, see Deych, 'O sblizhenii i razryve s narodovol'tsami', pp. 6–7; *idem*, 'K vozniknoveniyu Gruppy "Osvobozhdeniye truda"', *PR*, 4 (1923), p. 198; and Aksel'rod, *op. cit.*, pp. 387–8. See also Polevoy, *op. cit.*, pp. 138ff; and Samuel H. Baron, *Plekhanov: The Father of Russian Marxism* (London, 1963) (hereafter *Plekhanov*), pp. 78–88.

33 Plekhanov, *Nashi raznoglasiya*, *Soch.*, II, pp. 153ff; Marx and Engels, *Selected Works*, I, p. 386.

34 Plekhanov, *Sotsializm i politicheskaya bor'ba*, *Soch.*, II, p. 47; *idem*, *Nashi raznoglasiya*, pp. 286, 113; see also p. 271.

35 *Idem*, *Nashi raznoglasiya*, pp. 110, 205, 210ff, 221, 233–4, 238–9, 256, 260, 271 (Plekhanov's italics in quotation).

36 *Idem, Sotsializm i politicheskaya bor'ba*, pp. 83, 87–8; *idem, Nashi raznoglasiya*, pp. 263, 332, 349. See also the group's programme, reprinted in Plekhanov, *Soch.*, II, pp. 357–62.

37 Marx, 'Preface to a Contribution to the Critique of Political Economy', in Marx and Engels, *Selected Works*, I, p. 363.

38 Plekhanov, *Sotsializm i politicheskaya bor'ba*, p. 79.

39 *Idem*, *Nashi raznoglasiya*, pp. 271, 337.

40 *Idem*, *Sotsializm i politicheskaya bor'ba*, p. 86.

41 Baron, *Plekhanov*, p. 70.

42 Marx and Engels, *The Communist Manifesto*, *Collected Works*, VI, p. 493.

43 See Baron, *Plekhanov*, pp. 125–9.

44 L. G. Deych, 'Pervyye shagi gruppy "Osvobozhdeniye truda"', *GOT*, I, p. 11. See also, for example, Plekhanov, *Soch.*, IV, p. 277.

45 See Plekhanov, *Soch.*, II, pp. 361–2; see also *Nashi raznoglasiya*, pp. 349, 350n.

46 Letter from Deych to Aksel'rod, *GOT*, I, pp. 169–70.

47 Marx and Engels, *Perepiska*, pp. 309–10.

48 Baron, *Plekhanov*, p. 135.

49 D. Blagoyev, *Kratki belezhki iz moya zhivot* (Sofia, 1949) (hereafter *Kratki belezhki*), pp. 33ff.

50 V. Kharitonov, 'Iz vospominaniy uchastnika gruppy Blagoyeva', *PR*, 8: 79 (1928), p. 160.

51 See *IRS*, II, pp. 187ff.

52 The main sources on the Blagoyevtsy are: Blagoyev, *Kratki belezhki*, pp. 33–76; and Kharitonov, *op. cit.*, pp. 152–63; see also the letter by Kugushev in *PR*, 8: 79 (1928), pp. 164–5. The paper *Rabochiy* is reprinted in N. L. Sergiyevsky's edition, *Rabochiy:*

gazeta partii russkikh sotsial-demokratov (blagoyevtsev), 1885 (Leningrad, 1928). The reading programme is published in *KL*, 7 (1923), pp. 275–84. For secondary accounts, see Sergiyevsky, *Partiya russkikh sotsial-demokratov. Gruppa Blagoyeva* (Moscow–Leningrad, 1929); Polevoy, *op. cit.*, pp. 283–314; and S. A. Ovsyannikova, *Gruppa Blagoyeva. Iz istorii rasprostraneniya marksizma v Rossii* (Moscow, 1959).

53 Kharitonov, *op. cit.*, p. 156.

54 The programme drafted by the group was sent to the émigré Social Democrats and the émigré Narodovol'tsy for their perusal. It is reprinted, together with the covering letters to the two émigré groups, in *Byloye*, 13 (1918), pp. 43–52; see esp. pp. 47, 49.

55 *Ibid.*, pp. 44, 46.

56 The articles contributed by the émigrés were Plekhanov's 'Sovremennyye zadachi russkikh rabochikh' (see *Soch.*, II, pp. 363–72), and Aksel'rod's 'Vybory v germanskiy reykhstag i sotsial-demokraticheskaya partiya'. See *IRS*, II, p. 191, for the émigrés' letter to the Blagoyevtsy.

57 See Figner, *op. cit.*, I, p. 91.

58 Blagoyev, *op. cit.*, pp. 46–7, 64.

59 See *Byloye*, 13 (1918), pp. 43ff.

60 *Ibid.*, p. 44.

61 *Ibid.*, pp. 43, 44.

62 *Ibid.*, p. 44.

63 *Ibid.*, pp. 48, 49.

64 Kharitonov, *op. cit.*, p. 153.

65 See *Byloye*, 13 (1918), p. 48.

66 *Ibid.*, p. 50; Ol'minsky, 'Davniye svyazi', *Ot gruppy Blagoyeva*, p. 69. See also I. I. Popov, 'Revolyutsionnyye organizatsii', p. 59.

67 See *Byloye*, 13 (1918), p. 48.

68 See *IRS*, II, p. 189.

69 *Byloye*, 13 (1918), pp. 46–7; *Rabochiy*, p. 34.

70 *Byloye*, 13 (1918), p. 47.

71 Blagoyev, *op. cit.*, p. 64.

72 *Rabochiy*, pp. 21ff.

73 *Ibid.*, pp. 49ff.

74 D. Blagoyev, *Sŭchineniya* (20 vols., Sofia, 1957–64), I, p. 72.

75 See *KL*, 7 (1923), pp. 275ff.

76 *Byloye*, 13 (1918), p. 45.

77 On this strike, its main participants and related events, see especially P. A. Moiseyenko, *Vospominaniya starogo revolyutsionera* (Moscow, 1966); *Rabocheye dvizheniye*, ed. A. M. Pankratova, III, Part I, pp. 123–302; and the collections of documents and articles, *Morozovskaya stachka 7–13 (19–25) yanvarya 1885 g.*, ed. D. Ryazanov (Moscow, 1923), and *Morozovskaya stachka, 1885–1935*, with foreword by Pankratova (Moscow, 1935). Comprehensive secondary accounts are given by N. I. Tolokonsky, *Orekhovo-Zuyevskaya stachka 1885g.* (Moscow, 1956); and P. I. Kabanov and R. K. Yerman, *Morozovskaya stachka 1885 goda* (Moscow, 1963).

78 On conditions in the factory, see Tolokonsky, *op. cit.*, pp. 19–42; and Kabanov and Yerman, *op. cit.*, pp. 20–8.

79 See Pankratova, *op. cit.*, III, Part I, p. 123.

80 *Ibid.*, pp. 188–9.

81 *Moskovskiye vedomosti*, 146, 29 May 1886.

82 See Plekhanov, 'Zabastovka v Rossii', *Soch.*, II, pp. 390–2.

83 On Tochissky's group documents are very scarce. See the police report, 'Doklad departamenta politsii ministru vnutrennikh del' in *KL*, 7 (1923) (hereafter 'Doklad departamenta politsii'), pp. 344–88; and the memoirs of A. Breytfus, 'Tochiskiy i yego kruzhok', *ibid.*, pp. 324–39. See also M. Lebedeva [Tochisskaya], 'K biografii P. V. Tochisskogo', *IRS*, III, pp. 296–9. For secondary accounts, see especially Polevoy, *op. cit.*, pp. 323–36; R. A. Kazakevich, *Sotsial-demokraticheskiye organizatsii Peterburga* (Leningrad, 1960), pp. 31–76; N. K. Lisovsky, *P. V. Tochisskiy – odin iz organizatorov pervykh marksistskikh kruzhkov v Rossii* (Moscow, 1963).

84 Lebedeva, *op. cit.*, p. 297.

85 Breytfus, *op. cit.*, p. 325.

86 See Pipes, *Social Democracy and the St Petersburg Labour Movement, 1885–1897* (Cambridge, Mass., 1963) (hereafter *Social Democracy*), pp. 10–11. There is a lengthy Soviet riposte to Pipes' book: R. A. Kazakevich and F. M. Suslova, *Mister Payps fal'sifitsiruyet istoriyu* (Leningrad, 1966).

87 See Breytfus, *op. cit.*, pp. 326–8, 332–3.

88 *Ibid.*, pp. 325–6.

89 'Doklad departamenta politsii', p. 356. Danilova's testimony to the police would not in itself be conclusive: it was prudent for detainees to dissociate themselves from terrorism, which the police continued to view as the most heinous political offence.

90 Breytfus, *op. cit.*, p. 326; 'Doklad departamenta politsii', p. 349.

91 N. L. Sergiyevsky, 'O kruzhke Tochiskogo', *KL*, 7 (1923), p. 340.

92 See, for example, Polevoy, *op. cit.*, p. 325.

93 Breytfus, *op. cit.*, p. 338.

94 *Ibid.*, p. 335; *Literaturnoye naslediye G. V. Plekhanova*, I, pp. 255–6.

95 Lebedeva, *op. cit.*, p. 297. See Breytfus, *op. cit.*, p. 338, on Tochissky's lukewarm attitude towards a St Petersburg workers' association.

96 Lebedeva, *op. cit.*, p. 297.

97 *Ibid.*, p. 298; Breytfus, *op. cit.*, p. 326.

98 'Doklad departamenta politsii', pp. 355–6.

99 Breytfus, *op. cit.*, pp. 327–9.

100 Original material on Fedoseyev's circle is also very scarce. See especially the memoirs of M. G. Grigor'yev, 'Vospominaniya o fedoseyevskom kruzhke v Kazani', *PR*, 8: 20 (1923), pp. 55–66; and Sergiyevsky's articles, based on archive material: 'O fedoseyevskom kruzhke 1888–89 gg.', *KL*, 5 (1923), pp. 340–3; 'Fedoseyevskiy kruzhok 1888–1889 gg.', *ibid.*, 7 (1923), pp. 285–321, and 9 (1924), pp. 169–76; and 'Tak chto zhe takoye Fedoseyevskiy kruzhok 1888–1889 gg.', *IRS*, I, pp. 67–96. For secondary accounts, see especially Polevoy, *op. cit.*, pp. 349–58; and Shcheprov, *op. cit.*

101 Quotations from Nafigov, *Pervyy shag*, p. 203. See also Mitskevich, *Na grani dvukh epokh*, pp. 79–85; and Grigor'yev, *op. cit.*, p. 61.

102 See N. Ye. Fedoseyev, *Stat'i i pis'ma* (Moscow, 1958), p. 35.

103 Sergiyevsky, 'Tak chto zhe takoye Fedoseyevskiy kruzhok 1888–1889 gg.', pp. 71–2.

104 Grigor'yev, *op. cit.*, p. 61; Mitskevich, *Na grani dvukh epokh*, p. 79.

105 I. Lalayants, 'Nekotoryye dopolneniya k biografii N. Ye. Fedoseyeva', in *Fedoseyev Nikolay Yevgrafovich: Odin iz pionerov revolyutsionnogo marksizma v Rossii (Sbornik vospominaniy)* (Moscow–Petrograd, 1923), p. 28.

106 See *KL*, 7 (1923), p. 295.

107 See Fedoseyev, *op. cit.*, pp. 218–19; Gor'ky, *Moi universitety*, pp. 63–4.

108 See *KL*, 7 (1923), p. 306.

109 *Ibid.*, 9 (1923), pp. 175–6.

110 Fedoseyev, *op. cit.*, p. 92.

111 See V. V. Vorovsky's record, made in 1919, of a conversation which took place in 1904. The record was first published by N. Valentinov [N. V. Vol'sky] (who had copied extracts from it when it was sent to him for his perusal by Vorovsky), in his article, 'Chernyshevskiy i Lenin', *Novyy zhurnal*, 26 (1951), pp. 197–200, esp. p. 197. This transcript is reprinted in Valentinov's book, *Vstrechi s Leninym* (New York, 1953), pp. 106–9, which is translated as *Encounters with Lenin* (Oxford, 1968) (see pp. 66–8).

112 On the journals available to Ul'yanov, see D. Ul'yanov's verbal recollections published in *Vospominaniya o Vladimire Il'iche Lenine* (5 vols., Moscow, 1969–70), I, p. 93; Valentinov, 'Chernyshevskiy i Lenin', pp. 197ff; and Ul'yanova-Yelizarova, 'Vospominaniya ob Il'iche', p. 22.

113 N. K. Krupskaya, *Memories of Lenin*, tr. E. Verney (London, 1930), p. 198.

114 Valentinov, 'Chernyshevskiy i Lenin', pp. 194, 199.

115 Krupskaya, *op. cit.*, pp. 34, 202.

116 See Valentinov, 'Chernyshevskiy i Lenin', p. 198.

117 *Ibid.*

118 *Ibid.*, p. 194.

119 See Ivansky, *op. cit.*, pp. 422–3.

120 Krupskaya, *op. cit.*, p. 204.

121 Chernyshevsky, *Chto delat'?*, in *PSS*, XI, p. 210.

122 Valentinov, 'Chernyshevskiy i Lenin', p. 196. See also *idem*, *Vstrechi s Leninym*, pp. 114ff.

123 Ul'yanova-Yelizarova, 'Vospominaniya ob Il'iche', p. 25.

124 Valentinov, 'Vstrecha Lenina s marksizmom', *Novyy zhurnal*, 53 (1958), pp. 189–90.

125 Polevoy, *op. cit.*, p. 362; *Vladmir Il'ich Lenin: A Biography*, p. 27. See also Nafigov, *Pervyy shag*, p. 174.

126 Lenin, 'Neskol'ko slov o N. Ye. Fedoseyeve', in *Fedoseyev Nikolay Yevgrafovich*, p. 5 (also in *PSS*, XLV, pp. 324–5).

127 Trotsky, *op. cit.*, pp. 129–30.

128 Ul'yanova-Yelizarova, 'Vospominaniya ob Il'iche', p. 25.

129 See Ivansky, *op. cit.*, p. 468.

130 *Ibid.*, p. 469. Mandel'shtam's recollections were first printed in *Moskva*, 4 (1958), pp. 55–7.

131 Ul'yanova-Yelizarova, 'Vospominaniya ob Il'iche', p. 25.

132 Ivansky, *op. cit.*, pp. 468–9.

133 Ul'yanova-Yelizarova, 'Vospominaniya ob Il'iche', p. 25.

134 Krupskaya, *op. cit.*, p. 42.

135 Trotsky, *op. cit.*, p. 125.

136 Lenin, *Chto delat'?*, in *PSS*, VI, pp. 180–1.

137 Krupskaya, *op. cit.*, p. 43.

138 See Ivansky, *op. cit.*, p. 467.

139 Lalayants, 'O moikh vstrechakh s V. I. Leninym', p. 49.

140 Krupskaya, *op. cit.*, p. 11.

141 Ol'minsky, 'Davniye svyazi', p. 73.

142 On the workers' circles, see especially the memoirs of workers themselves: K. Norinsky, 'Moi vospominaniya', *Ot gruppy Blagoyeva*, pp. 10ff; Bogdanov's memoirs, partly reprinted in *ibid.*, pp. 39ff; and [V. A. Shelgunov], 'Vospominaniya V. A. Shelgunova', *ibid.*, pp. 55ff. See also Golubev, *op. cit.*, pp. 108ff; V. B[artenev], *MG*, 10 (1908), pp. 190ff; and V. V. Svyatlovsky, 'Na zare Rossiyskoy sotsial-demokratii', *Byloye*, 19 (1922), pp. 142ff.

143 See Svyatlovsky, *op. cit.*, p. 144.

144 *Ibid.*, p. 142.

145 See, for example, V. B[artenev], *MG*, 10 (1908), p. 193.

146 There is much material on the Brusnev group. See V. B[artenev], *MG*, 10 (1908), pp. 169–97; Golubev, *op. cit.*, pp. 105–21; Svyatlovsky, *op. cit.*, pp. 139–60; M. I. Brusnev, 'Vozniknoveniye pervykh sotsial-demokraticheskikh organizatsiy', *PR*, 2: 14 (1923), pp. 17–32; *idem*, 'Pervyye revolyutsionnyye shagi L. Krasina', in *Leonid Borisovich Krasin ('Nikitych')*, ed. M. N. Lyadov and S. M. Pozner (Moscow–Leningrad, 1928) (hereafter *Krasin*), pp. 59–81; L. B. Krasin, 'Dela davno minuvshikh dney (1887–1892 gg.)', *PR*, 3: 15 (1923), pp. 3–28; *idem*, 'Iz vospominaniy peterburgskogo tekhnologa', in *Krasin*, pp. 49–59; V. Karelina, 'Leonid Borisovich – propagandist i organizator rabochikh kruzhkov', in *Krasin*, pp. 86–92; and the articles of Norinsky and Bogdanov in *Ot gruppy Blagoyeva*. See also the documents published in *Ot gruppy Blagoyeva*, pp. 79–96. Secondary sources on the group are Polevoy, *op. cit.*, pp. 375–95; Kazakevich, and Pipes, *Social Democracy*, pp. 22–39.

147 Pipes, *Social Democracy*, pp. 10–11.

148 [V. A. Shelgunov], *op. cit.*, p. 55.

149 Norinsky, *op. cit.*, p. 10.

150 Bogdanov, *op. cit.*, p. 40.

151 See *Ot gruppy Blagoyeva*, pp. 85–6.

152 Bogdanov, *op. cit.*, p. 40.

CONCLUSION

1 Arthur P. Mendel, *Dilemmas of Progress in Tsarist Russia: Legal Marxism and Legal Populism* (Cambridge, Mass., 1961), p. 118.

2 Oliver H. Radkey, *The Agrarian Foes of Bolshevism: Promise and Default of the Russian Socialist Revolutionaries, February to October 1917* (New York and London, 1958), p. 3.

3 Franco Venturi, 'Russian Populism', in his *Studies in Free Russia*, tr. Fausta Segre Walsby and Margaret O'Dell (Chicago and London, 1982), p. 240.

4 Robert Service, 'Russian Populism and Russian Marxism: two skeins entangled' in *Russian Thought and Society, 1800–1917: Essays in Honour of Eugene Lampert*, ed. Roger Bartlett (Keele, 1984), p. 221.

5 Leopold H. Haimson, *The Russian Marxists and the Origins of Bolshevism* (Cambridge, Mass., 1955), p. 111.

6 See Mendel, *op. cit.*, p. 121.

7 Radkey, *op. cit.*, p. 5.

8 Haimson, *op. cit.*, p. v.

❧ SELECT BIBLIOGRAPHY

Entries may be listed under an author's pseudonym, which is given in the index of names.

PRIMARY SOURCES (collections of documents, police reports, testimonies, journals, theoretical writings, programmes, memoirs, etc.)

Adoratsky, V. 'Za 18 let (Vstrechi s Vladimirom Il'ichom)', *PR*, 3: 26 (1924), pp. 92–106

[Aksel'rod, P. B.] 'O zadachakh nauchno-sotsialisticheskoy literatury ("pis'mo k tovarishcham")', *GOT*, II, pp. 87–102

    Perezhitoye i peredumannoye, Berlin, 1923

Alekseyev [Yu. A. Bunin] 'Neskol'ko slov o proshlom russkogo sotsializma i o zadachakh intelligentsii', *IRS*, III, pp. 187–202

Anan'ina, L. I. 'Pervoye marta 1887 goda', *NV*, I, pp. 151–9

[Annensky, N. F.] 'Sotsializm i narodnichestvo', *IRS*, III, pp. 225–41

Aptekman, O. V. *Obshchestvo 'Zemlya i Volya' 70-kh godov*, Petrograd, 1924

Argunov, P. A. 'Moskovskiy kruzhok "Militaristov"', *NV*, I, pp. 87–96

    'Yeshcho ob "Obshchestve perevodchikov i izdateley"', *KS*, 9: 106 (1933), pp. 72–85

'Arkhivnyye dokumenty k biografii V. I. Lenina (1887–1914)', *KA*, 1: 62 (1934), pp. 55–74

Ashenbrenner, M. Yu. *Voyennaya organizatsiya Narodnoy Voli i drugiye vospominaniya*, ed. N. S. Tyutchev, Moscow, 1924

Baddeley, John F. *Russia in the 'Eighties'*, London, 1921

Bakh, A. N. *Zapiski narodovol'tsa*, Leningrad, 1931

[Bakunin, M. A.] *Archives Bakounine*, ed. Arthur Lehning, 7 vols. published, Leiden, 1961– *IS*, 5 vols., Petersburg–Moscow, 1919–21

    Selected Writings, ed. Arthur Lehning, London, 1973

    Sobraniye sochineniy i pisem 1828–1876, ed. Yu. M. Steklov, 4 vols., Moscow, 1934–5

B[artenev], V. 'Vospominaniya peterburzhtsa o vtoroy polovine 80-kh godov', *MG*, 10 (1908), pp. 169–97, and 11 (1908), pp. 168–88

Bazilevsky, B. [V. Ya Yakovlev] (ed.) *Gosudarstvennyye prestupleniya v Rossii v XIX veke*, 3 vols., I, St Petersburg, 1906, II, Stuttgart, 1904, III, Paris, 1905
Revolyutsionnaya zhurnalistika semidesyatykh godov, Paris, 1905

Berezin, M. Ye. *et al.* 'Vospominaniya iz zhizni narodnicheskikh kruzhkov v Kazani (1875–1892 gg.)', *KS*, 10: 71 (1930), pp. 111–36

Bervi, V. V. *Izbrannyye ekonomicheskiye proizvedeniya*, 2 vols., Moscow, 1958–9
Tri politicheskiye sistemy: Nikolay Iyy, Aleksandr IIoy i Aleksandr IIIiy. Vospominaniya, [Geneva], 1897

Blagoyev, D. *Kratki belezhki iz moya zhivot*, Sofia, 1949

Bodayev, V. A. 'N. M. Flyorov i "Podgotovitel'naya gruppa partii Narodnoy voli"', *NV*, II, pp. 15–23

[Bogoraz, V. G.] *Bor'ba obshchestvennykh sil v Rossii*, [Novocherkassk], 1886

Borzyakov, Gr. 'Revolyutsionnaya molodyozh' v Odesse v 1882–1884 gg.', *KS*, 8–9: 57–8 (1929), pp. 129–58

Braginsky, M. A. 'Aleksandr Il'ich Ul'yanov', *KS*, 32 (1927), pp. 43–52
'Iz vospominaniy o voyenno-revolyutsionnoy organizatsii (1884–1886 gg.)', *NV*, II, pp. 113–27

Bramson, M. V. 'Otryvki iz vospominaniy (1883–1886 gg.)', *NV*, I, pp. 81–6

Breytfus, A. 'Tochiskiy i yego kruzhok', *KL*, 7 (1923), pp. 324–39

Bukh, N. K. 'Pervaya tipografiya "Narodnoy Voli"', *KS*, 8–9: 57–8 (1929), pp. 54–94
Vospominaniya, Moscow, 1928

Bukhbinder, N. A. 'K istorii sotsial-demokraticheskogo dvizheniya v Kiyevskoy gubernii', *KL*, 7 (1923), pp. 263–84

Bulanova, O. 'A. P. Bulanov', *KS*, 5: 12 (1924), pp. 291–6
'"Chornyy peredel"', *GOT*, I, pp. 112–22

Burtsev, V. L. 'Iz moikh vospominaniy', *Svobodnaya Rossiya*, 1 (1889), pp. 48–56

Bychkov, A. 'Delo o revolyutsionnykh kruzhkakh v Kiyeve v 1879, 1880 i 1881 g.g.', *LR*, 2: 7 (1924), pp. 39–62

Bykhovsky, N. Ya. 'Bulochnik Aleksey Maksimovich Peshkov i kazanskaya revolyutsionnaya molodyozh' kontsa 80-kh gg.', *Byloye*, 4: 32 (1925), pp. 202–19

Charushin, N. A. *O dalyokom proshlom*, Moscow, 1973

Chaykovsky, N. V. 'Cherez pol stoletiya: Otkrytoye pis'mo k druz'yam', *Golos minuvshego na chuzhboy storone*, 3: 16 (1926), pp. 179–89

Chebotaryov, I. N. 'Vospominaniya ob Aleksandre Il'iche Ul'yanove i peterburgskom studenchestve 1883–1887 gg.', *AIU*, pp. 239–54

Chernyavskaya-Bokhanovskaya, G. F. 'Avtobiografiya', *KS*, 4: 41 (1928), pp. 7–22, 5: 42 (1928), pp. 49–67, and 6: 43 (1928), pp. 20–36

Chernyshevsky, N. G. *PSS*, 15 vols., Moscow, 1939–50

Chornyy peredel 5 nos., London–Minsk, 1880–1

Debagoriy-Mokriyevich, Vl. *Vospominaniya*, Paris, 1894

Delo 1-ogo marta 1881 goda, St Petersburg, 1906

Denisenko, V. P. 'Khar'kovskaya gruppa partii "Narodnoy voli" (1885–1887 gg.)', *NV*, II, pp. 128–42

Deych, L. G. 'Aaron Zundelevich (odin iz pervykh sotsial-demokratov v Rossii)', *GOT*, II, pp. 185–216

'G. V. Plekhanov, "O bylom i nebylitsakh"', *PR*, 3: 15 (1923), pp. 29–44

'O sblizhenii i razryve s narodovol'tsami (K istorii vozniknoveniya gruppy "Osvobozhdeniye truda")', *PR*, 8: 20 (1923), pp. 5–54

'Pervyye shagi gruppy "Osvobozhdeniye truda"', *GOT*, I, pp. 9–49

'Pis'ma k Aksel'rodu', *GOT*, I, pp. 148–99

Rol' yevreyev v russkom revolyutsionnom dvizhenii, Berlin, 1923

Russkaya revolyutsionnaya emigratsiya 70-kh godov, Petersburg, 1920

'Vmesto bibliografii', *GOT*, III, pp. 340–70

'Ya. V. Stefanovich sredi narodovol'tsev', *GOT*, III, pp. 96–121

Za polveka, 2 vols., Berlin, 1923

Deych, L. G. (ed.) *Gruppa 'Osvobozhdeniye truda'*, 6 vols., Moscow, 1924–8

Dikovskaya-Yakimova, A. D. *et al.* (eds.) '*Narodnaya volya' v dokumentakh i vospominaniyakh*, Moscow, 1930

'Narodnaya volya' pered tsarskim sudom, Moscow, 1931

Narodovol'tsy posle I-go marta 1881 goda, Moscow, 1928

Narodovol'tsy 80-kh i 90-kh godov, Moscow, 1929

Narodovol'tsy, sbornik III, Moscow, 1931

Dobrolyubov, N. A. *SS*, 9 vols., Moscow–Leningrad, 1961–3

'Doklad departamenta politsii ministru vnutrennikh del', *KL*, 7 (1923), pp. 344–88

Drey, M. I. 'Zametka o rabochem dvizhenii v Odesse v 1880–1881 gg.', *KS*, 5: 12 (1924), pp. 73–7

Dzhabadari, I. S. 'Protsess 50-ti (Vserossiyskaya sotsial'no-revolyutsionnaya organizatsiya 1874–1877 g.)', *Byloye*, 8: 20 (1907), pp. 1–26, 9: 21 (1907), pp. 169–92, and 10: 22 (1907), pp. 168–97

Fedorchenko, L. S. 'Pervyye shagi sotsial-demokratii v Kiyeve', *KS*, 6: 27 (1926), pp. 21–33

Figner, V. N. 'M. N. Trigoni', *GM*, 7–8, 1917, pp. 198–211

'Yuriy Nikolayevich Bogdanovich', *KS*, 7 (44), 1928, pp. 169–75

Zapechatlyonnyy trud, Moscow, 1964 (2 vols.)

Flerovsky, N. [V. V. Bervi] *Polozheniye rabochego klassa v Rossii*, St Petersburg, 1869

Fokin, M. D. *et al.* 'Istoricheskaya zapiska o taynom obshchestve "zagovorshchikov"', *KS*, 12: 49 (1929), pp. 49–58

Frederic, Harold *The New Exodus: A Study of Israel in Russia*, London, 1892

Freyfel'd, L. V. 'Iz zhizni narodovol'cheskikh organizatsiy kontsa 80-kh godov', *NV*, II, pp. 143–56

'Svetloy pamyati Sof'i Mikhaylovny Ginsburg', *KS*, 5: 12 (1924), pp. 259–71

'Zapozdalaya popravka', *KS*, 4: 113 (1934), pp. 122–8

Frolenko, M. F. *SS*, 2nd edn, 2 vols., Moscow, 1932

Gedeonovsky, A. V. 'Yaroslavskiy revolyutsionnyy kruzhok 1881–1886 gg.', *KS*, 3: 24 (1926), pp. 95–109

Gertsen, A. I. [Herzen] *SS*, 30 vols., Moscow, 1954–65

Getsov, I. 'Tipografiya "Chornogo peredela"', *GOT*, I, pp. 123–32

Golovkin, V. N. 'Iz vospominaniy narodnika', *NV*, III, pp. 213–32

Golubev, V. S. 'Stranichka iz istorii rabochego dvizheniya', *Byloye*, 12 (1906), pp. 105–21

Golubeva, M. [Yasneva] 'Moya pervaya vstrecha s Vladimirom Il'ichom', *Vospominaniya o Vladimire Il'iche Lenine*, Moscow, 1956–60, I, pp. 96–9

'Vospominaniya o P. G. Zaichnevskom', *PR*, 6–7: 18–19 (1923), pp. 27–31

Gor'ky, Maksim [A. M. Peshkov] *Moi universitety*, *PSS*, 25 vols., Moscow, 1968–76, XVI, pp. 7–137

Gots, M. R. 'Moskovskaya tsentral'naya gruppa partii "Narodnaya volya"', *NV*, I, pp. 97–108

Govorukhin, O. M. 'Vospominaniya ob A. I. Ul'yanove, P. Ya. Shevyryove, V. D. Generalove i P. I. Andreyushkine', *AIU*, pp. 211–38

Grigor'yev, M. G. 'Vospominaniya o fedoseyevskom kruzhke v Kazani', *PR*, 8: 20 (1923), pp. 55–66

Ignatova, Ye. N. 'Brat'ya V. N. i I. N. Ignatovy', *GOT*, I, pp. 101–11

'Moskovskiye narodniki kontsa 70-kh godov', *GOT*, V, pp. 45–52

Ivanchin-Pisarev, A. I. *Khozhdeniye v narod*, Moscow–Leningrad, 1929

[Ivanov, S. A.] 'Iz narodovol'cheskikh vospominaniy S. A. Ivanova', *NV*, II, pp. 24–65

'Iz vospominaniy o 1881 gode', *Byloye*, 4 (1906), pp. 228–42

'K kharakteristike obshchestvennykh nastroyeniy v Rossii v nachale 80-kh godov', *Byloye*, 9: 21 (1907), pp. 193–207

Ivanova-Boreysho, S. A. *Pervaya tipografiya 'Narodnoy voli'*, Moscow, 1928

Ivanovskaya, P. S. 'Pervyye tipografii "Narodnoy voli"', *KS*, 3: 24 (1926), pp. 32–57

Ivansky, A. I. *Molodoy Lenin: Povest' v dokumentakh i memuarakh*, Moscow, 1964

Molodyye gody V. I. Lenina. Po vospominaniyam sovremennikov i dokumentam, Moscow, 1957

'Iz pokazaniy N. I. Rysakova', *KA*, 6: 19 (1926), pp. 178–94

Iz rabochego dvizheniya za Nevskoy zastavoy v 70-kh i 80-kh godakh (Iz vospominaniy starogo rabochego), Geneva, 1900

'K biografii S. M. Ginsburg', *KS*, 3: 24 (1926), pp. 211–32

'K biografiyam A. I. Zhelyabova i S. L. Perovskoy', *Byloye*, 8 (1906), pp. 108–29

'K istorii otnosheniy chernoperedel'tsev i narodovol'tsev', *IRS*, II, pp. 389–411

'K istorii protsessa 21', *KA*, 5: 36 (1929), pp. 122–79, 6: 37 (1929), pp. 102–37, 1: 38 (1930), pp. 70–108

'K istorii sabunayevskoy revolyutsionnoy organizatsii 1889–1890 godov', *NV*, III, pp. 248–63

'K istorii voyennoy organizatsii "Narodnoy Voli"', *KS*, 5: 18 (1925), pp. 210–40

Karatayev, N. K. (ed.) *Narodnicheskaya ekonomicheskaya literatura*, Moscow, 1958

Kharitonov, V. 'Iz vospominaniy uchastnika gruppy Blagoyeva', *PR*, 8: 79 (1928), pp. 152–63

Khlebnikov, Semyon. 'Vospominaniya ob Aleksandre Il'iche Ul'yanove, 1886–1887 g.', *AIU*, pp. 261–8

Kogan, Z. V. 'Tul'skaya tipografiya partii "Narodnoy voli"', *NV*, II, pp. 105–12

Koval'skaya, Ye. *Yuzhno-russkiy rabochiy soyuz*, Moscow, 1926

Koz'min, B. P. (ed.) *Nechayev i nechayevtsy*, Moscow–Leningrad, 1931

Kravchinsky, S. M. *Smert' za smert'*, St Petersburg, 1878

Krol', M. A. 'Vospominaniya o L. Ya. Shternberge', *KS*, 8–9: 57–8 (1929), pp. 214–36

Kropotkin, P. *Memoirs of a Revolutionist*, 2 vols., London, 1899

Krupskaya, Nadezhda K. *Memories of Lenin*, tr. from the 2nd Russian edn by E. Verney, London, 1930

Kulakov, A. A. 'Dopolneniye k vospominaniyam B. D. Orzhikha', *NV*, III, pp. 177–82

'"Narodnaya volya" na yuge v polovine 80 gg.', *NV*, I, pp. 140–4

Kulyabko-Koretsky, N. G. *Iz davnikh let: vospominaniya Lavrista*, Moscow, 1931

'L. G. Deych i Narodnaya volya', *Byloye*, 25 (1924), pp. 280–8

Lalayants, I. 'Nekotoryye dopolneniya k biografii N. Ye. Fedoseyeva', in *Fedoseyev Nikolay Yevgrafovich: Odin iz pionerov revolyutsionnogo marksizma v Rossii*, Moscow–Petrograd, 1923, pp. 25–34

'O moikh vstrechakh s V. I. Leninym za vremya 1893–1900 gg.', *PR*, 1: 84 (1929), pp. 38–70

Lavrov, P. L. *Filosofiya i sotsiologiya: Izbrannyye proizvedeniya*, 2 vols., Moscow, 1965

Izbrannyye sochineniya na sotsial'no-politicheskiye temy, 4 vols. published, Moscow, 1934–

Narodniki-propagandisty 1873–78 godov, St Petersburg, 1907

'Vospominaniya o Sof'ye Mikhaylovne Ginsburg', *GM*, 7–8 (1917), pp. 225–56

[Lebedev, V. S.] 'Programma vospominaniy chlena Isp. k-ta "Nar. Voli" V. S. Lebedeva', *NV*, I, pp. 160–5

Lebedeva, M. [Tochisskaya] 'K biografii P. V. Tochisskogo', *IRS*, III, pp. 296–9

Lenin [V. I. Ul'yanov] *PSS*, 5th edn, 55 vols., Moscow, 1958–65

Lion, S. Ye. 'Ot propagandy k terroru (Iz odesskikh vospominaniy semidesyatnika)', *KS*, 5: 12 (1924), pp. 9–24, and 6: 13 (1924), pp. 9–24

Literatura partii Narodnoy voli, Moscow, 1907

Literaturnoye naslediye G. V. Plekhanova, 8 vols., Moscow, 1934–40

Loyko, Lidiya [Kvashnina] *Ot 'Zemli i voli', k VKP(B)*, Moscow–Leningrad, 1929

Lukashevich, A. 'V narod! (Iz vospominaniy semidesyatnika)', *Byloye*, 3: 15 (1907), pp. 1–45

Lukashevich, I. D. *I marta 1887 goda*, Petersburg, 1920

Lyubatovich, O. S. *Dalyokoye i nedavneye*, Moscow, 1930

Makarevsky, Aleksey. 'Iz istorii revolyutsionnogo dvizheniya 1885–1887 godov', *LR*, 2: 7 (1924), pp. 63–93

'Rabochiy narodovolets P. L. Antonov (Vospominaniya)', *KS*, 5: 12 (1924), pp. 272–81

'Revolyutsionnyy Khar'kov v 1882–1885 gg.', *LR*, 5 (1923), pp. 64–97

Martynov, A. 'Vospominaniya revolyutsionera', *PR*, 11: 46 (1925), pp. 262–83

Marx, Karl. *Letters to Dr Kugelmann*, London, 1934

Marx, Karl and Engels, Friedrich. *Collected Works*, 18 vols. published, London, 1975–

Correspondence, 1846–1895, London, 1934

Perepiska K. Marksa i F. Engel'sa s russkimi politicheskimi deyatelyami, 2nd edn, Moscow, 1951

Selected Correspondence, Moscow, 1953

Selected Works, 2 vols., Moscow, 1962

Mazurenko, S. 'Ot "Chornogo peredela" do kommunisticheskoy partii', *Puti revolyutsii*, 2–3: 5–6 (1926), pp. 5–27

Mikhaylovsky, N. K. *Sochineniya*, 6 vols., St Petersburg, 1896–7

Mirtov, P. L. [Lavrov] *Istoricheskiye pis'ma*, St Petersburg, 1870

Mitskevich, S. 'Kazantsy v Nizhnem', *Puti revolyutsii*, 2 (1922), pp. 11–14

Na grani dvukh epokh: ot narodnichestva k marksizmu, Moscow, 1937

Revolyutsionnaya Moskva, 1888–1905, Moscow, 1940

Moiseyenko, P. A. *Vospominaniya starogo revolyutsionera*, Moscow, 1966

Morozov, N. A. *Povesti moyey zhizni*, 2 vols., Moscow, 1961

Terroristicheskaya bor'ba, London, 1880

Moshinsky, I. N. [Yu. Konarsky] 'Devyanostyye gody v kiyevskom podpol'ye', *KS*, 5: 34 (1927), pp. 7–24

Na putyakh k 1-mu s'yezdu RS-DRP (90-ye gody v Kiyevskom podpol'ye), Moscow, 1928

Nadin, P. 'Strel'nikovskiy protsess 1883 goda v Odesse (Otryvok iz vospominaniy gosudarstvennogo prestupnika)', *Byloye*, 4 (1906), pp. 84–102

Nevsky, V. I. (ed.) *Istoriko-revolyutsionnyy sbornik*, 3 vols., Moscow–Petrograd, 1924–6

Nikonov, S. A. 'Iz vospominaniy ob A. I. Ul'yanove', *PR*, 2–3: 85–6 (1929), pp. 172–90

'Zhizn' studenchestva i revolyutsionnaya rabota kontsa vos'midesyatykh godov', *AIU*, pp. 135–81

N[ovopolin], G. 'Iz istorii rabochikh narodovol'cheskikh kruzhkov', *KS*, 8–9: 57–8 (1929), pp. 203–13

Novorussky, M. V. 'Aleksandr Il'ich Ul'yanov', *AIU*, pp. 199–208

Zapiski shlissel'burzhtsa, 1887–1905, Petersburg, 1920

Obshchina, 9 nos., Geneva, 1878

Obzory vazhneyshikh doznaniy proizvodivshikhsya po delam o gosudarstvennykh prestupleniyakh v zhandarmskikh upravleniyakh imperii, I–XVI (1881–91), housed in the Central State Archive of the October Revolution (TsGAOR), *fond* no. 102, *opis'*, no. 252, *yed. khr.* 1–12

Ol'minsky, M. [M.S. Aleksandrov] (ed.) *Ot gruppy Blagoyeva k 'Soyuzu bor'by', 1886–1894 gg.*, Rostov-on-Don, 1921

Orzhikh, B. D. 'V ryadakh "Narodnoy voli"', *NV*, III, pp. 75–172

'Ot izdateley', *IRS*, III, pp. 219–25

Pankratov, V. S. *Iz deyatel'nosti sredi rabochikh v 1880–1884 gg.*, Moscow, 1906

Vospominaniya. Kak prikhodilos' rabotat' sredi rabochikh v 1880–1884 godakh, Moscow, 1923

Pankratova, A. M. (ed.) *Rabocheye dvizheniye v Rossii v XIX veke*, 4 vols., Moscow, 1951–63

Perazich, V. *Yu. D. Mel'nikov*, Khar'kov, 1930

'Yuvenaliy Mel'nikov i Khar'kovskiy rabochiy kruzhok', *LR*, 3 (1923), pp. 108–15

Peshekerov, P. K. 'Propaganda narodovol'tsev sredi rabochikh v Rostov-na-Donu v 1882–1884 g.g.', *NV*, I, pp. 116–28

'Rabochiy-narodovolets G. G. Rudomyotov', *KS*, 11: 60 (1929), pp. 164–71

'Pis'mo Ispolnitel'nogo Komiteta "Nar. Voli" k zagranichnym tovarishcham', *GOT*, III, pp. 143–51

Plekhanov, G. V. *Sochineniya*, 24 vols., Moscow–Leningrad, 1923–7

Podbel'sky, Yu. 'Papiy Podbel'skiy', *KS*, 3: 52 (1929), pp. 41–62

'Pokazaniya N. I. Kibal'chicha, T. Mikhaylova, S. L. Perovskoy, N. I. Rysakova, pokazaniya i zayavleniye A. I. Zhelyabova', *Byloye*, 4–5: 32–3 (1918), pp. 230–304

Polonskaya, M. N. [Oshanina] 'K istorii partii Narodnoy Voli', *Byloye*, 6: 18 (1907), pp. 3–10

Polyakov, M. M. 'Razgrom yekaterinoslavskoy narodovol'cheskoy gruppy v 1886 g.', *NV*, I, pp. 145–50

Popov, I. I. 'F. V. Olesinov', *KS*, 5–6: 114–15 (1935), pp. 227–30

Pyotr Filippovich Yakubovich, Moscow, 1930

'Revolyutsionnyye organizatsii v Peterburge v 1882–1885 godakh', *NV*, I, pp. 49–80

Popov, M. R. *Zapiski zemlevol'tsa*, Moscow, 1933

Pribylyova-Korba, A. P. '*Narodnaya Volya*'. *Vospominaniya o 1870–1880-kh gg.*, Moscow, 1926

Pribylyova-Korba, A. P. and Figner, V. N. (eds.) *Narodovolets Aleksandr Dmitriyevich Mikhaylov*, Leningrad, 1925

'Programma pervogo v Rossii s-d kruzhka', *Byloye*, 13 (1918), pp. 43–52

'Protsess 20-ti narodovol'tsev v 1882 g.', *Byloye*, 1 (1906), pp. 227–301

Protsess 193-kh, Moscow, 1906

'"Rabochiy" – Rostovskiy zhurnal 1883 goda', *LN*, 2 (1932), pp. 75–100

Rabotnik, 15 nos., Geneva, 1875–6

Rusanov, N. S. *Iz moikh vospominaniy*, Berlin, 1923

Sapir, Boris (ed.) *Lavrov: Gody emigratsii: arkhivnyye materialy v dvukh tomakh*, 2 vols., Dordrecht, 1974

   '*Vperyod!*', *1873–1877: Materialy iz arkhiva Valeriana Nikolayevicha Smirnova*, 2 vols., Dordrecht, 1970

Serebryakov, E. A. *Revolyutsionery vo flote*, Petrograd, 1919

Sergiyevsky, N. L. (ed.) *Rabochiy: gazeta partii russkikh sotsial-demokratov (blagoyevtsev), 1885*, Leningrad, 1928

Shebalin, M. P. 'Kiyevskiy protsess 12 narodovol'tsev v 1884 g.', *NV*, II, pp. 66–80

   Klochki vospominaniy, Moscow, 1935

   'Peterburgskaya narodovol'cheskaya organizatsiya 1882–1883 gg.', *NV*, I, pp. 40–8

Shebeko, General (ed.) *Chronique du mouvement socialiste en Russie 1878–1887*, St Petersburg, 1890

Shekhter-Minor, A. N. 'Yuzhno-russkaya narodovol'cheskaya organizatsiya', *NV*, I, pp. 131–9

Shelgunov, N. V. *Sochineniya*, 3rd edn, 3 vols., St Petersburg, [1905]

   Vospominaniya, Moscow–Petrograd, 1923

Shilov, A. A. (ed.) *German Aleksandrovich Lopatin (1845–1918)*, Petrograd, 1922

[Shternberg, L. Ya] 'Politicheskiy terror v Rossii 1884', in Sapir (ed.), *Lavrov: Gody emigratsii*, II, pp. 572–94

Sklyarevich, Vl. 'O kiyevskoy "gruppe zagovorshchikov" 1885–1892 gg', *KS*, 5: 42 (1928), pp. 68–71

Smirnov, F. V. 'Otgoloski "Narodnoy voli" v Yaroslavle i Rybinske v 1882–1887 godakh', *NV*, III, pp. 233–47

Starik [S. Kovalik] 'Dvizheniye semidesyatykh godov po Bol'shomu protsessu', *Byloye*, 10 (1906), pp. 1–30, 11 (1906), pp. 30–72, and 12 (1906), pp. 56–81

[Stefanovich, Ya. V.] ['Russkaya revolyutsionnaya emigratsiya'], *GOT*, III, pp. 278–91

Stepnyak, S. M. [Kravchinsky] *Podpol'naya Rossiya*, in *Izbrannoye*, Moscow, 1972

Sukhomlin, V. I. 'Iz epokhi upadka partii "Narodnaya volya"', *KS*, 3: 24 (1926), pp. 75–89, 4: 25 (1926), pp. 29–45, 6: 27 (1926), pp. 65–87, and 7–8: 28–9 (1926), pp. 61–103

Svyatlovsky, V. V. 'Na zare Rossiyskoy sotsial-demokratii', *Byloye*, 19 (1922), pp. 139–60

Tan [V. G. Bogoraz] 'Povesti proshloy zhizni', *Russkoye bogatstvo*, 9 (1907), pp. 107–31, and 10 (1907), pp. 150–64

Tarnovsky, V. [G. G. Romanenko] *Terrorizm i rutina*, London, 1880

Tezyakov N. I. 'Iz perezhitogo–studencheskiye gody', *Kazanskiy meditsinskiy zhurnal*, 5–6 (1930), pp. 496–507

[Tikhomirov, L. A.] *Vospominaniya L'va Tikhomirova*, Moscow–Leningrad, 1927

Timofeyev, M. A. 'Perezhitoye', *KS*, 8–9: 57–8 (1929), pp. 94–117

Tkachov, P. N. *Izbrannyye sochineniya na sotsial'no-politicheskiye temy*, ed. B. P. Koz'min, 5 vols. published, Moscow, 1932–

   Sochineniya, ed. A. A. Galaktionov *et al.*, 2 vols., Moscow, 1975–6

Ul'yanova-Yelizarova, A. I. (ed.) *Aleksandr Il'ich Ul'yanov i delo 1 marta 1887 g.*, Moscow–Leningrad, 1927

Valk, S. N. (ed.) *Arkhiv 'Zemli i voli' i 'Narodnoy voli'*, Moscow, 1930

Valk, S. N. *et al.* (eds.) *Revolyutsionnoye narodnichestvo 70-kh godov XIX veka*, 2 vols., Moscow–Leningrad, 1964–5

Veden'yev, I. 'V khar'kovskikh revolyutsionnykh kruzhkakh 1882–1889 gg.', *LR*, 5 (1923), pp. 98–111

Vestnik 'Narodnoy voli', 5 nos., Geneva, 1883–6

Volkov [I. I. Maynov] 'Narodovol'cheskaya propaganda sredi moskovskikh rabochikh v 1881 godu', *Byloye*, 2 (1906), pp. 176–83

Vospominaniya o Vladimire Il'iche Lenine, I, Moscow, 1956

Vospominaniya rodnykh o Lenine, Moscow, 1955

Witte, Count. *The Memoirs of Count Witte*, tr. and ed. Abraham Yarmolinsky, London, 1921

Yakovenko, Ye. I. 'O vtorom 1-ye marta', *KS*, 32 (1927), pp. 7–42

Zalkind, L. S. 'Vospominaniya narodovol'tsa', *KS*, 3: 24 (1926), pp. 90–4

Zerno, no. 2, *KA*, 6: 37 (1929), pp. 219–30

'"Zerno", Rabochiy listok', *IRS*, II, pp. 353–88

SECONDARY SOURCES

Alston, Patrick L. *Education and the State in Tsarist Russia*, Stanford, 1969

Anatol'yev, P. 'Obshchestvo perevodchikov i izdateley', *KS*, 3: 100 (1933), pp. 82–141

Annensky, N. F. *et al. Gallereya shlissel'burgskikh uznikov*, St Petersburg, 1907

Antonov, V. *Russkiy drug Marksa. German Aleksandrovich Lopatin*, Moscow, 1962

Baron, Samuel H. 'The first decade of Russian Marxism', *SR*, 14: 3 (1955), pp. 315–30
   Plekhanov: The Father of Russian Marxism, London, 1963

Berlin, Isaiah. *Russian Thinkers*, London, 1978

Billington, J. H. *Mikhailovsky and Russian Populism*, Oxford, 1958

Bogucharsky, V. Ya. [V. Ya. Yakovlev] *Aktivnoye narodnichestvo semidesyatykh godov*, Moscow, 1912
   Iz istorii politicheskoy bor'by v 70-kh i 80-kh gg. XIX veka, Moscow, 1912

Carr, E. H. *Michael Bakunin*, New York, 1961

Cole, G. D. H. *A History of Socialist Thought*, vols. I and II, London, 1953–4

Filippov, R. V. *Iz istorii narodnicheskogo dvizheniya na pervom etape 'khozhdeniya v narod', 1863–1874*, Petrozavodsk, 1967

Florinsky, Michael T. *Russia: A History and an Interpretation*, 2 vols., New York, 1953

Footman, David. *Red Prelude: A Life of A. I. Zhelyabov*, 2nd edn, London, 1968

Ginev, V. N. *Narodnicheskoye dvizheniye v srednem povolzh'ye*, Moscow–Leningrad, 1966

Greenberg, Louis. *The Jews in Russia*, New Haven and London, 1965

Haimson, L. H. *The Russian Marxists and the Origins of Bolshevism*, Cambridge, Mass., 1955

Harding, Neil. 'Lenin's early writings – the problem of context', *Political Studies*, 23 (1975), pp. 442–58
   Lenin's Political Thought, 2 vols., London, 1977–81

Hardy, Deborah. *Petr Tkachov: The Critic as Jacobin*, Seattle, 1977

Itenberg, B. S. *Dvizheniye revolyutsionnogo narodnichestva*, Moscow, 1969

Itenberg, B. S. and Chernyak, A. Ya. *Zhizn' Aleksandra Ul'yanova*, Moscow, 1966

Kazakevich, R. A. *Sotsial-demokraticheskiye organizatsii Peterburga kontsa 80-kh – nachala 90-kh godov*, Leningrad, 1960

Kazakevich, R. A. and Suslova, F. M. *Mister Payps fal'sifitsiruyet istoriyu*, Leningrad, 1966

Keep, J. L. H. *The Rise of Social Democracy in Russia*, Oxford, 1963

Khait, G. Ye. 'V kazanskom kruzhke', *Novyy mir*, 4 (1958), pp. 189–93

Kheyfets, M. I. *Vtoraya revolyutsionnaya situatsiya v Rossii: konets 70-kh – nachalo 80-kh godov XIX veka*, Moscow, 1963

Kon, Feliks. *Istoriya revolyutsionnogo dvizheniya v Rossii*, Khar'kov, 1929

Korbut, M. K. *Kazanskiy gosudarstvennyy universitet*, 2 vols., Kazan', 1929–30

  'Kazanskoye revolyutsionnoye podpol'ye kontsa 80-kh godov i Lenin', *KS*, 8–9: 81–2 (1931), pp. 7–27

Korol'chuk, E. A. *Severnyy soyuz russkikh rabochikh i revolyutsionnoye rabocheye dvizheniye 70-kh godov XIX v. v Peterburge* Leningrad, 1946

Koz'min, B. P. *Iz istorii revolyutsionnoy mysli v Rossii*, Moscow, 1961

  P. N. Tkachov i revolyutsionnoye dvizheniye 1860-kh godov, Moscow, 1922

Kusheva, Ye. 'Iz istorii "Obshchestva Narodnogo Osvobozhdeniya"', *KS*, 4: 77 (1931), pp. 31–56

Kuz'min, Dmitriy. *Narodovol'cheskaya zhurnalistika*, Moscow, 1930

Lampert, Evgeny. *Sons against Fathers: Studies in Russian Radicalism and Revolution*, Oxford, 1965

  Studies in Rebellion, London, 1957

Laue, Theodore H. von. 'The fate of capitalism in Russia: the Narodnik version', *SR*, 13: 1 (1954), pp. 11–28

Levin, Sh. M. *Obshchestvennoye dvizheniye v Rossii v 60–70-ye gody XIX v.*, Moscow, 1958

Levitsky, V. '"Narodnaya volya" i rabochiy klass', *KS*, 1: 62 (1930), pp. 48–66

  Partiya 'Narodnaya volya'. Vozniknoveniye. Bor'ba. Gibel', Moscow–Leningrad, 1928

Livshits, S. 'Podpol'nyye tipografii 60-kh, 70-kh, i 80-kh godov', *KS*, 4:41 (1928), pp. 23–33, 6: 43 (1928), pp. 60–78, 1: 50 (1929), pp. 64 80

Malinin, V. A. *Filosofiya revolyutsionnogo narodnichestva*, Moscow, 1972

Mat'yas, O. A. *Nachalo revolyutsionnoy deyatel'nosti V. I. Lenina*, Moscow, 1956

Meijer, J. M. *Knowledge and Revolution*, Assen, 1955

Mendel, Arthur P. *Dilemmas of Progress in Tsarist Russia: Legal Marxism and Legal Populism*, Cambridge, Mass., 1961

  'N. K. Mikhailovsky and his criticism of Russian Marxism', *SR*, 14: 3 (1955), pp. 331–45

Nafigov, R. I. *Pervyy shag v revolyutsiyu. V. I. Ul'yanov i kazanskoye studenchestvo 80-kh godov XIX veka*, Kazan', 1970

Nevsky, V. *Ocherki po istorii rossiyskoy kommunisticheskoy partii*, 2nd edn, I, Leningrad, 1925

Offord, Derek. 'Political terrorism in Russia in the 1880s: the Fenian lesson', *Irish Slavonic Studies*, 5 (1984), pp. 27–31

  'Revolutionary Populist Groups in Russia in the 1880s', unpublished PhD thesis, University of London (LSE), 1974

Ovsyannikova, S. A. *Gruppa Blagoyeva. Iz istorii rasprostraneniya marksizma v Rossii*, Moscow, 1959

Pipes, Richard. 'Narodnichestvo: a semantic enquiry', *SR*, 23: 3 (1964), pp. 441–58

  'The origins of Bolshevism: the intellectual evolution of young Lenin', in *Revolutionary Russia*, ed. Pipes, Cambridge, Mass., 1968, pp. 26–52

  'Russian Marxism and its Populist background', *The Russian Review*, 19 (1960), pp. 316–37

  Social Democracy and the St Petersburg Labour Movement, 1885–1897, Cambridge, Mass., 1963

Polevoy, Yu. Z. *Zarozhdeniye marksizma v Rossii: 1883–1894 gg.*, Moscow, 1959

Pomper, Philip. *Peter Lavrov and the Russian Revolutionary Movement*, Chicago, 1972
  The Russian Revolutionary Intelligentsia, New York, 1970
  Sergei Nechaev, New Brunswick, 1979
Rashin, A. G. *Formirovaniye rabochego klassa Rossii*, Moscow, 1958
Reuel', A. L. *Russkaya ekonomicheskaya mysl' 60–70-kh godov XIX veka i marksizm*, Moscow, 1956
Schapiro, Leonard. 'The role of the Jews in the Russian revolutionary movement', *SEER*, 40: 94 (1961), pp. 148–67
Sedov, M. G. *Geroicheskiy period revolyutsionnogo narodnichestva*, Moscow, 1966
  '"Narodnaya volya" pered sudom istorii', *Voprosy istorii*, 12 (1965), pp. 45–62
  'Nekotoryye problemy istorii blankizma v Rossii', *Voprosy istorii*, 10 (1971), pp. 39–54
  'P. L. Lavrov v revolyutsionnom dvizhenii v Rossii', *Voprosy istorii*, 3 (1969), pp. 55–72
Senchakova, L. T. *Revolyutsionnoye dvizheniye v russkoy armii i flote v kontse XIX – nachale XX v.*, Moscow, 1972
Sergiyevsky, N. L. '"Chornyy peredel" i narodniki 80-kh godov', *KS*, 1: 74 (1931), pp. 7–50
  'Fedoseyevskiy kruzhok 1888–1889 gg.', *KL*, 7 (1923), pp. 285–321, and 9 (1924), pp. 169–76
  'Gruppa "Osvobozhdeniye truda" i marksistskiye kruzhki', *IRS*, II, pp. 86–167
  'Narodnichestvo 80-kh godov', *IRS*, III, pp. 148–84
  'O fedoseyevskom kruzhke 1888–89.', *KL*, 5 (1923), pp. 340–3
  Partiya russkikh sotsial-demokratov. Gruppa Blagoyeva, Moscow–Leningrad, 1929
  'Tak chto zhe takoye Fedoseyevskiy kruzhok 1888–1889 gg.', *IRS*, I, pp. 67–96
Service, Robert. 'Russian Populism and Russian Marxism: two skeins entangled', in *Russian Thought and Society, 1800–1917: Essays in Honour of Eugene Lampert*, ed. Roger Bartlett, Keele, 1984, pp. 220–46
Seton-Watson, Hugh. *The Decline of Imperial Russia, 1855–1914*, London, 1952
  The Russian Empire, 1801–1917, Oxford, 1967
Shcheprov, S. *Vydayushchiysya revolyutsioner N. Ye. Fedoseyev*, Moscow, 1958
Teodorovich, I. A. 'Istoricheskoye znacheniye partii "Narodnoy voli"', *KS*, 8–9: 57–8 (1929), pp. 7–53
  'Sotsial'no-politicheskaya mysl' chernoperedel'chestva i yeyo znacheniye v nashem proshlom', *KS*, 4–5: 101–2 (1933), pp. 5–54
Theen, Rolf H. W. *Lenin: Genesis and Development of a Revolutionary*, London, 1974
Thun, A. *Istoriya revolyutsionnogo dvizheniya v Rossii*, Leningrad, 1924
Tkachenko, P. S. *Moskovskoye studenchestvo v obshchestvenno-politicheskoy zhizni Rossii vtoroy poloviny XIX veka*, Moscow, 1958
  Revolyutsionnaya narodnicheskaya organizatsiya 'Zemlya i volya', 1876–1879 gg., Moscow, 1961
Troitsky, N. A. *Bol'shoye obshchestvo propagandy: 1871–1874*, Saratov, 1963
Trotsky, Leon. *The Young Lenin*, tr. Max Eastman, Newton Abbot, 1972
Tvardovskaya, V. A. 'Organizatsionnyye osnovy "Narodnoy voli"', *Istoricheskiye zapiski*, 67 (1960), pp. 103–44
  Sotsialisticheskaya mysl' Rossii na rubezhe 1870–1880 gg., Moscow, 1969
Ulam, Adam B. *Lenin and the Bolsheviks*, London, 1966
Utechin, S. V. 'The "Preparatory Trend" in the Russian revolutionary movement in the 1880s', *St Antony's Papers*, 12 (1962), pp. 7–22

Valentinov, N. [N. V. Vol'sky] 'Chernyshevskiy i Lenin', *Novyy zhurnal*, 26 (1951), pp. 193–216, and 27 (1951), pp. 225–49

Encounters with Lenin, Oxford, 1968

'Ranniye gody Lenina', *Novyy zhurnal*, 36 (1954), pp. 220–37, 37 (1954), pp. 211–33, 39 (1954), pp. 212–31, 40 (1955), pp. 200–16, 41 (1955), pp. 176–96

The Early Years of Lenin, University of Michigan, 1969

'Vstrecha Lenina s marksizmom', *Novyy zhurnal*, 53 (1958), pp. 189–208

Valk, S. N. 'G. G. Romanenko. (Iz istorii "Narodnoy Voli")', *KS*, 11: 48 (1928), pp. 36–59

'Molodaya partiya Narodnoy voli', *Problemy marksizma*, 1: 3 (1930), pp. 95–119

'Rasporyaditel'naya komissiya i "Molodaya partiya Narodnoy voli"', *KS*, 2: 75, pp. 98–137

Venturi, Franco. *Roots of Revolution: A History of the Populist and Socialist Movements in Nineteenth-Century Russia*, London, 1960

Vilenskaya, E. S. *N. K. Mikhaylovskiy i yego ideynaya rol' v narodnicheskom dvizhenii 70-kh – nachala 80-kh godov XIX veka*, Moscow, 1979

Vilensky-Sibiryakov, Vl. *et al.* (eds.) *Deyateli revolyutsionnogo dvizheniya v Rossii. Bio-bibliograficheskiy slovar'*, 5 vols., Moscow, 1927–34

Volin, B. *Lenin v Povolzh'ye*, 2nd edn, Moscow, 1956

Volk, S. S. *Karl Marks i russkiye obshchestvennyye deyateli*, Leningrad, 1969

Narodnaya Volya, 1879–1882, Moscow–Leningrad, 1966

Walicki, Andrzej. *A History of Russian Thought from the Enlightenment to Marxism*, Oxford, 1980

The Controversy over Capitalism: Studies in the Social Philosophy of the Russian Populists, Oxford, 1969

Woodcock, George. *Anarchism*, Harmondsworth, 1970

Wortman, R. *The Crisis of Russian Populism*, Cambridge, Mass., 1967

Yarmolinsky, A. *Road to Revolution*, New York, 1959

Zayonchkovsky, P. A. *Krizis samoderzhaviya na rubezhe 1870–1880-kh godov*, Moscow, 1964

Rossiyskoye samoderzhaviye v kontse XIX stoletiya. Politicheskaya reaktsiya 80-kh – nachala 90-kh godov, Moscow, 1970

Zdobnov, N. V. *Istoriya russkoy bibliografii do nachala XX veka*, 2nd edn, Moscow, 1951

Zil'bershteyn, I. 'Nekotoryye voprosy biografii molodogo Lenina', *KS*, 1: 62 (1930), pp. 7–23

 *INDEX*

Titles of works are listed under the names of their authors.

Abaza, A. A., 37
Afanasyev, F. A., 156
Aksakov, S.T., 90
Akselrod, P. B., 26, 46, 84–5, 111, 125
Alexander II, 28–9, 36–7, 39, 41–6, 64, 68, 72, 117, 123–4, 131
Alexander III, xi, 36–7, 54, 73, 98, 139
Andreyushkin, P. I., 72–3, 98, 101–2
Annenkov, P. V., 118
Annensky, N. F., 107–11
Antonov, P. L., 55–6
Aptekman, O. V., 26–7
Arkadakskaya, L. V., 141
armed forces, revolutionary activity in, 28, 30, 33, 49–50, 83, 86, 114
Arshaulov, P. P., 132
Association of St Petersburg Artisans, 141–5, 155–6, 165, 167

Bakh, A. N., 53, 56, 58, 63, 92
Bakunin, M. A., 2, 9, 11–13, 15–17, 20–1, 33, 118, 122, 160, 163; *Statism and Anarchy*, 12
Balabukha, S. P., 88, 90, 93
Balakirev, M. A., 90
Baramzin, Ye. V., 94
Barannikov, A. I., 26, 39
Baron, Samuel H., xi
Baudelaire, Charles, 79
Bazhin, N. F., *History of an Association*, 8
Bekaryukov, D. D., 88, 93–4, 98, 112–16, 145, 148–9, 163

Belinsky, V. G., 40
Belyayev, N. N., 76
Berezin, M. Ye., 148, 154
Bervi, V. V. (pseudonym N. Flerovsky), 2–3, 5, 7, 137; *The Condition of the Working Class in Russia*, 5
Blagoyev, D. N., 130–2, 134, 137, 156, 167
Blagoyevtsy, 130–8, 155–6, 165, 167
Blanc, Louis 85, 135, 137; *The Organisation of Labour*, 137
Blanquism, *see* Jacobinism
Bodayev, V. A., 52–3, 57, 61
Bogdanov, N. D., 156, 158
Bogdanovich, Yu. N., 41, 47–8, 64
Bogoraz, L., 101, 105–7, 115–16, 147
Bogoraz, V. G. (pseudonym Tan), 64–9, 101, 106, 168; *The Struggle of Social Forces in Russia*, 65–6, 68–9, 106
Boldyrev, I. P., 115–16
Borodin, N. A., 132
Breytfus, A. L., 141, 143–4
Brusnev, M. I., xiii, 157
Bunin, Yu. A., 88–9; *A Few Words on the Past of Russian Socialism*, 88
buntari, 17, 20, 23, 34, 113
Burachevsky, I. K., 157
Butsevich, A. V., 50–1
Buyanov, V. V., 141, 156
Byron, Lord George, 79

capitalism, 2–3, 5–6, 9, 14, 19, 31, 66, 68, 74,

80–2, 84–5, 108–11, 121–5, 127–9, 133–4, 146, 169

Charushnikov, I. P., 93, 107, 111–12

Chaykovtsy, 16–17, 19, 21–2, 34, 55, 78, 163

Chebotaryov, I. N., 71, 104

Chekhov, A. P., 64, 78; *Ivanov*, 78

Chekin, A. V., 94

Chelyabinsk index, 93

Chernov, V. M., 169

Chernyavskaya, G. F., 58

Chernyshevsky, N. G., 3, 6, 8, 59, 68, 82, 102, 121–2, 125, 137, 150–2, 155; *What is to be done?*, 8, 151–2, 155

Chervinsky, P. P., 80

Chetvergova, M. P., 153–4

Chirikov, Ye. N., 153–4

Chizhevsky, I. K., 86

Chornyy peredel (The Black Partition), 27

commune, 1–3, 5, 10, 12, 33, 73, 79 81, 108, 110–11, 121–2, 124–5, 128, 146, 161–2

coup d'état, see seizure of power

Danielson, N. F. (pseudonym Nikolay -on), 5, 80, 82, 118–19; 'The Capitalisation of Agricultural Income', 80

Danilova, Ye. A., 141, 144–5

Degayev, S. P., 56–7, 62

Delyanov, I. D., 97

Dembo, I. V., 75

Derenkov, A. S., 94

Deych, L. G., 20, 26, 47, 125, 130

Dickens, Charles, 79

Dikovskaya, *see* Yakimova

Diksztajn, Sz., *What does a man live on?*, 158

Dobrolyubov, N. A., 3, 70, 86

Dobrolyubov demonstration, 70–1, 86, 97–8

Dostoyevsky, F. M., 34, 40, 77; *The Brothers Karamazov*, 34

Druzhinin, V. P., 49

Dühring, Karl, 85, 119

Dushevsky, P. G., 86

Dzyubenko, S. M., 89

'Emancipation of Labour' group, xi, 84, 87, 125–33, 144, 158

Engelgardt, A. N., 79

Engels, Friedrich, 5, 14, 59, 74, 84–5, 111, 117–26, 130–1; *The Origin of the Family, Private Property and the State*, 149; *Socialism: Utopian and Scientific*, 84; *The Condition of the Working Class in England*, 5, 84; *The Housing Question*, 84; *see also* Marx and Engels

Fedoseyev, N. Ye., 146–9, 152–4, 164, 167

Figner, V. N., 26, 46–8, 51, 57, 85, 92, 134

Flaubert, Gustave, 79

Flerovsky, N., *see* Bervi

Flyorov, N. M., 52–3, 57, 59, 61–2

Fokin, M. D., 93–4, 112–13, 148–9, 163

Fomin, V. V., 156

Fourier, Charles, 10

Foynitsky, F., 76

Frederic, Harold, 43–4

Freyfeld, L. V., 75

Frolenko, M. F., 26, 34, 39

Fyodorov, *see* Omulevsky

Galkina, S. N., 98, 101

Garfield, James, 41

Gelfman, G. M., 39, 44

General Students' Union, 83

Generalov, V. D., 72–3

Gerasimov, A. A., 132

Geyking, 23

Ginsburg, S. M., 75–6

Gizetti, A. V., 87

Goldenberg, G. D., 23

Golitsynsky, A. P., 4

Golubev, P. A., 92–3, 147

Golubev, V. S., 156

Goncharov, V. A., 53, 89

Gorky, *see* Peshkov

Govorukhin, O.M., 71–3

Grabovsky, P. A., 89

Grachevsky, M. F., 26, 41, 48, 51

Grazhdanin (The Citizen), 87

Grigorovich, D. V., 137

Grigoryev, M. G., 147

Grinevitsky, I. I., 29, 37

Haimson, Leopold H., 168 9

Harding, Neil, 106

Haxthausen, Baron A. von, 2

Heine, Heinrich, 75

Henry, Emile, 34

Herzen, A. I. (Gertsen), 2–3, 122

Hugo, Victor, 79

Ignatov, V. N., 126

Ignatyev, N. P., 37, 43–4

Iordan, N. V., 88–9

Isayev, G. P., 39

Ishutin, N. A., 15

Itenberg, B. S., x

Ivanov, S. A., 56, 58, 63

Ivanov, V. I., 139

Jacobinism (Blanquism), 16, 32–4, 47–8, 68–9, 106, 126–7, 152, 154, 168; Jacobins, 21, 31–2, 34, 47–50, 105–7

Jews, participation of in revolutionary movement, 44, 64

Kablits, I. I. (pseudonym Yuzov), 80
Kacharovsky, 76, 101
Karaulov, N. A., 57
Karpenko, A. I., 54–5
Katkov, M. N., 140
Kautsky, Karl, *The Economic Teaching of Karl Marx*, 149
Kazakevich, R. A., xi
Kerensky, F. M., 100
Khalturin, S. N., 22
Kharitonov, V. G., 132
Kibalchich, N. I., 39
Kiyevlyanin (The Kievan), 45
Klements, D. A., 24
Kletochnikov, N. V., 39
Klimanov, Ye. A., 141, 156
Kogan, Z. V., 64–5
Kolodkevich, N. N., 26, 39
Kondoyanaki, N., 101
Kondratenko, A. F., 115
Korba, A. P. (Pribylyova), 41, 46–8, 51
Korolenko, V. G., 107
Kotlyarevsky, M. M., 23
Kovalevsky, M. M., 98
Kovalik, S. F., 17
Kovalskaya, Ye. N., 28
Kovalsky, I. M., 23–4
Kramskoy, I. N., 4, 8
Kravchinsky, S. M. (pseudonym Stepnyak), 23–4; *A Death for a Death*, 24
Krivenko, S. N., 57
Krol, M. A., 64
Kropotkin, D. N., 23, 25
Kropotkin, P. A., 10, 17, 46
Krupskaya, N. K., 150–1, 154–5, 168
Kudryashov, V. N., 54–5
Kudryavtsev, P. F., 94, 154
Kugushev, V. A., 132
kulaks, 18, 45, 146
Kushchevsky, I. A., *Nikolay Negorev*, 8
Kvashnina, L. P. (Loyko), 92
Kvyatkovsky, A. A., 26

labour movement, xi, 21, 139–42, 155–6
Lafargue, Paul; *The Religion of Capital*, 158
Lalayants, I. Kh., 155
Lassalle, Ferdinand, 85, 134–5, 144
Latyshev, P. A., 132
Lavrov, P. L., 2, 7, 9–11, 13, 15–17, 20–1, 33–4, 46, 58, 91, 118–19, 126, 137, 141, 160, 162–3; *Historical Letters*, 7, 10; *The State Element in the Future Society*, 10
Lazarev, D. V., 141, 145
Lazareva, V. V., 141
Lebedev, V. S., 41, 44, 46, 50
Lebedeva, *see* Tochisskaya

Lelevel, B. F., 157
Lenin, *see* V. I. Ulyanov
Levin, Sh. M., x
Levinsky, I. S., 53
Levitov, A. I., 4, 137
Lopatin, G. A., 5, 58–60, 62–3, 86, 92, 118–19, 132
Loris-Melikov, M. T., 37
Lukashevich, I. D., 71–3

Machiavelli, Niccolò, 16
Makarenko, A. A., 88
Makarevsky, A. N., 89
Maksimov, S. V., 4, 137
Malthus, Thomas, 87
Mandelshtam, M. L., 153–4
Manucharov, I. A., 88–9
Martynov, S. V., 41, 46, 50
Marx, Karl, 5, 13, 19, 59, 74, 87, 109, 111, 116–27, 129–30, 134, 137, 146, 149, 153–4, 158; *Capital*, 5, 59, 73, 103, 118–19, 137, 148, 152; *Contribution to the Critique of Political Economy*, 149; *Outlines of a Critique of Political Economy*, 84; *The Civil War in France*, 84; *The Poverty of Philosophy*, 118, 149; *Wages, Price and Profit*, 84; *Wage Labour and Capital*, 84
Marx, Karl and Engels, Friedrich, *The Communist Manifesto*, 118, 124–5, 130, 137
Mazurenko, S. P., 89
Mefodiyev, G. A., 156
Melnikov, Yu. D., 114–15
Mendel, Arthur P., 164
Merkhalev, N. A., 88, 90
Meshchersky, V. P., 87
Mezentsov, N. V. 23–4
Mikhaylov, A. D., 21, 26, 39
Mikhaylov, T. M., 39
Mikhaylovsky, N. K., 2–3, 5–7, 29, 34, 36–7, 78–9, 118–19, 122–3, 137, 170; 'What is Progress?', 6
militarists, 83–6, 94, 154, 163
Milovsky, S. N. (pseudonym Yeleonsky), 94
Milyutin, D. A., 37
Minsky (pseudonym of N. M. Vilenkin), 75
mir, 10, 12, 18; *see also* commune
Mitskevich, S. I., 147
Moiseyenko, P. A., 139–40
Mordovtsev, D. L., 4, 137; *Signs of the Times*, 8
Morozov, N. A., 25–6, 31–2, 39
Morozov, Savva, 138
Morozov, T. S., 139–40
Morozov strike, 138–41
Moskovskiye vedomosti (Moscow Gazette), 140
Motovilov, N. A., 98, 101, 105, 107, 115–16, 147

Muscovites, *see* Pan-Russian Social-
Revolutionary Organisation
Musorgsky, M. P., 4
Myasoyedov, G. G., 4

Nabat (The Tocsin), 14–15, 31
Nafigov, R. I., 102, 105
Narodnaya volya (The People's Will), 29, 31, 41,
45, 48—9, 60, 62, 65, 67–8
Naumov, N. I., 4, 137
Nechayev, S. G., 15
Nefyodov, F. D., 4
Nekrasov, N. A., 4, 8, 52, 77, 137
Nemisty, 86
Nikolay -on, *see* Danielson
Norinsky, K. M., 158
North-Russian Workers' Union, 22, 139
Novorussky, M. V., 72

Obnorsky, V. P., 22
Oboleshev, A. D., 20
Obshchina (The Commune), 111
Olesinov, F. V., 63
Olovennikova, Polonskaya, *see* Oshanina
Omulevsky (pseudonym of I. V. Fyodorov),
Step by Step, 8
organisation, revolutionaries' views on, ix–x,
15–16, 18–21, 30–1, 35, 51, 60–1, 83, 93–4,
112–14, 163, 168
Orzhikh, B. D., 63–5, 67
Oshanina, M. N. (Olovennikova, Polonskaya),
26, 32, 34, 41, 48–9, 51, 58, 68
Osinsky, V. A., 23, 26
Osipanov, V. S., 71–3, 98
Otechestvennyye zapiski (Notes of the Fatherland),
37, 39, 79, 81, 83, 122
Ovchinnikov, M. P., 56–7, 59
Owen, Robert, 10

Pankratov, V. S., 115
Pan-Russian Social-Revolutionary Organisation
(Muscovites), 19, 22
Paprits, Ye. E., 84
peasant revolt, 13, 19–20, 29, 43, 86
peasantry, ix, 1–6, 9–10, 12, 14–16, 18–20, 27,
30, 33–5, 42, 52, 67, 74, 79–81, 88–9, 91–4,
108–11, 114, 120, 128–9, 135–6, 141, 144,
146, 161, 168
Pechorkin, Ye. F., 92, 107
Perazich, V. D., 114
Pereverzin, 158
Perov, V. G., 4
Perovskaya, S. L., 26–7, 34, 39, 49, 52, 54, 98,
135
Peshekerov, P. K., 54
Peshkov, A. M. (pseudonym Maksim Gorky),
94, 149

Pipes, Richard, xi, 105, 142, 157–9
Pisarev, D. I., 162
Plekhanov, G. V., xi, 19, 21, 26–7, 90, 110–11,
125–31, 133, 137, 140, 146, 148, 162, 164,
166–9; *Our Differences*, 106, 127–9, 144, 149;
Socialism and Political Struggle, 84, 127, 129
Pobedonostsev, K. P., 36–7, 41
Podbelsky, N. P., 98
pogroms, 43–6, 64
Polevoy, Yu. Z., xi, 102, 105
Popko, G. A., 23
Popov, M. R., 26
positive hero, 7–8, 131, 134, 151–2
Preobrazhensky, G. N., 26
Pribylyova, *see* Korba
Proudhon, Pierre-Joseph, 118–19
Pugachov, Ye. I.,13

Rabochaya gazeta (Workers' Paper), 28, 42
Rabochiy (The Worker) (paper of the
Blagoyevtsy), 132–3, 136–8
Rabochiy (The Worker) (paper of Rostov
workers' group), 54
Radkey, Oliver H., 166
Raspopin, V. T., 83–5, 163
Ravachol, 34
Razin, S. T., 13
Repin, I. Ye., 4
Reshetnikov, F. M., 4, 14, 137
Ricardo, David, 5, 87
Rodzevich, G. M., 157
Rogachov, D. M., 17
Rogachov, N. M., 49
Romanenko, G. G., (pseudonym Tarnovsky),
31, 45–6
Rudomyotov, G. G., 56
Russkoye bogatstvo (Russian Wealth), 57
Russo-Turkish War, 24, 29, 123
Rysakov, N. I., 39, 42
Ryurik, 62

Sabunayev, M. V., 58, 76, 85
Sakharova, O., 98
Salova, N. M., 58–9, 62
Saltykov-Shchedrin, M. Ye., 78, 83, 90
Sanin, A. A., 149
Sazonov, G. P., 86
Sazonov, N. I., 118
Schäffle, Albert, 90
Sedov, M. G., x
seizure of power, 15, 27, 30, 34, 47–9, 69, 83,
85–6, 90, 94, 105–6, 114, 135
Semevsky, V. I., 87
Serebryakov, E. A., 58
Sergeyeva, Ye. D., 48, 51
Sergiyevsky, N. L., 144

Service, Robert, 166
Shalayevsky, I. A., 141
Shatko, P. P., 132
Shchapov, A. P., 4, 137
Shchedrin, N. P., 28
Shcheprov, S. V., 102
Shekhter, A. N., 64
Shelepenko, I. F., 89
Shelgunov, N. N., 86
Shelgunov, N. V., 79, 159
Shelgunov, V. A., 141, 158
Shevyryov, P. Ya., 71–3
Shternberg, L. Ya., 64, 67–9
Skvortsov, A. G., 101, 105, 107
Skvortsov, P. N., 146–7
Slavophiles, 2, 141
Sleptsov, A. A., 118
Sleptsov, V. A., 4
Smith, Adam, 87
Society for the Liberation of the People, 31
Society of Translators and Publishers, 83–5, 89, 167
Sokolov, N. V., *Renegades*, 8
Solovyov, A. K., 25
Sotsialisticheskoye znaniye (Socialist Knowledge), 84–5
South-Russian Workers' Union, 28
Southern Social Society, 88
Sovremennik (The Contemporary), 151
Spencer, Herbert, 59
Spielhagen, Friedrich von, 134
Stasov, V. V., 4
Stefanovich, Ya. V., 20, 26, 46–50
Stepnyak, *see* Kravchinsky
Stepurin, K. A., 58, 62
Stoyanovsky, S. L., 75
Strelnikov, F. Ye., 51, 91
Struve, P. B., *Critical Notes*, 169
student circles, 28, 164–5; in Kazan, 91–5, 98, 101, 147–9, 152–4; in Kharkov, 51, 75, 88–90; in Kiev, 51, 112–14; in Moscow, 83–5; in Odessa, 51; in St Petersburg, 58, 70–1, 75–6, 86–7, 101, 156–7
student disturbances, 22–3, 42, 53, 58, 86–8, 95–9, 101, 165
Sudeykin, G. P., 57, 61, 91
Sukhanov, N. Ye., 39
Sukhomlin, V. I., 58, 62

Taine, Hippolyte, 59
Tan, *see* Bogoraz, V. G.
Tarnovsky, *see* Romanenko
Tellalov, P. A., 41–2, 44, 48
terrorism, 23, 26–7, 31, 33, 38, 45, 77, 83, 85, 88, 90, 105, 113, 115, 123–4, 130, 135–6, 143–4, 154–5, 161, 167; acts of, 23, 25, 28,

42, 51, 53, 57, 67, 71–2, 75, 97–8; 'economic', 28, 56, 61–3, 88–9; motives advanced for, 24–5, 28–9, 41, 67, 73–4
Theen, Rolf H. W., 106
Tikhomirov, L. A., 25–6, 30–3, 41, 47–9, 51, 58, 66–8, 79, 85, 106, 127–8
Timofeyev, I. I., 141, 156, 158
Tkachenko, P. S., x
Tkachov, P. N., 2, 9, 13–16, 29–32, 34, 48, 55, 78, 107, 118–19, 121–2, 127
Tochisskaya, M. V. (Lebedeva), 141
Tochissky, P. V., 141–5, 155–6, 163, 165, 167
Tolstoy, D. A., 37, 50, 67, 139
Tolstoy, L. N., 10, 77, 79, 84, 90; *Anna Karenina*, 77; *Confession*, 79; *My Faith*, 79; Tolstoyanism, 79, 164
Trepov, F. F., 23–4
Trigoni, M. N., 39
Trotsky (L. D. Bronshteyn), 104, 153–4
Tsivinsky, V. F., 157
Turgenev, I. S., 7, 59, 77, 86, 103; *Fathers and Children*, 7; *On the Eve*, 7
Tvardovskaya, V. A., x

Ulyanov, A. I., 70–5, 87, 100–4, 151–2, 154, 167–8
Ulyanov, V. I. (Lenin), xi–xiii, 70, 85, 98, 100–7, 146–7, 149–55, 166–8; *The Development of Capitalism in Russia*, 169; *What is to be done?*, 154, 168
Ulyanova, A. I., 103, 152–5
Ulyanova, M. I., 103
Union of Youth of Narodnaya Volya, 58
Uspensky, G. I., 52, 59, 78, 161
Uspensky, N. I., 4
Utechin, S. V., xi

Vaillant, Auguste, 34
Valentinov, N. (pseudonym of N. V. Volsky), 151–2
Vasilyev, N., 141–2
Venturi, Franco, x, 166
Veretennikov, N., 100
Vershinina, 92, 107
Vestnik 'Narodnoy voli' (Herald of 'Narodnaya Volya'), 58, 126, 136
Viktorov, P. P., 42
Vilenkin, *see* Minsky
Volin, B. M., 105
Volk, S. S., x
Volkov, V. S., 139–40
Volsky, N. V., *see* Valentinov
Volzhskiy vestnik (The Volga Herald), 146
Vorontsov, V. P. (pseudonym V. V.), 80–2, 128, 146; *The Fate of Capitalism in Russia*, 80–1

Vorovsky, V. V., 150–1
Voynaralsky, P. I., 17
Vperyod! (*Forward!*), 11, 118
Vygornitsky, K. A., 98, 101, 107

Walicki, Andrzej, x
Witte, S. Yu., 96
workers: urban, 16–17, 21–2, 33, 35, 38, 42,
    51–6, 61–3, 74, 109, 111, 120, 128–30, 133–4,
    136–45, 156–9, 163, 165, 167; relation to
    peasantry of, ix, 19, 22, 55, 129, 136, 144
workers' circles: in Kharkov, 28, 41, 53, 114–
    15; in Kiev, 28, 53; in Moscow, 28, 41; in
    Odessa, 28, 53; in Rostov 53–6, 115–16; in
    St Petersburg, 28, 52–3, 70, 132, 137, 141–5,
    155–9; in Yekaterinoslav, 54–5, 64

Yakimova, A. V. (Dikovskaya), 26, 39
Yakubovich, P. F., 57–63, 96
Yanovich, L. F., 83, 85
Yarmolinsky, A., x
Yasevich, L. F., 64
Yastrebov, S. M., 86
Yeleonsky, *see* Milovsky
Yeliseyev, G. Z., 5

Yevgrafov, P. Ye., 156
Yuridicheskiy vestnik (*The Legal Herald*), 146
Yuzhakov, S. N., 80–2; 'Forms of Agricultural
    Production in Russia', 81
Yuzov, *see* Kablits

Zaboluyev, P. L., 88
Zaichnevsky, P. G., 32, 49, 152
Zasodimsky, P. V., 4, 137
Zasulich, V. I., 23–4, 26, 124–5, 131
Zelenenko, V. V., 101, 105
Zemlya i Volya (Land and Liberty), 19ff, 26,
    39, 91, 94
Zemlya i Volya (*Land and Liberty*) (journal),
    24, 32
zemlyachestva, 83, 87, 98, 100–1
Zhebunyov, V. A., 45
Zhelyabov, A. I., 26–7, 34, 39, 49, 52, 54, 94
Zhenzhurist, I. M., 98
Zhukovsky, Yu. G., 118
Ziber, N. I., 5, 118, 146
Zlatopolsky, S. S., 44, 50
Zlatovratsky, N. N., *Foundations*, 79
Znaniye (*Knowledge*), 118
Zundelevich, A. I., 26, 34, 44